Happier Being

Happier Being

Your Path to Optimizing Habits, Health & Happiness

Tal Leead, PsyD

Cover and Design: HR Hegnauer
Editing: Noam Leead
Author's photo by: Shani Leead
Author's website: happierbeing.com

"This book exemplifies the ways in which we can all make happiness our greatest currency. The concept of following our "Inner Giggle" – that cross section between meaning and pleasure in life – speaks volumes about the kind of philosophy Dr. Tal is sharing with the world. I highly recommend this book to anyone searching to live happier and spread happiness onto others!"

—Luis Gallardo, MBA, Executive Director at No Barriers;
Founder of the World Happiness Foundation

"In this thoughtful book, Dr. Tal presents you with several tips, techniques, and time-proven principles to increase your well-being and joy in life. This book gives you a highly practical and integrated approach to live better and feel better."

—Giovanni Dienstmann, meditation teacher, coach,
and author of *Mindful Self-Discipline*

"As a clinician who supports those facing one of the most challenging health obstacles imaginable – cancer – I have found that those able to cultivate three things: joy, gratitude, and purpose, have better quality of life and better clinical outcomes. Dr. Tal's book, *Happier Being*, is an invaluable resource loaded with thought-provoking questions, tools, and tangible habit-creating exercises to help folks explore these three questions, helping them tap into their Inner Giggle and engage in a more meaningful and flourishing life."

—Nasha Winters, ND, FABNO, Executive Director
of The Metabolic Terrain Institute of Health

"*Happier Being* is brilliantly simple and powerfully effective. In a time where everyone wants to make everything complicated, Dr. Tal has gifted us with a complex systems blueprint for living a happier life. As I read her impactful perceptions and experience the suggested strategies, I feel the epigenetics of happiness moving through the human system, informing it of possibilities once believed to be out of reach. This is a must read for fully living Happier Being!"

—Dr. Mickra Hamilton, CEO, Aperion Zoh Corporation

"Relationships are key to success but that's not all, they are key to health and happiness too. I am thrilled to see Dr. Tal dedicate a whole chapter to the importance of deeper relationships and social connections in her practical, insightful, and entertaining book, *Happier Being*."
—Michelle Tillis Lederman, author of
The Connector's Advantage and *The 11 Laws of Likability*

"If you're searching for a road map to more meaning, connection, and laughter in your life, this book is for you. Using positive psychology, Dr. Tal shines a light on happiER. It's not about where you're starting, it's about how you learn to optimize your everyday well-being. If you want a jumpstart on happiness, I recommend this book."
—Louisa Jewell, MAPP, author of *Wire Your Brain for Confidence: The Science of Conquering Self-doubt*; Founder and President of the Canadian Positive Psychology Association

"This is a great step-by-step plan for building positive emotions. I like the way it guides you to dive deeper into the painful layers of your past in order to reframe your reality. The author's breadth of experience makes it fun to read."
—Loretta Breuning, PhD, Professor and Founder of the Inner Mammal Institute; author of *Habits of a Happy Brain*

"A compelling, practical, wisdom-filled read for anyone wanting to lead a more hopeful life. As happiness habits are our second key to Hope and cultivating a hopeful mindset, I can't stress enough how important it is to practice the habits of happiness. As hope is a known protective factor for anxiety and depression, this book is a great read for anyone struggling with mental health and/or other health issues. As a psychologist, Dr. Tal offers an inside look at research and strategies to improve your happiness levels, impacting all aspects of life. The book is filled with inspiring personal and professional stories and is accompanied by tools for anyone looking to become a happier being."
—Kathryn Goetzke, MBA, Founder at The Mood Factory, iFred, and Innovative Analysis; United Nations Representative for the World Federation for Mental Health

"This book is a landmark contribution to holistic mental health. After reading *Happier Being* you will think more consciously about the decisions you're making every day. For someone who has spent a lifetime coping with depression, anxiety, chronic stress and relationship issues, I truly believe Dr. Tal's book provides great tools to help live life with more ease and joy. A truly marvelous read filled with personal, inspiring accounts!"
—Trina Wyatt, MBA, Founder and CEO of Conscious Good

"In her well-researched yet lively and engaging book, *Happier Being*, Dr. Tal makes the case that happiness is rather built than found, and she provides her reader with clear guidelines on how to achieve that aspiration by aligning mind and body through nutrition, movement, and sleep. If you want a book that explains both the psychology of human behavior and the practical ways you can start applying positive habits, this is the book for you."
—Marc Philouze, Managing Director at Gnosis by Lesaffre

"If you are seeking a dazzling, innovative, and jubilant approach to sustainable happiness, if the answer is yes, then start reading *Happier Being* immediately. As Dr. Tal puts it, 'happier' is an internal process that is cultivated every moment. *Happier Being* offers you the psychological insights and the practical habits for achieving this state! The ripple effects of your newfound happiness will not only affect your personal success but the success of all those around you. This 'Inner Giggle' is transformative."
—Suresh Devnani, MBA, PhD, Consultant and Speaker on workplace happiness, well-being, and DEI; bestselling author

"Dr. Tal's book, *Happier Being*, is inspiring and insightful. The book presents scientific findings about happiness, ranging from Easterlin's Paradox to the latest research in neuroplasticity, in an accessible and useful format. Readers are given permission, rationale, and means for changing how they think, their habits, and their orientation towards happiness with Dr. Tal's concept of the Inner Giggle. This book feeds the intellectual side of the reader with its concise explanations of the latest research, and the emotional side with its guidance, encouragement, and tools for more happiness in life."
—Laura Musikanski, Executive Director of the Happiness Alliance

Most people hope to be happier.

This book is for those ready to actualize their Happier Being™.

Happier Being™ is both the how and the why for a life worth living. How? You become happier by intentionally optimizing your being every day. Why? Being happier is the ultimate booster to your success and satisfaction.

CONTENTS

Happiness Redefined:
Reclaiming Your Inner Giggle™

"We're Going In!"

The clear azure waters of the Mediterranean lapped at the rocks just a few feet from our table. There were few tourists in this little corner of Greece, and so we were dining in relative isolation at a secluded restaurant. The afternoon was stiflingly hot, but none of us had bathing suits; we hadn't planned to swim that day. Suddenly my husband and I locked eyes, and he said what I was thinking: "The water looks very inviting. Are we going in?" I replied with a smile. Before our two twenty-something daughters could stop us, we began stripping. Within moments we were in our underwear.

With our fifty-year-old bodies and fifteen-year-old mindsets, we tiptoed over the pebbles toward the surf. There, we plunged into the cool water with abandon and giggled, knowing our daughters were behind us looking for a rock to crawl under. Oh, the liberation and uninhibited joy we felt! It was like being kids again – fun and spontaneous and fully enjoying the moment together.

It also brought up a cascade of memories. My husband reminded me that I used to walk barefoot outside, sleep right by the water when we went camping, and swim with dolphins. How much more relaxed I was, he said. I listened to him and wondered where the woman he was talking about had gone.

Remembering Your Inner Giggle

What I realized that day, playing outside some Greek seaside restaurant whose name I'll never remember, was how much I'd missed my Inner Giggle™ – what I call that intuitive ability to be present and playful in the moment in a way that aligns personal meaning with pleasure. I hadn't lost it exactly, but I hadn't been prioritizing it either. As I'd moved through adulthood, I'd neglected to nourish the sense of joy that came so naturally when I was a child and young adult. I was very busy being a responsible, hardworking, and intermittently stressed-out psychologist and mother.

•   •   •

I was – we all are – born Happier Beings. We start out fully engaged in what we're doing, tuning out everything else, and as a result, we experience life more as a state of flow.[1] But something happens to us as we age. Perhaps we forget what kids know on an innate level – that being immersed in the present moment is good for us. Maybe we've learned things about life that sap our ability to have or even notice magical moments. Sometimes our thinking, feelings, and choices chip away at our ability to be happier. Sometimes our unhappiness is rooted in the stories we tell ourselves about life.

Inner Giggle experiences put us back in touch with that younger, more exuberant self – our original Happier Being. These moments don't have to be grand, or initiate an epiphany, in order to remind us of the pleasure of being in the present and invite us to visit more often.

Thinking about it, I realized I didn't know if I could sustain that expansive, joyful feeling of stripping and dashing into the sea. But I began to realize that giving myself permission to be freer, happier more often, no matter what else was going on, was something I wanted to reclaim. After spending more than twenty years working as a psychologist, there is one thing I'm sure of: everyone can augment their happiness. In Greece, on vacation, I was reminded that I am no exception.

I have been privileged to support and witness the remarkable ability of human beings to grow despite their struggles and to change regardless of circumstances. For years my clinical work as a psychologist focused on mentally ill patients whose emotional pain was severe enough to find themselves in and out of a hospital. It was hard work and I loved it. Eventually I moved to private practice, helping clients dealing with depression, anxiety, chronic physical stress and pain, and work or relationship issues. They were managing better than my hospitalized patients had been, but their low-grade, chronic emotional and physical pain was robbing them of happiness. It was a trend I could see not just among my clients but in the general population. I began to consider that their increasingly limited ability to recognize and experience moments of true joy had something to do with it.

I noticed that, though most of my clients made progress with their struggles, some of them didn't show increased happiness commensurate with that relief. Of course, suffering fewer negative emotions lifted their mood and increased their overall well-being, but they still didn't feel appreciably happier or more fulfilled. I came to realize that the important work here isn't just about what you take away – depression, anxiety, a broken heart – but what is added back in. Namely, what I decided to call the Inner Giggle. Once I began focusing on this work, I've been able to move my clients from simply functioning to flourishing. Flourishing is always the goal.

The Inner Giggle is the key to rediscovering your Happier Being. It's in what satisfies your inner purpose and brings joy to your life. This kind of happiness comes from trying and striving to do your best every day; from connecting to your intentions and feeling good. An easy way to think of your Inner Giggle is within the implications of those two words: "Inner" equating to your personal meaning and "Giggle" equating to pleasure.

Being happier is about learning to boost your positive emotions and energize whatever is working well. As you begin to recognize your strengths and talents, you'll discover what you might be lacking and what you can develop to help you thrive. That's why, throughout this book, we'll not only be looking at what needs to be taken out of your life but also – most importantly – at what you can add back into it to improve your happiness level. Happier Being is an all-encompassing concept that leads to optimism and feeling empowered to shift your mindset for growth. By developing your Inner Giggle, you will realize you have the control and autonomy to change – to become happier.

By the end of this book, you'll know that more joy is within your reach – within all of our reach – and that how to find it can come easily, once you learn some simple, happiness-boosting habits. This will, in turn, improve other aspects of your life – your relationships, work, and energy. There is so much research, which I'll be sharing with you, that proves happiness is the ultimate currency. I say use it. Make spending it your best habit!

If you want to more easily manifest and manage positive change in any aspect of your life, you'll want to learn how to be a Happier Being. And the exciting part is that the Inner Giggle concept is an example of how life needs to be. Combining the serious aspect of it, your inner world, with the fun aspect of it, that which can make you giggle.

Why Evolve Your Inner Giggle? Not Just Happiness

If being happier is the goal, the Inner Giggle is a tool to get there. But neither term represents a semantic shift. They are, instead, mental shifts that help you create your unique definition of happiness and your personal ways of boosting it. This is about tapping into what you find personally meaningful and pleasurable, about directing you away from merely pursuing general happiness to specifically pursuing the aspects of it *unique to you*. Your Inner Giggle becomes something you can almost reach out and touch: it becomes more tangible.

You feel this tangible response in your mind and body. And no matter how small or fleeting that response, it affects your energy – an unmistakable sign that you just got happier. You're in the moment, experiencing life through your own lens of happiness. Your Inner Giggle is your clear response to something that moved you, that made you stop and happily reflect for a few seconds longer. The Inner Giggle is really about the satisfaction of experiencing yourself giving it your all daily. You *feel* it. You are energized by the feeling. It immediately creates a warm physical sensation you know and love. It focuses your mind and mutes the unnecessary noises. It releases tension and softens your posture. It can bring back certain memories or inspire cherished dreams. Most importantly, it endures – even through hardship.

You probably know by now that you can't think your way to happiness. You can't meditate, shop, have sex, work, or gym your way to it either. You might feel happy when your favorite sports teams come out on top, but that's a more universal feeling. That kind of happiness is pleasurable and an important part of your Inner Giggle – but it's also fleeting and somewhat impersonal. The most effective parts of your Inner Giggle are inherently personal. Its meaning is uniquely yours and encompasses deeper parts within yourself. This kind of happiness is about striving to optimize who you are and who you can be.

So how do you know if you've felt this kind of happiness? Here's context that might help:

> **You feel the full scope of your Happier Being when your wishes, thoughts, and behaviors align with your values and character strengths – the things that mean the most to you and are integrally a part of you.**

This isn't about assembling a list of your psychological abilities. That's the old textbook way of thinking. Instead, this is about understanding what makes you tick: your thought patterns, your emotional makeup, your strengths, even your weaknesses and roadblocks, and using those aspects to charge your positive energy every day. Happier Being is a force for good in your life, so it's vital to prioritize it. This simple shift of the lens through which you operate holds amazing outcomes for you and makes every day much more enjoyable. Even when things aren't going well. Especially when things aren't going well.

Feeling Your Inner Giggle

What does your Inner Giggle feel like? Recognizing how you experience it in your body is important in order to further connect and integrate that feeling with your happiness. Your embodied Inner Giggle might start when something surprising, pleasant, funny, absurd, unexpected, meaningful, or interesting reaches your mind. From there, it travels down to your heart, where it causes you to feel emotionally different in a positive way. Finally, you have a physical sensation that changes the energy vibration throughout your whole body. This might make you giggle out loud, or you might feel it resonate within your being. This is your Inner Giggle.

**We all have experienced our Inner Giggle at some point,
though it might have been a while for you. I'd like you to pause
for a moment, close your eyes, and conjure up a moment
when you heard your Inner Giggle loud and clear.**

Can you remember it? Hold onto it. In fact, I encourage you to use this memory of what your Inner Giggle feels like as you work on your happiness levels using the ideas and practices in this book. Once you've adopted your version of your Inner Giggle, the inherent duality of the term – what brings you meaning and pleasure – symbolizes and identifies what you are striving for. You become aware of your inner world, enriching it, connecting to it, healing it, and never again neglecting to address and nourish your joy, your senses, and your energy.

You can also think of your "Inner" as referring to your darker self, darker in the sense that it is a less lit, less seen side of your personality. Because the deeper you dive into your psychology, the less light you have, initially. The Giggle is the lighter side, the sense of lifting yourself up. Therefore, your focus is on bringing some inner lightness into your life and acknowledging that you have the power to do this by choosing your mindset. This might sound complex, but it isn't, and this book will guide you through creating all the energy-boosting habits that promote your Inner Giggle and safeguard your Happier Being.

It's simple too. Although by simple, I don't mean easy, but instead I mean intuitive enough for anyone to follow. The process starts with self-awareness. You begin to focus on crafting your life with all the gifts and challenges handed to you through the lens of your Inner Giggle. You'll find that you get into the habit of asking yourself, is this going to energize my Happier Being? This conscious way of thinking, feeling, and acting to answer this powerful question, will guide you in your quest to reach a healthy balance between pleasure and meaning in your life – especially during hard times.

If this sounds good to you, I hope you delve into this book with enthusiasm and the goal of changing your mindset around your Happier Being. By developing your Inner Giggle, you'll begin to understand what Happier Being means to you, work toward it, and experience more fulfillment, connections, joy, and the energy to sustain it all.

Journal

On this journey to discover your Inner Giggle, I'd suggest keeping your preferred journal application or a notepad nearby, so you can make notes, use the journal prompts, and document the rise of your Inner Giggle and the changes it brings to your life.

Prioritizing Your Inner Giggle

I developed my concept of the Inner Giggle after I was diagnosed with Lyme Disease about a decade ago. Lyme is a tick-born disease, and its diagnosis is difficult to pin down, as the symptoms often mimic other conditions. After going from one expert to the other, and finally having been given the correct diagnosis, I still had no idea what contracting this disease meant for me or how long it would take to get better. I just knew I had migraines, body pain, and an annoying loss of cognitive function – more specifically, my ability to express myself. Words have always been important to me. I have always felt their power and loved to turn a phrase into something more significant or funny to make myself or others laugh. But suddenly, I had a hard time finding the words. I was often too tired to speak, and when I did, the words weren't at all what I meant to say. That's when I started to lose track of my Inner Giggle – and my connection to myself as a Happier Being.

One day a neighbor of ours, a cute little boy, rang our doorbell hoping to sell some candy bars to raise money for his school. He had an adorable little speech ready the moment I opened the door. Unfortunately, his vocal pitch was extremely high, and in his excitement he was speaking very loudly – almost to the point of shouting. Even more unfortunately, my husband was still sleeping, and I didn't want the little boy's top-of-his-lungs enthusiasm to wake him up.

I hurriedly told the boy that I'd be willing to buy one from him, but if so, he'd have to whisper. He looked at me funny, but he kept talking, hoping to seal the deal. I could not understand for the life of me why he was still talking loudly. Somewhat frustrated by the situation, I told him again: "Just please whisper!"

To my consternation, the boy immediately stopped shouting – and starting *whistling*. Now I was the one who was confused. After all my requests for quiet this little jokester started whistling! But the comparative quiet was a boon, so I rushed into the house, grabbed a couple bucks, swapped them for a candy bar, and sent the cute little whistling boy on his way.

My youngest daughter, who'd been home the whole time and was listening to the commotion approached me as I closed the door. She had the kind of subdued smile on her face every mother knows (the one that's itching to make fun of what you just did or said and holding back laughter at the same time). She then informed me that while I thought I was telling the boy to "whisper" I was actually begging him to "whistle"! I looked at my youngest for a few seconds, the keys turning in my brain until I heard a click, and I realized what just happened.

While this confusion was a result of my mental fatigue and chronic pain, we both erupted in unstoppable laughter. Eventually we collected ourselves enough to wonder if our little neighbor boy was still whistling his way around the neighborhood. I hoped I hadn't startled him too much! But he made his sale, and I got to laugh with my daughter. I think it was a win-win.

You can't control everything in your life, but you can make the choice to find your Inner Giggle in spite of your challenges. This is the goal.

Of course, it can be difficult to do at times. Compared to looking after your health and making sure your basic needs are met, happiness may sometimes feel like a bonus. However, research has documented that those who are happier live more pleasurable, meaningful, and purposeful lives.[2] That makes sense. And there's a significant cumulative effect. When you actively participate in allowing yourself to be happier more often – no matter at what point or stage of your life you are – you boost your experience of joy, contentment, love, pride, and awe, and improve your energy levels over time. Being happier improves your immune system, your engagement with work and with other people, and your physical and mental health. It boosts your confidence and self-esteem. At work, employers experience lower turnover with happier employees, more job satisfaction, and better performance leading to higher wages. It can also lead to better recovery from illness or injury. And on and on.

You don't have to be cheery and bubbly by nature to increase your experienced joy. You don't have to indulge in pleasant things all the time to be happier. You don't even have to be happy all the time! I feel unhappy, frustrated, hurt, and blue at times. It's not realistic to think you can avoid negative emotions 24/7 and live only in the positive ones. But if you take the time to prioritize your happiness, you can experience more positive emotions more often, making your life measurably better.

In fact, there is evidence that becoming happier first will bring rewards (like a better job, better relationship, better financial situation) that we usually think will make us happier only once we've achieved them. Shawn Achor, a professor at Harvard who studies happiness, claims that we need to reverse the happiness formula. He talks about our perception of becoming happy: Hard Work + Success = Happiness. When in reality, the order should be flipped: Happiness + Hard Work = Success.[3] In essence, happiness is not an end goal but something we need to prioritize first. If we prioritize happiness, we, in turn, do better work and can become more successful. At the end of the day, if you're not happy, it doesn't matter how successful you are.

In essence, Shawn Achor's work suggests that rather than getting what you want in order to be happy, you need to focus on your happiness to get what you need in life (once again, reversing the happiness formula). This is because happiness gives you an advantage, a leg-up on life, so to speak. When you prioritize happiness, you behave and act from a place of positivity and intention. You are more creative and can see solutions to your problems that you couldn't see before. You're also generally more productive and perform better when you're happier, leading to both greater satisfaction and success in life.

The advantage of reversing the happiness formula shows how vital it is to rethink the benefits of happiness. When you realize happiness is a resource you can tap into to achieve, produce, perform, and truly feel your best self, you're much more likely to prioritize it.

The truth? If you want to focus more on great results, happiness first will support any endeavor you choose to embark on.

This is extremely powerful knowledge, and your Inner Giggle will help you turn this around. You'll realize that while you can't control everything in your life, you can choose to find your Inner Giggle despite your challenges. The choice is yours, and this book will give you the tools to make a more joyful one.

ONE

The Winning Intersection of Happier Being:
Meaning and Pleasure

Prioritize Your Happiness *Now.*

You're probably thinking: *Of course I want to be happier every day — and now, not later. But there's a lot going on for me. How do I make happiness a priority?*

Here's the problem: When we don't prioritize happiness, we rob ourselves of day-to-day joy, put ourselves at a disadvantage, and suffer unnecessarily. I've seen this in my practice, where the people who come to me are dissatisfied with their lives but underestimate their power to change the circumstances that create this dissatisfaction. They are more willing to work on attaining some faraway but more tangible goal (say, buying a bigger house) than work on deepening their understanding of what makes life worth living. They neglect their Inner Giggle daily, then wonder why they are not happy.

Ask any parent what they hope for most for their child, and they tell you it's a happy life. But how often do we tell our kids that this is the most important expectation we have of them? And how about us, how often do we model this priority in our own behavior? Instead of behaving like we think happiness is the most important thing about life, we sacrifice today to busyness because we believe it will make us happier in the end. Unfortunately, it often doesn't.

But what if happiness became the new standard by which we judged our lives? What if happiness was declared the "new green"? What if you recognized the stark reality that not paying attention to your happiness will cause your health to decline, your relationships to deteriorate, and your productivity to diminish? What if that notion was codified in stone? Would you prioritize happiness then?

Doreen, a client of mine, was a busy wife and mother of four children. She worked in a job she hated, spending her days largely checked out and feeling unvalued and unfulfilled. She dreamed of being a writer and longed to feel that her voice mattered.

In our sessions, we identified that Doreen's adult life echoed her childhood growing up with seven siblings — and without a quiet place to call her own. Doreen didn't even feel she deserved a quiet place — that's just how things had always been. She was resigned to being unhappy until she had more time and space, but she wasn't motivated to create either for herself.

We worked on unpacking Doreen's routines, including how long she could keep working in an environment that wasn't nourishing her, or how many minutes she focused on herself (few to none at the time) every day. Slowly, she became more aware of just how long she was postponing being happier, in not just one but many aspects of her life.

Doreen began by changing her physical environment, as we agreed it was an obstacle to writing. She considered a few options, but an old empty barn on their property caught her eye. What if she could work bit by bit to create the space she had always dreamed of? By doing so, Doreen gave herself permission to have her own space, symbolizing and reinforcing the shift in her perspective on her formula of happiness. In essence, she dialed up her "deservability scale." She was deserving of this space, now, as she was deserving of her happiness, and she knew that slowly, she could make it work.

The barn was filled with old junk that needed clearing out before Doreen could get to work. Interestingly, Doreen was doing the same thing mentally — getting rid of old baggage about her having to postpone happiness. Doreen had finally given herself permission to prioritize her happiness, and nurturing her Inner Giggle meant she started deriving more meaning and joy in her life. So much so that Doreen quit her job and found work at a newspaper as a writer. The more connected she got to her inner world through the meaningful work she felt she was doing, the more pleasure she experienced, and the happier she became.

Like Doreen, you need to prioritize your Inner Giggle today, not tomorrow. Often, you push happiness aside, thinking it'll come later, and continue to do things you dislike because "that's just the way it is" or "others are worse off," or whatever words or phrases you like to chalk up your unhappy life situations to. You need to quit thinking that those time-deprived routines are acceptable and that one day you'll be happier, and instead make happiness an urgent and immediate goal. It's a psychological fact that you're likely to put off the tasks that may seem important but not necessarily urgent. I'm proposing that you make your happiness urgent. How often do you ask or say things like, "The car lease is up? Three years went by so quickly!" Or, "The kids are already off to college"? The answer is: too often.

Stop postponing. Bring happiness to the forefront of your life.

The Positive, Cascading Effects of Happiness

To help you further integrate the notion that you deserve happiness – engrave it in your DNA – I'd like to share some research into the benefits of Happier Being.

Sonja Lyubomirsky, in her book *The How of Happiness*, says happiness benefits not only those directly experiencing it but also those around them – family members, partners, and communities. Movie heroines who exude happiness (think Elle Woods in *Legally Blonde*) inspire the characters around her to become happier too, as well as the audience watching the film. This is because happiness is contagious.[4] When you prioritize happiness, you're giving yourself the chance to live the life you want – and you give others that opportunity too. Now, that's something worth trying!

Another study[5] from 2012 found that when employees from seven different Fortune 500 companies received an email with a gentle reminder to make happiness-enhancing decisions, they were far happier by the end of the week than those who didn't. Those decisions included going to their kids' baseball games, watching less TV, etc. Simple enough to do, but somehow the reminder to prioritize happiness encouraged them to make those decisions more often.

Happiness can even help you live longer. One study[6] looked at the lifespan of 178 nuns. It found that the happiest nuns lived an average of ten years longer than the least happy nuns. Additional research shows happiness can also help keep your immune system strong, help protect your heart from various diseases, and can even protect against strokes.

The Inner Giggle Is a Compass

Happiness is about the joy you get from opening up to your most enjoyable, meaningful potential in any given moment. It's not about reaching your potential per se, but like Doreen, being in the mode to optimize your experience. Your Inner Giggle zone is the relief within you that you did it: that tiny celebratory moment in which meaning and pleasure align to allow you a mental victory, be it big or small. This is especially true when you are challenged, out of balance, have health issues, or feel under emotional attack. It is then that being open to your best self increases your potential to feel happier.

What is the compass point or the North Star that keeps you moving in the direction of Happier Being? It is, of course, your Inner Giggle. When you learn to anticipate what triggers it, what types of things bring you joy, and what it feels like inside when you experience your Inner Giggle, it:

- Becomes your accountability partner, keeping you on track
- Protects you by flooding your mind and body with healthy energy
- Serves as positive emotional reinforcement that you did it right, again!
- Helps you not just do better but *be* better – *being happier*

Consider your Inner Giggle a mental compass that gently guides you toward Happier Being during the endless doing in your day. Like an ocean breeze, it oxidizes everything – it rejuvenates and refreshes but disturbs nothing. It creates a moment of clarity that helps you pause and bring relief — it feels good to act from your higher self. It reminds you to savor what connects you with how you want to show up in the world. Your Inner Giggle is happiness in its purest form: you think, feel, and experience yourself at peace. Realistically (reality being a space I hang out in often), we can't be at this optimal state all the time. So it's important to absorb, reflect on, and use your Inner Giggle as a compass any time you feel off. Use it to reboot and recharge yourself, changing your thinking and doing to keep striving for better so that you can keep tackling the goals/work/ path you're on.

Journal

Recognize when you are in your Inner Giggle zone by finishing these sentences:

- I am at my happiest when _______
- I feel I am following my inner meaning when I _______
- I enjoy myself the most when _______

Dispelling Happiness Fallacies

Happiness research makes a compelling case for prioritizing your Happier Being. But the literature and our culture are also full of happiness fallacies. Let's address them.

Fallacy #1: Born That Way
You may believe that people are born happy or unhappy, but that's not true. Happiness is a muscle, something you can strengthen, rather than being set or stagnant. Surely, some people are born with the ability to more easily build muscle — but anyone can increase their muscle strength if they have the right tools. In fact, research shows that your happiness set point, your innate set point for the capacity to be happy, accounts for about fifty percent of your happiness level. Your specific life circumstances amount to another ten percent. This leaves forty percent of your happiness being made up of your intentional behavior. This forty percent is where your Inner

Giggle finds its power, because within it you get to choose how to be, what to focus on, and how to follow your goals.

The part of your happiness you have direct control over lies in your daily intentional activities. Forty percent control is a high percentage, right? Knowing that your level of happiness can increase dramatically as a result of your intentional mindset and actions is a powerful motivator to work on your Happier Being. It is where you have room to maneuver – to increase or decrease your happiness levels by what you do and how you think every day. And the ripple effect of its positive influence on your life grows and expands as you move toward it.

So what are these habits? We'll learn about them in the chapters that follow.

Fallacy #2: Reaching a Milestone

You might believe that happiness means maximizing pleasure by self-indulgence. That's what the philosophers call hedonism – sex, drugs, and rock and roll might spring to mind. But we know that's fleeting happiness. It might be fun, and it is certainly important to experience, but it doesn't last or encompass all of what happiness is about. The term eudaimonic well-being, on the other hand, is a fancy way of describing the type of happiness that comes from living a life full of growth, purpose, and meaning. As it turns out, the Greeks who investigated the length of a good life discovered what current science has shown – pleasure and meaning are intricately linked. Moreover, living in line with your eudaimonic standards, practicing your values, and aspiring for excellence leads to flourishing living.

Does this mean you always have to operate from a place of eudaimonic well-being? Shouldn't you avoid the fun things that may be fleeting? Not at all! The brilliant part is that you don't have to choose just one way of life. It doesn't have to be an either/or situation – it can be both. By defining your Inner Giggle, you can tap into how life works best for you on both sides. The pleasure side and the meaningful side of life. The good life is a combination of optimizing both.

A common phenomenon is crucial to note here, namely, something called the hedonic adaptation. Humans tend to quickly return to their baseline level of happiness, even as they experience major positive or negative life events. We might buy the house we wanted, graduate college, or finally score that promotion, and get a boost of happiness – but it's doesn't last long. We tend to get used to that new, good thing faster than we think we will, and then find ourselves wanting more. A new happy thing. This is called "the hedonic treadmill," which brings me to the third fallacy.

Fallacy #3: Not Enough Money

Most of us think more money will bring us more happiness. Moreover, we assume that the increase in happiness level will be directly proportional to the increase in income. Research shows that beyond a certain point, however, that this simply isn't true. Studies in the US show that daily well-being does not show any statistically significant increases after someone reaches $75,000 of annual household income. While this figure has received a good deal of attention, people tend to miss that almost all the gains in daily well-being associated with income occur below $40,000.

Essentially, a certain income level is necessary for food, shelter, and preventing daily worries. But once you've reached that basic level of financial security, whatever that amount seems to be for you, the incremental growth in happiness levels is not proportionally correlated. That means that if your yearly income doubles from $40,000 to $80,000, you will feel a significant increase in overall well-being. But if your income is already $100,000 and doubles, your increase in happiness may not necessarily double, or be felt as significantly.

We see this in lottery winners. They return to their previous set point of satisfaction a few months to a couple of years after winning the big bucks. This is, again, due to the hedonic treadmill or hedonic adaptation, wherein we rather quickly return to a relatively stable level of happiness.[7] Winning the lottery may raise your standard of living but doesn't necessarily increase your happiness set point.

Baffling as these results may be (and personally, I often have a wave of skepticism reading these findings), I hope they make you pause and reevaluate any old ways of thinking about the fallacy of money and your happiness.

Surely, there will always be different life scenarios where more money will make a significant difference in your, or your family's, overall well-being. For example, if you have a child who would like to attend college and have no funds for it, extra money makes a big difference. Or if you have a loved one that fell ill, and the financial burdens have increased substantially, your well-being will suffer. Nevertheless, the point of all the above income-related statistics is to direct you away from falling blindly for the myth of the direct correlation between having more and more money and its potential effect on your happiness levels. More money can provide more security and a better sense of agency and ease in life, which can safeguard some level of well-being. And depending where you are globally, its effect on your well-being might differ. But regardless of culture, it does not guarantee the highest level of happiness. Happiness does not rise indefinitely with the rising of your income.

The good news is that more and more of us are awakening and understand that a life spent pursuing more and more money can, ironically, rob us of happiness. The shift from prioritizing money for its own sake to using it as a utility vehicle to expand our experiences or to make a difference in the world to lower suffering and enhance the good, is rising to the top of our collective happiness scale, and that is a good thing.

John had a house in Malibu overlooking the ocean and the most amazing cars you could imagine. His materialistic achievements were many; nevertheless, he worked really hard to upgrade what he already had. We often talked about the concept of the hedonic treadmill. He understood it, but he had a hard time getting off it. He often felt the need to conquer one more thing to feel complete.

During one session, John told me about an important meeting in Vegas he had to attend. He wanted to arrive on a private plane. If he could just step out of that plane to go to his meeting, he thought, he'd finally feel like he made it. But on the way to the airport, his car broke down, forcing him to get a taxi instead. At the airport, the pilot informed him they wouldn't take off until the next day due to some technical difficulties. So John decided to set up a nice limousine ride instead, as he could not afford to be late for his meeting. When he got into the limo, he realized he left his luggage in the taxi, and at that point, surrendered to any idea of showing up to the meeting the way he wanted.

Funny enough, in our next session, John told me that the TV screen in the back of the limo showed the same commercial over and over again, one featuring a woman running on a treadmill. Finally it clicked: it was a symbolic message. He could endlessly fantasize about the next best thing, trying to one-up himself, but in the end, he didn't need the extra flashiness to feel as though he had made it. Reflecting on the Inner Giggle he had just found, he smiled in our session and said, "I needed to stop chasing the next best thing. I was already there! So for the rest of the limo ride, I felt how everything from our sessions was crystalizing in that tiniest of TV screens in front of my eyes. One of the best commercials I have ever seen!"

For John, this moment became the reality check that he needed. His mood for the rest of our session vacillated between deep insight to self-entertainment as he allowed himself to enjoy his Inner Giggle. He was becoming a Happier Being.

Fallacy #4: Happiness Is Someplace You Reach

I hope you're starting to see that happiness – or your psychological wealth – is a process, not a place. You won't get it by acquiring your exact, fantasized circumstances or obtaining one more thing – whether that's money, marital status, or weight loss.

Happiness is truly an intrinsic journey. Instead of being conditioned solely by external circumstances, it's often conditioned by internal choices.

Such choices often align with things you care about (your values, your purpose) and allow you to feel a sense of joy and pleasure. The ultimate goal is then to successfully focus your attention on the meaningful parts of your life, despite challenges and setbacks.

If you approach your Inner Giggle from this optimal standpoint, you begin to make it your most important life habit. You guard it while using it to infuse your life with positive emotions, meaning, engagement, and pleasure. Approaching life satisfaction from this process mindset will also make it more likely you'll achieve your goals. This is because prioritizing your happiness necessitates the optimization of all aspects that matter most in life, including your health, wealth, and relationships.

In this process of gaining more control over your happiness, as I mentioned earlier, your Inner Giggle becomes your accountability partner. If you no longer feel it, you know that more work needs to be done in one aspect of your life or another in order to experience it more often. Your Inner Giggle informs you about the habits you have to create, and it also guides you through optimizing them. Your Inner Giggle is part of your routine every day. Granted, some days it may be easier to access, other days more complex. Nevertheless, it represents the subtotal of all the energy boosted by the right habits you practice. And we could all use more positive energy in our lives, physical and mental.

Fallacy #5: Not Deserving of Happiness

In order to become more energized by tapping into your Inner Giggle, you'll also need to become aware of any mental obstacles. Beyond the existential obstacles to happiness, such as the need for safety, shelter, food, health care, and the like, there are psychological obstacles too. Among these psychological obstacles are negative beliefs and misconceptions about happiness. You may not even realize you hold onto them, but these misconceptions are actually pretty common. For example, do you believe your happiness is selfish? Were you raised with the notion that happiness is earned only after sacrifice? Do you think that focusing on being happier makes you complacent? Do you sometimes wonder if it's moral to nourish your happiness when so many people are starving in the world or when there are countries engaged in armed conflict or during a global pandemic?! And what about pollution, discrimination, endangered species, global warming, and terrorism? The media constantly reinforces your sense of doom – with dire urgency. After all, positive news does not attract many media viewers. How can you possibly become any happier with all of that going on?

Okay, I'd like you to take a breath and know that someone else's suffering doesn't take away from your own (nor does your suffering diminish anyone else's pain). And as such, neither should take away from your privilege to be happy. Remember, these types of thoughts are negative beliefs and misconceptions about happiness, they're unconscious conflicts that you (and many of my clients) picked up somewhere along the way. At the heart of it, they're psychological obstacles to your flourishing. More so, your active practice of happiness will make you the best version of your happy self so that you can make a difference in the lives of others (save the planet, end child hunger, be a better parent, whatever your calling may be).

It is in challenging times that becoming a Happier Being through finding your Inner Giggle becomes even more important. This issue will be further elaborated later in the book.

To help you thrive, I will introduce tools that will assist you to become aware of the psychological obstacles you might be facing on your way to optimizing your happiness and self-actualization. You may need to break some old habits and adopt a new mindset to help you nurture your Happier Being, so let's explore that next.

Recap

- Your Inner Giggle is the experienced intersection of meaning (inner) and pleasure (giggle) in your life – it is the purest form of happiness.
- Unlike fleeting happiness, your Inner Giggle is based on intrinsic values and character strengths.
- Your Inner Giggle is a muscle that needs to be worked on, and a tool that can and should be utilized every chance you get.
- Stop postponing and start prioritizing experiencing your Inner Giggle more often. It will increase your positive emotions, and happiness will follow.
- Use your Inner Giggle as a mental compass that guides you through your day – optimizing both the ups and downs.
- Remember to dispel any fallacies you have about happiness (refer to the five fallacies) as they are roadblocks to optimizing your happiness – which is your birthright!

Bonus information and mental training exercises relating to this chapter can be found here: happierbeing.com/exercises

TWO

The Power of New Habits

Create Lasting Habits and Build Your Desired Identity

When was the last time you felt truly energized and ready to take on the world? When was the last time you felt the kind of energy that needs a deep and restful night's sleep to flourish? I bet it's been some time since you've felt fully charged. So let's explore the physical happiness habits you can develop to optimize your energy and energize your Inner Giggle. As it turns out, the way we treat our bodies has a huge impact on our ability to be happier, and there are three core practices that our bodies need to thrive. These Inner Giggle energy boosters are:

- Eating
- Sleeping
- Moving

If you choose to optimize your Inner Giggle energy boosters (which I'll be sharing later in the book), you'll begin to experience positive changes in your well-being – because when you have the energy to keep going, you'll be able to show up as your best self in mind, body, and soul. As someone who's dealt with chronic illness thanks to my challenges with Lyme Disease, I know what it's like to be energy depleted, and I know what it's like to regain energy. The shift in showing up in the world is tremendous.

Part of the reason I've learned to value boosting physical energy so much is because it's an Inner Giggle booster like no other. Regardless of your circumstance, everyone benefits greatly when boosting these fundamental eating, sleeping, and moving habits. The Giggle part of your Inner Giggle, the joy you experience from boosting it, happens in the present. Keep this pleasurable part front and center while working on your habits, as it is up to you to find that joy while practicing them. Moreover, it is a crucial aspect of your ability to sustain the new behavior.

And, as you will read in the energy booster chapters to come, when you optimize them, you give yourself a chance to thrive, you boost your resilience in life, and you narrow the gap between the present you and the happiest you.

The Anatomy of New Habit Creation

Habits are the behaviors you engage in every day without having to make a conscious decision. They are the choices you deliberately made at some point and the actions you want to keep doing. By repeating them often, you stop needing to contemplate whether to do them each day or not. You just do them automatically, like brushing your teeth every night or having that cup of coffee in the morning. At some point, you consciously chose to brush your teeth or drink coffee. Now they are habits.

Your Habits Make You Who You Are

According to researchers at Duke University,[8] habits account for about forty percent of our behavior on any given day. Therefore, we can argue that in a sense about half of our respective lives is spent performing different habits. This means that the different elements of life, from health to money-spending practices, are all the results of your habits.

Will Durant,[9] who was an American writer, historian, and philosopher, wrote: "We are what we repeatedly do. Excellence, then, is not an act, but a habit." His words were used as a simple way of explaining some of Aristotle's contributions to philosophy, and they couldn't be more relevant. What you repeatedly do – i.e., what you spend time thinking about and doing each day – shapes the person you are, the things you believe, and the character you portray. Though it might be true that elements of your character were inherited from your parents, your way of being in the world today starts with your habits, and those habits shape how you approach your own life every day.

If you want to optimize your days and energy, it follows that you would want to identify the primary components of a habit. Many researchers have proven that the process of creating a habit is a three-step loop, and it goes like this:

Reminder: the cue/ trigger/ prompt or stimuli that initiates the behavior.
Routine: the behavior itself, what you do, the act, the thought.
Reward: the advantage you gain from doing the behavior.

As an example of a common habit, let's look at the process of answering one's door:

Reminder/Cue/Trigger: Doorbell sounds, and you walk toward the door.
Routine: Open the door.
Reward: Now you know who is there (and hopefully it's a welcome guest).

To simplify habit formation for a moment, we can say that if you want to create new habits, you have to figure out your "reminders" and "rewards" and then create new "routines." In order to succeed in creating your new habits, things like frequency, repetition, or the familiarity of the cues for a particular behavior all matter. But all that is just a part of habit creation.

To create new habits, the habits themselves have to carry intrinsic motivation. In other words, if you want to create a habit, that habit has to align with your values and be meaningful enough to create lasting, positive change in your life. You don't want to try and create a habit just because it's the latest fad or to satisfy someone else's wishes for you (even if they're well-intentioned). You need to choose habits that are personally unique and self-motivating. In this way, the habits better align with your overall aim of boosting your Happier Being, and the reward will be worth your efforts. After all, connecting to your Inner Giggle, psychologically and physically, has the promised benefit of helping you be the best version of yourself.

Journal

Common sense does not always lead to common action. But does common knowledge make doing things easier? No, you still need to become strategic with your specific plans to execute your new and improved habits! Write it down, commit, and reap the benefits of your own behavior.

Overcoming Resistance

Increasing your Inner Giggle energy boosters by creating new habits can be a difficult process – and this is largely due to resistance to change. You've probably had the experience of setting a New Year's resolution, only to see it fall apart pretty quickly. Am I right? There was a part of you that set a goal, that really wanted the results of the new habit, but there was another part of you that dreaded doing it or struggled with the growing pains. Let us get acquainted with those two conflicting parts, and explore ways to reconcile them when you set out to create new habits.

These two parts of you/your brain are what social psychologist Jonathan Haidt calls the "elephant" and the "rider" (the rider of the elephant).[10] The elephant part of your brain's response is automatic, emotional, and irrational. This part thrives on short-term satisfaction – like eating a whole chocolate bar by yourself. The other part of your brain, the rider, has a response that is controlled, analytical, and rational. This part thrives on calculating your actions. For example, contemplating the amount of sugar or dairy in the bar and its effect on your weight.

The problem is that the elephant is so much larger that the rider often has a hard time steering it in the desired direction. Hence, the rider may conclude that it's better to have only a few pieces of chocolate, while at the same time the elephant is shouting at the rider, "Eat it all!" This is why it can be so hard to change your behavior. So how do you make the switch? How do you get the rider and elephant to work together? Haidt introduces three simple steps to begin changing our behavior. We'll be using these steps to change our habits:

First, you have to tell the rider where you want to go. Map out the cues of the behavior you want to change (What tools and techniques do you have to prepare to get there? Do you need to secure support?). Second, you have to motivate the elephant by tapping into your emotional side (any small reward or win along the way triggers positive emotions and motivates the elephant to continue). And lastly, remove any roadblocks that the rider and the elephant might experience on their path (eliminate temptations, distractions, and anything that makes it harder to stick to your long-term plan).

You might be thinking, *I've tried to stay on the path, but it's tougher for me than for others. Other people have better self-control and willpower than I do.* I hear you. But as much as I believe that there are some innate variabilities when it comes to self-control, the truth here might surprise you.

> **People with a lot of self-control don't necessarily have more willpower than others. They've simply learned not to rely on willpower alone to stick with a plan – especially during times of stress.**

Let me explain further: People with a lot of self-control use their willpower wisely. They might use some of it to initiate a new habit, but over time they trust the habit to reinforce itself and become automated. The automatic habit they've formed guides both elephant and rider and keeps them on their intended path. It's the automation that acts as the fuel that keeps them going, not their willpower. Worth repeating? Yes. Not their willpower.

Willpower in Decision-making and Habit Formation

It turns out that willpower is limited. You can run out of it! And you don't want to find yourself in that position. Have you ever noticed that you are able to eat well for most of the day but suddenly you don't have the willpower to resist temptations by midday or evening? Contrary to what you might have been told, it's not only due to the physiological drop of glucose in your bloodstream or your being weak. It has to do with the finite nature of willpower. The fact is that you only have a certain amount of willpower per day. It therefore makes sense to know how to keep track of it, what uses it up, and how you drain your willpower during the day.

One of the biggest willpower energy drains is decision-making. All day long, you make "who, what, where, when, why" decisions, from less important ones – such as what detergent to buy – to more important ones – like the choice to keep reading this section about willpower. It's no surprise that by the end of the day you are left with little willpower available to you.

How do you correct this energy depleting pattern? By automating your energy-boosting habits instead of having to dip into your "willpower reserves." In doing so, you develop better self-control. This means that by planning ahead, you can more easily and systemically go about your daily tasks – reserving energy and willpower for any unexpected tasks along the way.

Roy Baumeister and John Tierney put it nicely in their book *Willpower*:[11] "This freedom from making a decision, which comes from forming the habit, is crucial because when I have to decide – which often involves resisting temptation or postponing gratification – I tax my self-control."

Willpower is often associated with weight and eating habits. If you have weight issues, you may feel badly about your perceived lack of willpower and self-control over your appetite. But, as you now know, willpower isn't a hereditary trait that varies from human to human. You were not given less willpower to control your eating than the skinnier person next to you. Willpower is finite for everyone on every given day.

Those who might *seem* to have more willpower (perhaps they don't cave in to eating sweets at the end of the day) actually develop automatic habits to assist them in making better choices that are more in keeping with their health goals. These habits reduce the amount of tiring, daily decision-making from their lives and allow them to have better self-control. They learn how to create an environment that supports them. They figure out what pre-planning they need to put in place so they won't stray (see Chapter Six for more eating tips). This adaptation to healthier eating habits allows them – and can allow you – to consume the quantity and quality of food congruent with staying healthy.

As for those rainy days or bumps in the road when your habit formation is interrupted (and you know there will be days like this), you can take a small dip into your willpower reserves to navigate and regain control. Once you've worked on automating your habits, you'll have enough willpower left to carry you through – and then you'll get back on track. This insight is a significant force in your success in initiating and following your new habits. You must create them and feel your Happier Being emerging more and more every time you succeed. After all, this is what it is all about. You don't have to wait to become more self-disciplined. You are behaving as such by executing your habits.

A Quick Side Note: Taxing Your Willpower Under Physical Stress
If you're dealing with chronic physical stress (which we'll cover in Chapter Ten), this concept is critical. Unlike other people, you find yourself needing to make daily decisions regarding your health. That, as we've learned, taxes your willpower.

Let's use one of our energy fundamentals, moving, as an example. Suppose you start your day fatigued already. Since you have several different items on your to-do list, it will be tricky to rely on your few remaining willpower reserves to make good decisions about your commitment to move your body. But if you've already automated your movement routine, you have fewer decisions to make regarding your behavior and a better chance of following through. You know when, where, and how you expect yourself to move that day since you already established your preplanned/automated steps of action. That's why you must work on automating your energy-boosting routine – because, unlike your chronic physical stress, it is more in your control. I believe this is the only true way to get closer to the level of health you desire.

Sustaining New Habits and
Boosting Your Energy Fundamentals

Since your willpower is finite, it's important to pick only one habit at a time to start your transformation. Once you master a new habit to the point that it becomes automated and feels like second nature – whether it's an energy-boosting habit or something else – then you can move on to the next one. Don't try to master too many habits at once – this simply sets you up for failure. There may be small habits that you can work on simultaneously, but don't try to master more than three at a time.

Developing a new habit doesn't need to and probably shouldn't take up too much of your time. Numerous research studies show that if you practice a new habit for as little as ten minutes a week, it'll only take a few weeks to notice the difference.

Here are three hacks to help you on your way:

One-minute Habit

B. J. Fogg,[12] a behavior scientist at Stanford University, wrote a book called *Tiny Habits: The Small Changes That Change Everything*. In it, he outlines his theory of "tiny habits," based on breaking habits down into the smallest possible step – so small and simple that your brain will have a hard time negotiating you out of it. This is why I suggest the one-minute habit: a habit so easy to perform that you don't have to rely on motivation.

Let's say the energy fundamental you want to improve is sleeping. You decide you want to read before bed to relax instead of staring at your phone. Start by reading just a few paragraphs per night for a minute or less, and then gradually increase the number. This little bit of reading doesn't require much motivation, but it starts to get your brain accustomed to the routine.

Stacking Habits

You could also pair your new reading habit with an already automated habit – helping you anchor the new behavior by associating it with an existing one. If, for example, you always turn on your night light at bedtime, you could place your book next to it, thereby cuing yourself to read every time you go to turn it on. This is called stacking habits. As simple as it might seem, habit-stacking takes the decision-making process out of the equation, allowing you to preserve willpower, and automates the new habit. The more times you read before bed and feel refreshed in the morning, the more your brain reinforces the new habit, and the more you start craving that good feeling of also accomplishing your main goal: sleeping better.

Habit stacking is just another way to execute your "implementation intentions," an elegant term coined by psychologist Peter Gollwitzer.[13] Implementation intentions (when you make prior intentions of how you would implement your plan/goal) help you find anchors in your life that will increase the probability of performing any habit. They are often referred to as the "if/then" tool (i.e., if the kids brush their teeth, then it's time to pack their school lunches/read them a story). The more you design your habits around your daily routine, the more chances you'll have of following through on them.

Time and Place Habits

Cues/triggers for using the if/then tool can also be linked to a different aspect of your day, such as a specific location, time, your emotional state, or other people's influence. BJ Fogg suggests finding passive times, like waiting in the carpool to pick up your kids from school, waiting for your bus to arrive, or waiting for your hot water to reach the shower, and then spend it as a time to create a "meanwhile habit." Meanwhile habits are habits you can do as a quick add-on to things you plan to do – but in order to do these, you find yourself waiting for something to happen first. For example, one breath, one squat (though not in the shower!), one grateful thought. Any tiny behavior you can perform, or even part of the behavior you aspire to automate, can be practiced as a meanwhile habit. It can be used as a springboard moment to be doing something bigger than you did before.

Journal ⟶⟶

Make a list of the different tasks and habits you perform throughout the day—the things that trigger the if/then tool—and consider if there's a good time to either stack a habit or develop a habit into your routine. The more a part of your day-to-day and effortless you can make the new habit, the more automated it will become, and the more you'll be able to sustain it—even on those days you may be feeling more stressed than normal.

Your Pre-commitments

There is one more piece to sustaining habits, preserving willpower, and upgrading your Inner Giggle energy boosters – eating, sleeping, and moving energy fundamentals – and it is called your "pre-commitments." By these we mean the dos and don'ts when it comes to choices. Take, for example, eating habits. It's easier to avoid the temptation of sugary, processed food if it's not in your face, so don't buy a half tub of ice cream. Instead, buy your willpower at the store.[14] The same thing goes for when you're trying to create better sleeping habits, such as shutting off the TV before bed. Make sure the remote control is not easily accessible. Better yet, remove the TV from your bedroom.

These external pre-commitments to changing your environment will support your behavioral changes when forming a new habit. You pre-commit to making any negative behaviors as inconvenient as possible. That reduces temptation and increases your ability to reinforce the positive behavioral change you are aiming for. Another example, if you wanted to take a walk every morning, would be to lay out your walking gear (shoes, attire, water bottle, etc.) the night before. In doing so, you remove decision-making and negotiating with your motivation from the equation, and you're out the door faster.

By laying out your gear, you're laying out the path for yourself. I hope you're starting to pick up what I am laying down.

Being Consistent

There's another important pre-commitment to take into account: being consistent. Being consistent builds positive emotion, which in turn feeds your inclination to repeat a habit and positively shapes your identity. Let's look at how this works.

Build Positive Emotion to Help You Repeat the Habit
The more often you engage in your new habit, the more success you'll have. This, of course, feels fantastic. It also reinforces your behavior and drives you to repeat the habit. Interestingly the most important part of sustaining a habit isn't the mechanical act of repeating it – though it does, of course, play a big role. Instead, it's the positive emotions that arise from your successful, habitual behavior that create the automation and your ability to sustain it. So the better you are at eliciting this good feeling, the deeper the new behavior becomes grooved or wired into your brain. This, in turn, will make it a bit easier to do it the next time. It's a win-win loop. Celebrate any progress! This goes back to the third part of any habit loop, the reward, and

noticing the positive emotions derived from your success at building your habit is gold!

Building this kind of positive emotion – so you can build the new habit – is much easier when you avoid "cheat days." Your 100 percent commitment – which some call "bright lines" or "do or die" standards – makes it easier to feel good and follow through. For example, if you decide to hike every weekday, rain or shine, you *must* hike those five days. If you decide not to eat after 8 p.m., you don't eat after 8 p.m. Ever. It doesn't matter if you have guests over, if you're eating out or even traveling. These are your bright lines.

Yes, you are human, and life will have its bumps and stormy weather (hard to hike in a blizzard). Or there will be days where your attention will be pulled in different directions, (and you didn't get a chance to eat). But the aim is to make that 100 percent commitment despite it all. Having a total-commitment attitude will reinforce doing your best, despite the adversity you may be facing. Why? Because by staying committed to realistic goals, even on days you're struggling, you choose to keep focusing on your improvements, no matter how small they might be for the time being. Remember, there are plenty of scenarios where doing something is better than nothing (better to have gotten to bed as planned five days out of the week than none). But having the intention of one hundred percent creates the optimal framework to work from. The following section will elaborate on this.

Your pre-commitment to being consistent helps shape your identity

Consistency teaches you a lot about who you are. Just as observing others' behavior teaches you who they are, you learn about you by observing what you do. When you observe yourself engaging in habitual behavior, you watch your own transformation. Over time, you transform your self-perception, and your new habits start shifting your identity. This is huge! Every time you repeat the habit, you fill in the gap between your past and future selves.

> **Each time you experience yourself behaving as the type of person you want to be, you reassure and reinforce that identity formation.**

A handful of years ago I went to a positive psychology conference. I was in the midst of treatment for Lyme Disease, and it had been a particularly difficult month. But I felt it was important I attend. I saw it not as something that would drain my energy but as a way to improve myself and my practice, as well as connect with other like-minded professionals. That mindset helped me decide to go.

Every morning the hotel alarm clock would go off, signaling that it was time to practice ten minutes of meditation. Then I'd go downstairs, attend some lectures and workshops for the day, and mingle with others. It was physically challenging for me to sit for long periods of time on those uncomfortable conference room chairs, but I took breaks, I brought healthy snacks, and in between the days' events I practiced deep, diaphragmatic breathing for even just one minute at a time – no matter how badly I felt. I was practicing what I preach (which when successful, always makes me feel better).

On the very last day of the conference, and after a not-so-restful night's sleep, I came down to the main conference room. I was dressed for a winter storm, as usual (it's no secret that they freeze these rooms). I sat down next to a smiling lady, who looked at my garb and jokingly asked "Are you cold?"

We both chuckled and then got to chatting. Several minutes into the conversation, I learned that not only did we share being cold and being psychologists but that she also was struggling with chronic illness. I sympathized and ended up sharing my own struggles with her.

"Oh, so sorry you struggle with Lyme," she said.

"No," I responded, "I'm thriving with Lyme."

This surprised me a bit, in the moment, but in retrospect, I was glad to see that I was able to see myself through the lens of being a thriver. I had, after all, made it to the conference. I'd practiced my happiness habits of self-development. And I'd used my Inner Giggle to guide me. It was only by doing so that I saw myself as a functional, healthy, and even happier person – a person whose identity was now intertwined with *thriving*.

My story lays down the crux of what we call "self-perception theory," first posited by Dr. Daryl Bem.[15] The basic idea is that when you see yourself doing something, you figure "that is me." Previous to this theory, scientists believed that self-knowledge drove behavior – that if we knew who we were inherently/internally, we could choose behaviors aligned with our thoughts, beliefs, values, etc. But Dr. Bem proved that our opinions about ourselves are formed exactly like our opinions about others – by judging our behavior. He uses the classic example of a friend who is always late. After a time, you not only perceive him as someone who is always late, but you also eventually decide he is unpunctual and probably disrespectful.

Self-perception theory argues that you go through the same process of judging your own behaviors. That is in part why, when you are often late but you do not see yourself as someone who is always late, it causes you greater stress when you are, once again, late. (In a sense, you experience what is called cognitive dissonance. In other words, your belief and thoughts about yourself are inconsistent with your behavior). Thus, your identity is driven by your actions, and your actions build your identity. As John Dryden brilliantly says, "We first make our habits, then our habits make us."

Building Your Identity Using Habits

Habits, in general, follow an optimal order for identity transformation to occur. Forming your desired identity through habits is about taking action first – and that takes both courage and consistency. The way you act reinforces the right emotions, positively affecting the way you feel about the action you've taken. The order of this transactional chain is important because when you choose who you want to be (your identity), you can choose the actions and behaviors that align. Then you can experience the positive feelings generated.

Integrating and accommodating your new identity is not about trying to feel your way into it, contemplating perhaps I will do it today, or else – I will try tomorrow. It's about proving to yourself that you cannot only do it but that this is what you *are doing*. This is who you are. You are someone who is committed to optimizing your well-being, and in the process, you are becoming a Happier Being.

Every day you commit to your Happier Being by creating healthy habits, you also lay the foundations of your new life. You are charging your energy and boosting your feedback that this is the person you are now. If you've seen yourself eating your greens every day, you are now someone who is a healthier eater. If you observe yourself running every day, you are now a runner. It doesn't matter that you're not a competitive runner or a diet coach. It's not about accolades or occupation. It is about who you see yourself to be every day, and what identity is gradually forming.

If you're not confident in who you can be yet, what identity you want to build, or are still unsure of your ability to change, that's okay. Start by choosing a habit that will move you in a positive direction. During this process, executing may become hard. Even if your identity hasn't formed strongly yet, remember that your bright lines will guide you. The more you are able to be consistent, the greater your chances of experiencing the benefits of feeling good from it. And the more positive emotions you experience in the process of change, the less growing pains will stop you from consistently following your chosen path.

As Eric Greitens, a Navy Seal who wrote a great book called *Resilience*, says, "We need to discipline ourselves to be less interested in how we feel in any given moment and more interested in (and committed to) who we want to be! Then, act that way. Again and again and again."[16]

This is exactly what habits are: behaviors you repeatedly do. The more you practice them, the more they reinforce who you want to become — and, more accurately, who you are becoming. This is the magic dust for when your being starts transforming. Your habits expand your mindset about your ability to change as you see the evidence of an updated version of you forming.

> **You start experiencing yourself as not only someone who wants and anticipates the results of the habit (better diet, fitness, sleep) but who embodies the belief that you are your behavior.**

You are not just someone who wants to lose weight: you don't eat processed sugar. Period. You are not someone dreaming of a six-pack; you always train. Period. You don't just shut technology off at 6 p.m.; you routinely synchronize your day with a digital sunset. Period.

WOOPing Your Goals
with Mental Contrasting

It's clear that creating new habits requires action and dedication. There will be bumps along the road to building your identity. But contrary to what you may believe, there are ways to plan ahead for these challenges. One of the best tools to do so is mental contrasting. According to German psychologist Gabriele Oettingen,[17] mental contrasting is the process by which you compare and contrast positive future outcomes with the potential for obstacles along the way. This process sets up realistic expectations regarding your goals while also planning realistically for future challenges. In essence, to turn your dreams into reality, you have to rub them up against reality itself.

To aid your quest, Oettingen offers the "W.O.O.P" (Wish, Outcome, Obstacle, and Plan) tool. Each word in the acronym represents a step in the mental contrasting process that can help you stay true to reality's constraints, find your way through them, and sustain your goals.

Take a second to consider one of your goals, take out your journal, and answer these four questions from Oettingen:[18]

Wish: What do you want?
Outcome: Why do you want it?
Obstacle: What's in the way?
Plan: What will you do about it?

Now that you've WOOP-ed your goal, you'll be better prepared for future pain points. Still, there are no quick fixes or drive-through transformations. It takes time to master new habits. Whatever it is, and no matter how tiny you made it, watch out for your internal expectations. Thoughts and expectations like: "I should be able to do it better, it shouldn't take that long, it should not be so difficult," etc. will surface – and that's okay because now you can WOOP these as well!

Be patient with yourself and with the results. You are optimizing your well-being daily; what's the rush? View it as a marathon, not a sprint. After all, as we have discussed numerous times before, what is really important is to get committed to the process, enjoy the forward motion, the daily improvements, the forming of the best of you. These momentary gains are what really count and make us happier!

You're now also aware of the power of creating tiny habits by committing to *action* first. Then you can sustain these habits by eliminating decision-making, preserving willpower, and striving toward automation. In your commitment to all of the above, you know you'll experience the value of compounded small habit changes over time, such as positive emotions and Happier Being. This is the goal of optimizing your Inner Giggle energy boosters!

You are on a path to take control over your life, your health, and your happiness levels. It takes time, but it is happening – despite any adversity or chronic stress in your life. If, after all this, you are still playing around with the faulty concept of waiting for a "muse" to inspire you, *don't*. You have to be your own muse, because the reality is that if you start now, inspiration will follow. If you wait, your muse will too.

Developing Your Keystone Habit

Thus far, you've been equipped with an arsenal of scientifically proven methods and tools to embark on creating the best version of yourself through added habits. But where to begin?

A good way to start is by developing your keystone habit, the one habit that will provide the biggest impact on your livelihood. Imagine a beautiful arch made of ancient bricks. In the middle of it, there is a keystone that holds the arch together. Without it, the arch will fall apart. Can you see it in your mind's eye? Now, think about the arch's architectural structure, and consider it as your own biological structure, if you will. Ask yourself: what is my keystone habit? What habit will have the most significant influence on my day-to-day quality of life? This is the habit that, when committed to, you know will help you activate your best self!

In *The Power of the Habit*, Charles Duhigg[19] explains that practicing your keystone habit will have a domino effect on other behaviors – and he is referring to any habit at all. In essence, you see yourself dedicated to your routine. Therefore, you experience yourself as a self-disciplined person, and slowly you begin developing self-control in more aspects of your life. That is the biggest gain of choosing a keystone habit: you'll better execute all your Inner Giggle energy boosting habits. They are necessary for your better life, and they will become the moving force of your success.

As an example, let's say you decide to make daily exercise your keystone habit. From there, you might also start noticing your protein intake increases, and hence, eating habits improve, as well as your quality of sleep at night (since your body is tired). Thus, you have more energy and productivity in the daytime.

Instilling a keystone habit can also decrease other, unrelated bad habits, such as over-engaging on social media platforms. After all, you're spending more time at the gym, and because exercise elevates your mood, you'll operate from a more positive state. This positive state will decrease the need to escape reality in front of a screen, or waste time and mental energy gossiping about others.

Have you thought about which energy fundamental you want to make your keystone habit? Though experts differ on which of the trinity of health habits (eating, moving, or sleeping) is more beneficial, the choice is yours. You are the one who knows yourself best. You are the one who knows what will move that needle of health and happiness for you. You are the one who knows which brick in your personality arch has the most significance to you. Only you have the insight to choose your keystone habit – so don't think about it for too long. Pick and then go for it.

Even though I suggest starting with one habit, all three Inner Giggle energy boosters are interrelated and interconnected. If you improve one, chances are that you end up improving the other two. Accordingly, don't procrastinate with wanting to make sure you pick the right one first. Pick one and keep moving towards the *new you.* You are guided by finding your Inner Giggle and consistently becoming a Happier Being!

Later in the book I will provide you with some amazing data on the science behind these energy boosters, and the fundamental practices, and practical suggestions to follow.

Now you're ready to dive into some of the challenges that might prevent you from finding your Inner Giggle – namely perfectionism and your mindset.

Recap

- In order to optimize your Inner Giggle energy boosters (your eating, sleeping, and moving practices), you need to first learn how to create lasting, healthful habits.

- The process of creating a habit runs in a three-step loop: reminder (cue that signals), routine (behavior you perform), and reward (advantage gained from the behavior).

- Habits that stick are based on intrinsic motivation. You have to experience the pleasure from performing the habit in the present, not only in its future rewards. It's not easy to change your behavior, but getting your concrete rational and emotional sides to work together will make it possible.

- Willpower is not hereditary, and it's limited/finite to everyone, every day. Decision-making depletes your "willpower reserves." This is why it's so important to automate your energy boosting habits. By doing so, you increase your self-control.

- Hacks to help you create a new healthy habit include: the one-minute habit (start small), habit stacking ("if/then" implementation intentions), time and place habits, and your pre-commitments (clearing your physical environment of unhealthy temptations).

- Pre-commitments also help shape your identity: each time you experience yourself behaving as the person you want to be, you reassure and reinforce that identity formation. This is "self-perception theory," which enables you to see yourself as your behavior.

- Start with one keystone habit – the unique energy-boosting habit (whether it's eating, sleeping, or moving) that keeps your biological arch intact. The one thing you can do that will energize you the most and get you ready to rock! Don't think about it too much, start!

Bonus information and mental training exercises relating to this chapter can be found here: happierbeing.com/exercises

THREE

The Paradox of Perfectionism

A Not-So-Perfect State of Being

Can you really embrace being happier while trying to be perfect?

The answer depends on whether you're an extreme perfectionist or a realistic one. If you hold yourself to the extreme, unrealistic standard of perfectionism in every aspect of your being, are unable to accept failure, and deny that experiencing painful emotions is a daily reality, embracing your Inner Giggle is irrelevant. But hopefully, you fall somewhere on the continuum between an extreme perfectionist and a realistic perfectionist – like most people. At times, you are more extreme in your pursuit of perfectionism, and at other times more realistic in accepting the ups and downs of life with its inherent limitations.

Perfectionism is one of the biggest impediments to energizing your Happier Being, mostly because having a perfectionist view impacts your idea of what happiness should look like. If you hold an extreme assumption that boosting your Inner Giggle requires feeling only its positive results 24/7, then you have an unrealistic expectation that will devastate your effort to become a Happier Being. Life doesn't offer anyone the option of omitting the occasional blues, disappointments, jealousy, or other painful emotions. Holding such an unrealistic expectation only sets you up to feel these negative emotions even more strongly than you would have if you had not held the unrealistic expectation of being able to avoid it.

If you are an extreme perfectionist, then you derive your self-worth solely from your accomplishments. That, too, is a huge hurdle to happiness, since whatever your projects in life might be, your worth is not the sum of your accomplishments. Please know this:

You are always more than the sum of your parts.

Now, nobody wants to be caught unprepared for a work presentation or take a couple of wrong turns on the way to an important meeting. These are unpleasant events, but they are also forgivable – to everyone except the perfectionist. The need to be prepared and not make mistakes drives them to keep trying to perfect their behavior. The constant fear of failing themselves, or others, is a painful daily reality. The personal injury when things do not go as planned is devastating and drains their energy. Ironically, this intense fear of failure can ultimately hinder their performance and get in the way of their overall well-being.

Extreme perfectionists take an all-or-nothing approach to the things they do, including their self-evaluation. They have a hard time accepting their shortcomings and tend to deny the inevitability of behaving or producing anything short of perfect. They focus on the end result, yet once they get there, it's usually not good enough – much like how they view themselves. In that eagerness to perfect, they are aspiring for "a life that's not just happier, but perfect."[20] Unfortunately, no such thing exists.

Often, those who insist on making their lives perfect are trying to avoid pain. They either strive in the belief that they can dodge criticism or ridicule if they get things perfect, or they won't try things they aren't sure they'll be successful at. Perfectionism is used as a shield to avoid getting hurt – but in reality, it results in the opposite. Perfectionists often struggle with pain, disappointment, self-criticism, anxiety, chronic fatigue, depression, and relationship issues. So it seems that striving for perfectionism results in greater imperfections and hindrances toward being a more resilient, Happier Being. This is the paradox of perfectionism.

Discipline vs. Perfectionism
in Parenting and Early Childhood

Looking at children from an early age, it is obvious that some are more predisposed to perfectionism. You can recognize budding perfectionists by their defensiveness when confronted with failure. They have a harder time not only losing games but also enjoying their school projects – nothing is good enough or pretty enough. These children absorb the praise their parents lavish on them for winning or getting A's, as if praise was the only way to be appreciated, to matter, or to avoid rejection. Slowly, these kids start seeing their life through the "only a grade" lens in other things they do, and this mindset continues in adulthood. As author Brené Brown says, "Many people think of perfectionism as striving to be your best, but it is not about self-improvement; it's about earning approval and acceptance."

Additionally, some children take it a step further and conclude that perfection equals success and reflects their degree of belongingness, especially if others around them reinforce that message. The parent might say things like, "Your talent won you that school project, just like your father did." But what if the child were to be unable to repeat this success the following year? Will the child be left feeling less like their father, less like they belong? What if the parent saw the child's distress from "failing" that time and communicated, "It's good to feel bad because this will teach you a lesson to work harder next time"?

Embedded in this message is a devastating notion that the child internalizes, which is that feeling bad about their imperfect performance can somehow become a reinforcer for perfectionism next time or a "good" thing to experience. The negative feelings around imperfect life endeavors start to become habits that are rationalized as "okay" to experience. And, as children grow into adulthood, they continue thinking and behaving as if it's good to feel negative about their performances, and then pass that on to the people in their life – i.e., children – because it means they hold them to a higher standard. The judgment of their kids' imperfections is then construed as a motivator for doing better. Still, in reality, it is only continuing the cycle of negative emotions around the unrealistic pursuit of perfection. In real life, as we'll discuss in a later chapter, the reinforcing power of negative emotions, keeping yourself down to build yourself up, is not the best recipe for success, especially if you want to optimize your Happier Being.

There is a fine line between supporting children to excel and demanding excellence, where the intended messages can get very confusing for a child's ego. Even if your parent taught discipline, you might have absorbed this message as aspiring to perfect a goal and develop unrealistic expectations. That was the only thing that made sense to you as a young child totally dependent on your parents' care. As mentioned previously, you looked for affection and avoided disappointment or rejection (even if, in actuality, it was just perceived rejection). Unfortunately, later as this dynamic was internalized, you started to treat yourself the same way — creating unreachable standards for yourself and assuming others would think less of you if you didn't perform at your highest capacity every time. And of course, now, when you don't perform as expected (because you're human!), you face the most painful outcome of all: the cycle of self-criticism.

Self-criticism perpetuates dislike of any part of you that is less than perfect. Like a hawk, you zoom in on those disliked, unapproved, imperfect parts – only to subjectively blow them out of proportion. You magnify their importance and what these parts say about you. As Brené Brown says in her writings,[21] you struggle with perfectionism in areas where you might have the greatest fear of shame or are most vulnerable to shame. Paradoxically, you turn to your dysfunctional defense mechanism once again, perfectionism, hoping it will keep you from that shame, getting hurt, or being found as an imposter of your trade. But it results in the opposite. Now you're in a big entanglement of despair, stress, and the inability to show your true self to the world. This is, once again, the paradox of perfectionism.

A Quick Side Note: The Dangers of Severe Discipline

There are circumstances in which perfectionist parenting results in harsh emotional and/or physical abuse or neglect and leaves deep wounds. This is not the type of perfectionism I am discussing here. Abuse is abuse, and I reject any way of rationalizing it. Period. If you think you've experienced such, and the above resonates with your pain, my heart goes out to you — and I would encourage you to seek professional help. Don't wait for the "right" moment to invest in your happiness. Now is the best moment. You were born feeling good about yourself. You were born wanting to share your efforts with others. You deserve to live like this again. Feeling fantastic about yourself, imperfections, efforts, and all. As the American humorist Don Herold commented, "Babies are such a nice way to start people." Don't you agree?

The Consequences of Rigid Perfectionism on Your Happier Being

It's clear by now that perfectionism makes you feel disappointed in your reality and yourself far more often than necessary. You begin to think if this one thing isn't perfect, or if you aren't perfect, basically, you can't truly be happy. Any kind of criticism then becomes an assault on your ego, which becomes a direct attack on your Inner Giggle.

A perfectionist is often focused on what other people think. Perfectionists are rigid in their rules of engagement and focus on the half-empty glass. This mindset leads to an all-or-nothing approach to the world. Many perfectionists then wonder why they should do anything if they can't do it perfectly. The fear of not being able to be perfect can often lead to procrastination because if something is never started and/or finished, at least it can't be judged. For many perfectionists, procrastination is just another way to avoid failure. It's self-protection. Unfortunately, the procrastination zone provides temporary comfort but lasting stress, as well as other symptoms.

Additionally, perfectionism can also lead to burnout because working to perfect a project can take up a lot of time and creates a sense of chronic busyness. Being busy might give the illusion of creativity, but in reality, it doesn't always equate to productivity. Additionally, perfectionists always keep themselves externally motivated to show their version of success — measuring it against previous work and/or others' work, which can become a strenuous full-time job. This might mean getting the highest grades, sales, clicks on social media, or even compliments by all the right people. Perfectionists can create competition everywhere, choosing any metrics to measure success. But if you're a perfectionist, the main competitor you must watch out for is yourself.

Now, this isn't to say measurements aren't a useful tool – after all, if you don't measure progress, how can you tell if there is improvement? There are areas in your life where you must measure to improve. For example, if keeping a balanced budget is a goal, your expenses versus your income need to be calculated. That being said, other areas of your life are not as easy to measure – like how much time to spend with your loved ones to achieve a good work/life balance. Albert Einstein once said: "Not everything that counts can be countable, and not everything that can be counted, counts." Okay, so variations of the importance of different metrics do exist. However, the painful problem that many perfectionists face is that they move from wanting to create the perfect product to wanting to create the perfect self-image or perfect self.

Parkinson's Law

This term was coined by Cyril Northcote Parkinson in a humorous essay for the Economist in 1955,[22] explaining that work expands to fill its allotted time. If perfection is the project, then the time defined for it is endless. Put simply, if you're aiming for perfection, your project can be endless, and you'd have a hard time enjoying the journey while you are at it. As the saying goes, "Procrastination is the assassination of your destination."

It's no surprise that perfectionists face issues of procrastination as well as burnout. "Perfect" isn't a task that anyone can and/or should take on because failure is inevitable. Of course, it's okay to want to do your best, but remember Parkinson's Law and try and adhere to a predetermined timeline – or you're bound to face some negative consequences.

In my clinical work, I've seen rigid perfectionism revealed as the culprit behind depression, anxiety, eating disorders, losing business, and more. The underlying fear of failure beneath the dysfunctional perfectionist side becomes toxic energy that disables all good intentions. Unsurprisingly, some of the most successful people have failed the most, and that's because they've accepted imperfect failures and still keep trying. For example, anyone who has mastered a skill has failed many more times than most people have even attempted it.

Michael Jordan famously said, "I've missed more than 9,000 shots in my career. I've lost almost 300 games; 26 times, I've been trusted to take the game-winning shot and missed. I've failed over and over and over again in my life. And that is why I succeed."

Untangling Yourself from Rigid Perfectionism

By now, you surely understand there is no logic in narrowing your life to living by rigid perfectionism – at least, if you want to take care of your well-being. Becoming happier comes from slowing down momentarily and allowing yourself to simply be appreciative of where you are. Step-by-step progress needs to be rewarded by you. Every single percent you advance merits a pat on the back. The criteria of 100 percent perfection, 100 percent of the time, will render your daily life too dull or too stressful. Too dull if you give up challenging yourself to get out of your comfort zone and develop in an area where you are not guaranteed to be the "best." And too stressful if you aim extremely high without the chance of ever reaching that elusive mountain peak of success – according to your unrealistic expectations.

You are in charge of the metrics you impose on yourself. Many are relevant and important to achieving overall success. Concentrate on the benefit of getting feedback rather than viewing it as criticism. Feedback is a natural thing to receive if you avoid being hijacked by your ego. Let's say, for example, that you worked hard on a project at work and got promoted. You were given positive feedback for your efforts. But what if you did the same work and didn't get promoted? Were you wrong in putting in the effort, contributing, creating? Did you waste your time? Granted, it is disappointing not to have been promoted, but to assume the reason it happened was that you "failed" to perfect your project isn't the full picture here. Judging yourself from this narrow perfectionist lens is unrealistic, inaccurate, and certainly not vital for your well-being.

Be Watchful of Society Perpetuating Perfectionism

In addition to untangling your own tendencies toward perfectionism, you have to be watchful of others too. Society is built to reward perfectionism at the expense of our Happier Being.

As explained earlier in this chapter, perfectionistic behavior can start when adults tell their kids, "You are so smart," or "You are so beautiful," and children begin to think they have to prove those things are true. If they don't live up to those expectations, their self-image suffers. A typical school environment, with the immediate social comparisons of "good" vs. "bad" grades, or "popular" vs "unpopular," continues to reinforce these ideals. As children become teens, endless advertisements touting the perfect body, skin, flat stomach, six-pack, etc. lead to people creating the perfect presentation of their lives on social media. You get the picture.

By the time you reach adulthood, you've been bombarded with self-help programs that promise expedited health and wealth, i.e., "be happy now" or "get rich quick." And when you try these and feel that you can't just be happy every second or get rich by the end of the summer, you think perhaps something is wrong with your ways of doing things, or worse, with yourself – which might result in doubling down on perfectionism and exacerbated self-deprecation.

It's easy to see that society worships perfectionism. Take, for example, a job interview, when an employer asks the interviewee to name a weakness, and they say, "I am a perfectionist," as if it were a strength in disguise. Why might they offer such a response? Because, from the outside looking in, we may see perfectionists as bright, ambitious, conscientious, and hardworking. Those all seem like great qualities. My argument, though, is that indeed these are fantastic characteristics, and a major part of perfectionistic people's personality. But to some degree, the pressure to maintain the intensity of only positive personality traits and continuously perform perfectly eventually tips to a negative outcome and becomes toxic.

The challenge is in keeping up these positive characteristics without the unpleasant side effects such as low self-esteem and unhappiness that rigid/extreme perfectionist aspirations leave you with. The challenge is becoming a functional perfectionist and not a dysfunctional one. I refer to this as becoming a healthy striver, with your Inner Giggle (metric) leading the way.

Moving from Perfectionist to Healthy Striver

Becoming a healthy striver means finding balance in doing your best. A healthy striver is focused on internal or intrinsic motivation. They want to be the best they can be for the sake of feeling prouder of themselves. That is a big part of their motivation to excel. They are still very much focused on optimizing their final product, their performance, but the motive for doing that doesn't solely depend on others' feedback. It is an internal, inner drive to strive for growth. They derive meaning from pursuing it and pleasure in putting their best foot forward. The healthy striver also accepts that achievement, whether in life, at work, or in a relationship, isn't a linear process. They expect that there will be setbacks and are determined to learn from them. They keep an open mind with their flexible thinking and focus on realistic and unconditional acceptance of what they must work with.

Done Is the New Perfect

A mind shift that can free you from the tyranny of perfectionism is to train your brain to accept that done is better than perfect. Pause for a moment, and see how this feels. Can you stomach it? Is your perfectionist voice starting to argue back?

The resistance to change is probably building up inside you, but just for a moment, can you begin to see the advantage of sharing your work now without fearing that it isn't perfect? Even marketing guru Seth Godin[23] advocates releasing work with known flaws. He calls on creators to behave more like computer programmers, advocating "shipping out minimum viable products and improving them in real-time, because done is better than none." Can you see the trend here?

Reinforcing this new mantra, "done is better than perfect," and training your mind to accept that less than perfect is helpful because there is always more that can be done. The need to make your project 100 percent perfect should not be a defense mechanism in disguise – like procrastination from fear of being prematurely done and subsequently given feedback. Remember that procrastination means standing on the other side of "done!" If you don't bust through it, you'll never finish your project. Try and live with the notion of "as good as it gets today" because being done with your project today is better than it being perfect and never seeing the light of day.

Oliver was a perfectionist, to a fault. Living with him, by his own admittance, was not easy. Working with him, as a successful cinematographer, was even harder.

In our sessions together, we first covered how Oliver's emotionally abusive parents played a part in developing rigid perfectionism. Throughout his childhood, Oliver was told that his efforts were never good enough, leaving him continuously agitated and anxious as well as intermittently depressed. He had learned to embrace and accept negative emotions, and to belittle positive ones. His pursuit of perfection continued into adulthood.

As Oliver and I continued to unpack the paradox of perfectionism, he realized just how much his perfectionistic ways had become hindrances in both his personal and professional life. He became determined to let go of the small stuff so that he could experience more joy and reconnect with the creative, engaging process of cinematography – instead of obsessing over the end result. Since I knew he also loved photography, one of the ideas we came up with was to develop photos the old-fashioned way in a darkroom. With the endless amount of digital applications and details available in today's world, I suggested we turn it on its head, and got Oliver excited about developing black and white film. With a nostalgic spirit, he turned one of his offices into a darkroom, and the challenge (not surprising that perfectionists love a little self-competition) was on.

After working in the darkroom for a bit, Oliver showed me some of the still photos he'd developed. "It's an exercise of learning to be more patient and in the moment," he said.

I agreed, adding that it was also a way to focus on the beauty of the creative process itself. Gaining a more realistic take on the process of being creative indirectly and positively impacted the anxiety and depression he felt in the past. This was very different from those times when he was so hard on himself and focused mostly on his work's imperfections.

Interesting, while not every still photo would come out perfect (because developing black and white films, without the digital aspect of endless variations, had its limitations), Oliver found this okay. Instead of being caught in an endless process of perfectionism, this more limited work forced him to intentionally accept the final developed photo as "good enough." The result helped Oliver avoid the procrastination zone and accept that done was better than perfect.

As Oliver continued to develop films, he learned to more easily let go of the small things in other areas of his life. He learned to ship his work[24] more quickly. He started accepting and adjusting the gray areas in between the black and white – metaphorically speaking. He began to better accept the gray areas of life. The irony of the concept of a "darkroom" did not escape me – or Oliver, for that matter. It was the darkness in him that he hoped to transform by exposing himself to change – just like the process of exposing film.

Don't let perfectionism become a reason to keep yourself in the dark. The procrastination zone is a dangerous, depressive place. Put in the time while creating and enjoy the process, but don't make time work against you or find reasons why your project is not yet good enough. Embrace the notion that even when you feel your creation or project is not yet perfected, you can follow the predetermined timeline you allowed yourself. Setting strict time limits for your project is like having a boss let you know that it's time to release your work. No matter how unfinished it might feel, it's time to let it go. It's like crossing the street. You can check for incoming traffic 100 times, but you eventually accept your assessment and decide to cross the street. Done!

Journal

Fire the Committee. Think about those people in your life who demand unrealistic perfectionism from you. Who are they? What function do they hold in your life? Please fire them! The stress they are causing is too high for your well-being.

Tools for Overcoming a Perfectionist Mindset

Naturally, there are times when an unfulfilled desired outcome is discouraging. If you shipped a product and it didn't deliver correctly, or if you prepared for a get-together and the actual party wasn't as great as you hoped, you might be disappointed. But to the perfectionist, this kind of failure can be devastating. Making mistakes can feel like emotional injuries. What helps? How can you go about moving the needle from perfectionist to someone who holds a realistic perception of their own accomplishments? How can you move from perfectionist to a healthy striver?

First, start by thinking of a time when it felt like you failed. Yeah, ouch. But no worries – we'll turn that failure around by using the tools below.

*Reframing "Failure": Action Steps for Past, Present,
and Future Perfectionist Thinking*

Accept what's in the past

The first step is to accept and appreciate reality. You failed, lost, messed up
– whatever happened, things didn't go the way you wanted them to. Accept
it for what it is; life happened for you (notice I didn't write "to you"). It's
part of being alive, part of being an active participant of life. Accept that
it already happened. It's in the past, and only you can stop any negative
downward spiraling, self-blame, or self-talk that occurs as a result. You are
in charge. It's up to you to stop self-attacking and maintain an objective
point of view. Being ambitious is great, but becoming trapped in defeat
from your own challenges is foolish.

Reality check in the present

Become a benefit finder with your perceived outcome. Get out your journal
and ask yourself:

- What did you learn?
- What new opportunities did failure bring?
- What is the worst thing that happened because of this failure?
- Are you appraising it that way because your ego took a bit of a hit?
- Are you using your perfectionist glasses to drive you to this
  conclusion?

And lastly, though I am not one of those who believe that everything
happens for a reason, I do believe you can find some good out of even the
most unwelcome situation (no matter how small that good might be). Shift
your focus away from finding the downsides to finding the upsides. It's
worth it.

Point of view for the future

Think about the long-term impact of this failure. Does it really make sense
to be worried about it for so long? Will you really be worried about it a year
from now? This is a good chance to project to your future and ask:

- Will you keep allowing your perfectionism to hurt your self-esteem or your relationships?

Or:

- Will you focus on your dedication and the hard work you put in?

After you ask yourself these questions, your emotional response can start to align with your best self. Reward yourself for the courage to have taken those risks and start planning for your next steps. Looking to the future, starting anywhere between now to tomorrow, where you can apply lessons you've learned. Be the person who appreciates the opportunity to improve and develop yourself for the benefit of you and those who love you.

I'd like to leave you with this last point and way of digesting the action steps above: You need to "coat" your thinking. The way we think coats the world we experience – everything from our accomplishments to our emotional life. Your thinking coats the reality you see. And the rigid perfectionist way of thinking, in black and white, allows you to assess yourself harshly, coating your days with bitter toppings. I suggest different toppings – like coating your perception with your Inner Giggle. Imagine your Inner Giggle as a delicious, dark, chocolatey outer layer. Everything underneath would taste a little better, right?

If we work to adjust our perceptions of the world around us, if we aim to coat our thinking with our Inner Giggle, we can change how we feel about what goes on in our heads and around us.

Allow Yourself to Be Human –
Move Away from "Superhuman" Perfectionism

To encourage your Happier Being, give yourself permission to be human.[25] To acknowledge you can't be good at everything, or anything all the time, is to acknowledge your human experience. Not everyone will love you. You'll have good days and bad days. Weeks of high achievement and less productive weeks. You'll gain some and lose some. Err and prevail. And yes, here it comes; you will also fail. Sometimes. You don't have to like it, but you can learn to accept it as part of life, and grow.

You also need to give yourself permission to be a beginner. "If you can't make a mistake, you can't make anything," as American educator Marva Collins[26] says. If you never want to try something you aren't already perfect at, you limit your potential before you even start. You might look at people who are already good at something and feel bad about yourself. But the truth is, you can only measure yourself against yourself. You need to allow yourself room to struggle and grow. Realistic expectations are your friend, and if your standards are based in reality, success is attainable. So yes, aim high, as high as you want, but if you're just starting out, you can't expect yourself to be an expert. That doesn't mean you suck, or you'll never get it – you just haven't developed that skill yet. You're human!

In addition to this tidbit, internalize the notion that needing assistance isn't a weakness. Give yourself permission to ask for help. This applies to everything – from domestic projects to work, hobbies, parenting, etc. Because although self-sufficiency and autonomy are great character strengths, when overused they – like any strength – become weaknesses. You can only get so far on your own, but by allowing others to recommend and share their experiences, strategies, and insights, you will be able to go further. Most great leaders had great teachers, role models they looked up to, and others who helped them along the way.

Humans err, that's what we do, but we also have the option of reaching out to others. Open your perfectionist mind and heart to receive. It doesn't make the task at hand any less yours if you've asked for assistance. Besides, we aren't supposed to endure life and its challenges by ourselves. In the end, trying to be overly independent can keep you isolated. By allowing yourself to ask for help, you're becoming a stronger, healthy striver, not weaker – so don't be afraid to ask for it!

Give yourself permission to have off days

Not every day will go as planned, and you need to accept that some days you will feel more off, bothered by work, or just "not in the mood." Though having 100 percent commitment to practicing your habits daily is a beneficial goal, life challenges everyone at times. Recall that it's all about realistic expectations. No one can run on 100 percent contentment all the time. While you can't avoid all the mundane or annoying parts of life, you can make sure you include pleasurable, meaningful things in your day. Maybe that means spending time with your family, swimming, or taking a cooking class. If you practice this, you'll be a healthy striver, and I can tell you that you will not only succeed more often, but also feel happier more often.

Derive Pleasure from the Process:
Perfectionism and the Hedonic Treadmill

I trust you can connect how the paradox of perfectionism feeds right into the hedonic treadmill we discussed earlier. Perfectionists often think, "If only I can do everything correctly," "the right way," and "create the best, newest, or never been seen before" product, then I can prove to others I'm not a fraud – and I'm worthy. What gets lost here is the benefit of working toward a goal. In addition, you should take into consideration the fact that the Inner Giggle – your means to your Happier Being – is awoken by the process of working hard toward something you want, like, or love – rather than only the result. The conviction of "inner" is as important as "giggle." You see, happiness is not just increased by reaching your goals, it is increased merely by having those goals and experiencing the joy derived in the process of achieving them. And ironically, the more you pursue perfectionism, the more likely it is that not only your happiness but perfection itself also starts fading away.

Robin entered our first session wearing a stunning scarf matching her boots. She scanned the room and sofa before she sat down and then precisely placed her handbag next to her. Much of what she wore, as I soon learned, was designed and made by her. There was a sense of pride as she described the ideas behind her fabric choices, colors, and designs. She detailed how the garment was stitched with meticulous attention to detail, quality, and style. She shared that she'd been working hard toward her dream of becoming a celebrated fashion designer.

Nevertheless, Robin felt discouraged that her work had only taken her so far. She received great feedback from her close friends and family but didn't think she could break into the "real world" of fashion. It was clear that she was suffering from the paradox of perfectionism, on the hedonic treadmill, and losing her ability to enjoy the process of what she loved to do. As we delved deeper into Robin's inner struggles, it seemed that another big obstacle was her false belief that other designers had succeeded faster. She concluded that if she didn't make it big by her early forties, it would be time to give it up, as that's as far as her talent could take her.

Together, Robin and I explored her perfectionist ways of thinking and the fixed mindset of having reached her limit, of guessing that others did not struggle as much or rose to the top faster. Slowly, she was able to connect that expanding her mind to accept more failures, imperfections, shortcomings, and creative possibilities would allow her to embrace the process of becoming a creative fashion designer. Over time, Robin learned to adopt a growth mindset (the focus of the next chapter) instead of a fixed one.

As Robin explored more of the behind-the-scenes history and attitudes held by some of her favorite designers, she began trusting her own process of growth. Being more dedicated to her vision of how to express her craft and being guided by her Inner Giggle led to better results. She began to feel that changing course midway or acquiring new skills to finish a piece of artistic clothing was training her mind to know that growth was good, and gave her an advantage. With the expectations that bumps were undeniable, she appreciated the levels of her designs where they are today.

In doing so, Robin gave herself permission to be human. She shifted her self-image from failure to learner, and became more focused on present goals as opposed to the past or future. As she moved from a perfectionist to a healthy striver, she was able to better enjoy the creative process of designing (awakening her Inner Giggle!) and became a happier designer. And of course, the cherry on top: Robin became more successful too.

Robin's story illustrates why it's crucial to keep your focus on your Happier Being via your Inner Giggle – that intersection between meaning and pleasure in your life – in its entirety. As a perfectionist, your Inner Giggle is the metric by which you need to measure progress in all your endeavors (recall that it is your internal compass). Often it is wise to have realistic standards and make adjustments to your Inner Giggle metric to keep your motivation and abilities aligned. This will help keep you balanced and focused on what's really important, bring you to your next step in work/life, and help you feel proud, accomplished, and happy along the way.

One of the reasons it's so hard to let go of being a perfectionist is that you value the positive aspects of operating this way; not only the end results, but the self-perception of being a perfectionist. For example, it boosts your ego to know you are an ambitious person. It makes you proud of being reliable, like always being on time. You take pleasure in your attention to details, since it expands your experiences. Doing a cost analysis of your perfectionism can ease you out of the all-or-nothing mentality and open the door to embracing your positive traits of perfectionism when the situation merits it. List all the traits that make you feel good about your perfectionism. Next to each of the traits you wrote down, write out its advantage and disadvantage. List traits such as being meticulous, driven, paying attention to details, being on time, being task-oriented, being reliable, or being reality-focused. Then list the cost of operating like this 100 percent of the time. The cost to you, your partner, family, work. Noticing a pattern?

Your behavior can change your perfectionist attitude. If you act like optimizing your life is the primary focus, then you can be more relaxed, more engaged in seeking feedback rather than criticism, and look for the best in a situation. Even if transitioning to holding such a healthy striver attitude does not yet feel cozy to you, practice it as often as you can. The more you approach it as creating a new habit, the easier it will get, and the attitude change will follow. If you keep your realistic expectations switched on and your self-criticism off, you'll protect your Happier Being and boost your resilience. You'll be more likely to strengthen weaker talents and become better equipped for life's inevitable challenges. This requires a shift in thinking, and we'll explore the power of mindset in the next chapter.

Moving from a perfectionist to a healthy striver applies to how you need to feel about yourself as well. Open your mind and heart, accept that you cannot truly ever reach perfection, that it's more of a Hollywood movie fantasy than human reality. It will take until the end of time and the end of your time on earth to reach perfection – yes, I'm extreme, but so are perfectionists! It's not worth your time!

Recap

- Perfectionism is one of the biggest impediments to energizing your Inner Giggle.
- Rigid perfectionism increases your fear of not being perfect, perpetuating procrastination in order to avoid judgment from others and/or yourself.
- As a perfectionist you move from wanting to create the perfect product to wanting to create the perfect self-image or perfect self, which simply does not exist. The unrealistic pursuit of perfection becomes a mentally and physically depleting process that results in greater hindrances. The paradox of perfectionism thus lies within the fact that perfectionism is used as a shield to avoid getting hurt – but in reality, results in the opposite. The more you pursue perfectionism, the more likely it is that not only your happiness but the ability to be perfect itself also starts fading away.
- Untangling yourself from rigid perfectionism means understanding that you're human, and you don't need to feel negative emotions about an imperfect performance or appearance (something partly acquired in early childhood that society perpetuates into adulthood).
- As a perfectionist, you can become a healthy striver by remembering tips like "done is the new perfect," accepting the past (moving on from failure faster), reality checking in the present, and looking towards the future (appreciating the opportunity to improve).
- Healthy strivers enjoy the process of having and working toward a new goal that they want, like, or love – rather than only the result (which rigid perfectionists focus on). This is because healthy strivers are guided by their Inner Giggle, and place value in their meaningful and pleasurable experiences (regardless of the result or what happens if they failed).
- As a perfectionist, you have to use your Inner Giggle as the metric that guides you to focus on what's really important. Coat your thinking with your Inner Giggle, and you can change how you feel about what goes on in your head and around you to become happier.

Bonus information and mental training exercises relating to this chapter can be found here: happierbeing.com/exercises

F O U R

Growing Into a New Mindset

Using Your Inner Giggle to Change Your Self-perception

Growth is uncomfortable because it usually involves doing things you've never done before and putting yourself in new, vulnerable situations. Allowing this newer version of you to arrive expands what you know about your abilities. But beware of the cycle of despair – the continuous ups and downs – that comes with growing beyond your comfort zone. It's easy to get caught in, at least until you've put on your Inner Giggle glasses. Like the thinking caps we were told to put on before a test when we were kids, your Inner Giggle glasses will help you spot the joy, the pleasure, and the reasons to lighten up every time you think to put them on. If you want to include more pleasure in your days, for example, by definition you have to expand your mind's view to explore creative ways to include it. Often, it feels not as structured or familiar as your comfort zone does, but this is the goal of putting your Inner Giggle glasses on.

And do you know what else they'll do?

They'll help you stop discounting the evidence all around you of the things that make you happier right now. So, rather than belittle the job assignment you were given because it makes for more work, you actually acknowledge that finally you have achieved recognition of deserving more responsibilities at work. And though a small step toward the promotion you still long for, you can choose to notice those happier moments of being proud, validated, and grateful. Allow yourself a moment of heartfelt celebration; smile, step to the break room performing a small happy dance. Any personal gesture that feels good to you. You acknowledge the difference in your state, a change to a happier moment for you right now. You experience that you can be a serious employee, and still break into a dance at the break room. Give it a try next time any joyous reason comes around.

We all want to be more successful in our lives. But many of us wrestle with a fixed mindset when we would be better off developing a growth mindset. Let's examine the difference between the two.

Growth Mindset vs. Fixed Mindset

People with a fixed mindset, tie their self-worth to the outcome. They want to avoid failure at all costs, even if that means never trying something new. If they fail, they see it as proof of their lack of talent. But mostly, they believe they are born with a certain amount of intelligence or talent. That is why it is referred to as a fixed mindset: If they fall short at something, they believe they always will. It is fixed, set in stone.

Contemplate for a moment where your thoughts express a fixed mindset about your abilities. Some examples might be thoughts like, "I'm not a good communicator, and I will never be"; "I can't do math, better not try it"; "Even if I post 100 times a day, I'll never get enough likes"; or "That project looks hard, I'll just do my own thing."

People with a growth mindset embrace new challenges even if it might mean failing a couple times, or needing to adjust their methods, or rethinking their original plan. They know that's how they eventually grow. For them, the only failure is not going for their goals and learning along the way – they value cultivating new and deeper understanding. People with a growth mindset believe that what they were born with is just the starting point – and that with diligence, patience, and effort, their potential is vast.

They enjoy expanding their abilities and expect to improve from there. They adopt an attitude of a learner. Above all, they view their character and their circumstances as changeable. They remain flexible to the ebbs and flows of life and open to the challenges that may present themselves. They think in terms of growth.

Journal

Think about yourself for a moment. Where and when do you feel you express more of a growth mindset? Examples of a growth mindset may include thoughts like: "I love that painting, I'm going to work on my art!"; "I really appreciate the feedback, I can improve next time"; "That job description seems challenging, I think I should apply"; or "Progress has been slow, but I'll get there!" Are there other areas in your life in which you could better develop a growth mindset?

A big part of developing your growth mindset is getting comfortable saying the words "not yet." Maybe you want to climb a mountain peak, but right now, you can only do the first mile. It's not like your muscles will never be able to carry you that far, or your heart can never adjust; they just need time and exercise to develop. So when you eventually reach a point halfway to the summit, you reassure yourself you haven't reached the peak – yet. You enjoy your improvement so far, whatever distance you have conquered on this mountain. Your growth mindset inspires confidence and motivation. Should you choose to train more and allow the time it takes, you will reach the top of the summit.

Carol Dweck, PhD, is among the world's leading researchers in the field of motivation. A psychology professor at Stanford University, her research centers on why people succeed and foster success. In her book, *Mindset: The New Psychology of Success,* Dweck explains that people with a fixed mindset often don't believe in effort.[27] In that fixed mindset, failure means you aren't smart or talented. In a growth mindset world, your efforts, not the results of them, make you smart and talented. This is key! Effort through self-development, no matter what stage of life you're in, will allow you to grow toward success and happiness. If you thought you were doomed to fail because you weren't born with talent or because you lost some ability due to a chronic disease or accident, it would be difficult to keep your Inner Giggle healthy and vibrant.

When I began to tackle the process of healing from Lyme Disease, I decided to get into sculpting. I didn't consider myself an artist by any means, but I was looking for something to get myself out of the monotonous rut I'd found myself in. I needed a daily self-care practice outside of making treatment decisions that would lift my spirits. I turned to art as therapy, and I knew early on that I wanted to work with clay. I liked the idea that I could use the clay as a grounding experience, as well as the simplicity of having only one medium, the clay, to manipulate. I was excited to devote energy to a creative outlet.

Soon enough I found a class close to where I live and taught by an acclaimed sculptor who had some of her art pieces exhibited outdoors in the surrounding neighborhoods. On the first day, I found myself awkwardly holding a big, bulky piece of clay while the teacher went around the room and the students introduced themselves. It became clear that I was the only one with no prior experience. I wasn't within my comfort zone or in my natural habitat. What was I doing here? I wasn't an artist, let alone a sculptor. Nonetheless, I felt excited by the challenge.

The drive to learn and engage in this new modality helped me overcome my thoughts of self-doubt and connected me to the pleasure of being there. When I was able to let go of the uneasy feeling of being a newbie, I began to just enjoy the process – the pure, tactile aspect of touching and shaping the clay. By the end of the class, the clay was in a different shape – and so was I. The transformation, first in myself and then in my sculpture, was only possible due to a growth mindset.

After the class was over, I continued sculpting at home. Sculpting any shape of the human body seemed to be the most relevant to my self-healing journey. While choosing a pose to sculpt, I ventured deep into my soul and found one. The pose was a female torso with her hand hugging herself. I called it "Self-love," and every time I worked on it, I felt my Inner Giggle bubble up and my Happier Being soar. I watched as the powerful pose helped me re-frame the frustration I felt about my body getting sick into an acceptance pose that symbolized how hard I was working to view my body for what it really was: an ally in helping me get better.

Once sculpted, clay pieces get fired in a kiln under high heat. Although I would've liked to report that "Self-love" came out of the kiln as a beautiful piece, it did not. In fact, my cherished "Self-love" sculpture completely exploded while in the kiln.

My initial reaction was, of course, sadness and frustration (yes, I'm a psychologist, but I'm also human). But then I thought to myself: "Gosh, can one really love oneself too much? I guess my sculpture held onto herself too tightly!" All kidding aside, and despite the initial disappointment, it was a great reminder of the importance of the creative process, and not just the end result. The real therapeutic work was being done every day with my hands and with my mind, while warming up my soul – and no doubt, I would find additional ways to keep practicing self-love (more on this in Chapter Five).

The Focus Gap

I believe you can cultivate your mindset, connect, and grow your Happier Being because while you may think you have a talent gap (i.e., not being "artistic enough" to create a clay sculpture), you are probably suffering more from a focus gap.

The focus gap turns your attention toward what you think you can't achieve rather than focusing on how you can learn and grow. When you focus on what isn't working within you instead of focusing on your ability to change, you rob yourself of the chance to improve. Of course, improvement depends in part on your ability to assess your areas of strength and weakness and know which parts need a boost. Indeed, the growth mindset absolutely acknowledges the gap between where you are now and where you want to be. But the point of focus is essential here. You need to expand your mind to your potential; adopt the core belief that you can, that it is doable. Then you can do it.

A Quick Side Note: Great Things Happen

Great things happen when you expand your mind and your thinking about the bounds of your potential. Take, for example, running a four-minute mile. It was believed to be impossible until 1954 in Oxford, England, when a professional athlete and neurologist Roger Bannister cracked track and field's most notorious barrier. What's interesting is how it influenced other athletes' mindsets about what was possible. The year after the record was broken, eight more runners ran a sub-four-minute mile, and the following year fifty-four more runners did it. Bannister's achievement (his own growth mindset) led other athletes to expand their thinking about what was possible. Their mindset moved from fixed to growth, and with practice, the sub-four-minute mile became a reality for many. And if you're curious, at the time of writing this book, the current world record mile-time is held by Moroccan runner Hicham El Guerrouj at 3:43.13.

Finding Your Giggle Glasses Through Neuroplasticity

The more you engage your Inner Giggle, the more you increase your ability to be a Happier Being. So can you cultivate the growth mindset that allows that to be possible? As perhaps you're beginning to recognize, every belief can be changed, even your core beliefs about your own nature, talents, and abilities. This is a very powerful point! Believing that you can change and don't have to be extraordinary to do so is crucial. You have the ability to make positive changes in your life by becoming someone who forever learns – and therefore forever grows. Your choices matter. Your existing talents and skills are your starting point. You might not have reached your desired level *yet*, but through perseverance, repetition, and dedication, you will succeed.

The good news is there is a science to support that belief, and it illuminates a fascinating fact about your flexible brain. For many years, it was believed that the brain's anatomy was fixed and incapable of changing past a certain age. It was also believed that our number of neurons was finite – no new ones could form. Scientists believed that the only real change the adult brain was capable of was the long, slow degradation of the aging brain. That's all changed. Since then, neuroscientists have shown that the brain is flexible and capable of incredible change. In the field, we call this neuroplasticity.

Neuroplasticity means that the adult brain is not permanently hardwired or set in its ways – instead, it can create new neuron pathways and learn new patterns. The neurological circuitry is changeable, and our behavior influences its constant ability to form. As neurological expert Donald Hebb says, "Neurons that fire together, wire together." Meaning, you form your psychological resources by repeating the same experiences that build your repertoire, and those experiences turn into stronger neural connections that change your brain. Ultimately, that means you can change your behavior (and thereby change your brain) – even if you have done things the same way a thousand times before.

The changing brain is important when you prioritize being the best version of yourself. Your beliefs, your thoughts, matter. A thought is an electro-chemical reaction. It is a chemical response initiated by your thoughts, resulting in nerve cells transmitting impulses that drop specific neuro-transmitters in your synapses. From the synapse, it moves to the next neuron. The repetition of this electrochemical reaction strengthens this neural connection, and this, in turn, strengthens the thought or action being repeated.

Consequently, if you hold on to a growth mindset long enough, even if you were operating more from a fixed mindset before, your brain will open up neural pathways and help you think that way. When you repeatedly stimulate your growth mindset circuit in your brain (so to speak), you make that pathway thicker, deeper, and stronger. Your nerve cells, dendrites, synapses, all work to create the right chemical exchange so that your axons (long fiber-like roads that conduct impulses to move messages along) can run the neurons to the next nerve cells faster and inform your brain of your wishes. Your habitual thoughts and habits are crucial if you want to change.

Neuroscientist Eleanor Maguire of University College London (U.C.L.) conducted a study[28] that showed the brains of London taxicab drivers literally changing as they learned to successfully navigate the complicated networks of city streets. Their brains grew significantly thicker in the hippocampus region, an area of the brain associated with spatial navigating memory, proving that more new neural networks were forming and enlarging the busier this region got. The more experience the drivers had, the larger this area of the brain was found to be. This changing brain aided in their ability to retain all the ins and outs of the difficult structure of London streets – which, if you've ever visited, you know is not an easy task.

Your brain works for your benefit, leading you to new behaviors. It's an invigorating reinforcement loop. And if you can change your brain for the better, you can also change your beliefs, thoughts, and behavior. If the brain is constantly upgrading itself, then you have a lot of control in terms of directing its shape and influencing your life.

Cultivating a Growth Mindset

The following are some practical ways that will help you activate your newly cultivated growth mindset.

Refocus on Investing in Efforts

Whether it's a major issue like losing your job or a small one like bombing a presentation, look at the setback from all angles to determine where you need to invest your efforts next. Then focus on developing and growing what is in your control and expanding your repertoire to include it as part of the solution. For example, maybe the manuscript you've written is rejected. Does that mean you quit writing forever and conclude you are not good at writing and never will be? Or will you ask for feedback, keep editing, and pitch until someone likes it? All these things are within your power and control – and you can build them up to improve your manuscript and situation moving forward.

Your brain is just like any other muscle – it needs to be trained to grow. By refocusing on the process of learning, the need to receive feedback on your manuscript is appraised by your brain more neutrally. Since growth necessitates feedback, it is being assessed by your brain as something less threatening. Because less stress is produced, there is more energy to deal with the issue and try new approaches to succeed. This is growth. By discounting the emotional response of being disappointed by rejection and separating the feedback from who you are, you preserve your self-worth in the process.

Consequently, you view this phase of growing pains as a stepping-stone in building your writing skills, and that is exactly how you train your brain to expand and allow your skill to grow. Breaking down the steps into practical and manageable challenges will allow you to feel some improvement every time you tackle another aspect on your road to mastery. And that is the reinforcing loop that rewards your brain and motivates you to seek it out again.

It takes intentional focus and effort to build new habits and develop new patterns – as you learned in Chapter Two. The more you train your brain to accept that change is possible, the more you will be able to learn – and the better chance you have of reaching your desired outcome. In the example I shared earlier about sculpting, I made sure not to question the relevance of being in the sculpting class or whether or not I was given the "artistic gene." This would no doubt have hindered my abilities to sculpt. Instead, I refocused on the process so that I didn't lose out on the positive, reinforcing feedback inherent in the joy of creating.

Developing new skills, as well as a new mindset, takes a lot of dedication, practice, and patience. It's important to remind yourself that you won't develop expert-level status right away. Similarly, you can't change your mindset from a fixed one to a growth one instantly. But for both, with the persistence of doing and with the acceptance that most important things in life take time and effort, you will prevail.

I encourage you to reassure your questioning mind (the part of your mind that likes to believe others have it easier because of their talents) that this is not the whole story of their success. They, too, worked hard and long before their moment of success.

If you give yourself the time and invest in your work, one day at a time, persist and persevere, you have a tremendous chance of success waiting for you.

I want to point out that those who have a growth mindset certainly don't believe that everyone can become anything. As Carol Dweck explains, without proper motivation or education, no one can become Einstein or

Beethoven. But, she writes, "a person's true potential is unknown; and (further) that it's impossible to foresee what can be accomplished with years of passion, toil, and training."[29] A diligent, patient, and persistent effort will get you where you want to go.

The only way you can know how much you can grow is by taking action. Thinking won't suffice.

You can't water your seeds once and then hope they'll grow. You have to be realistic about it and take time to provide them with the best conditions to thrive. You are full of seeds – the seeds of success, the seeds of resilience – so take consistent action to water them so that they can sprout and grow to their fullest potential.

Intentionally Acknowledge Your Progress – Real Results
Embracing a growth mindset means stepping out of your comfort zone and facing daily challenges as opportunities. That is the best way to reach your highest potential. But you have to bear in mind that even when consistently stretching your edges, the progress can be little.

Journal
Take some time each day to acknowledge the progress you've made. Did you make even one percent progress toward your goal of writing your book, fixing up the house, or learning a new skill? What changes did you make, or new patterns did you follow to improve your situation? Document it in your favorite note app.

The hard work you put into something should always be rewarded before the inherent skill. The talent is extra. The practice matters more. That is why it is not the degree of talent that assures your success; it is the extent of your growth mindset with its inherent tendency to keep learning and growing that will get you there. Perhaps not yet, not today, but soon enough if you continue to learn, practice, and feel proud of your progress.

Many growth mindset experts will warn you to beware of the false growth mindset: praising empty progress. Be honest about whether you've chosen the right path to learning. Check in with your progress often. Do not insist and persist with an ineffective learning strategy because you are now "focused" on effort, i.e., practicing your growth mindset. Be cognizant of seeing actual growth results, no matter how small they might be. True progress is the goal, even if you need to adjust your methods at some point – and I guarantee you that time will come, and likely more than once. But luckily, with a growth mindset, you are equipped to do just that.

My client, Rachel, was well-known and well-respected at work for her market research and writing skills, but when it came time for her to give a big presentation, she was overwhelmed by anxiety. In exploring why, I learned that Rachel, though she had a growth mindset in some areas of her life, had a fixed mindset with others. (Does that sound familiar to you? It sure does to me!) She told me that she wasn't good at public speaking, that she was uncomfortable in front of people, and that she wasn't fast on her feet talking to groups.

As we dove into the issue, we discovered this hesitance came from the messaging she'd absorbed as a child. Early on, Rachel learned not to do things she wasn't already good at, and speaking her mind was not something she'd practiced growing up. Her perception of her speaking abilities was formed in contrast to her family's opinions of her older brother's skill. Their parents called him a "born salesman," and he often dominated family conversations, much to young Rachel's dismay.

The upcoming presentation at work and its potential for feedback and criticism scared her. She was so worried about being hurt that she took the self-defeating stance of believing she was unable to change or grow as a public speaker. We talked about her expectations. She might never be an outstanding public speaker, but she could get better. Certainly she could get good enough to present something solid without fear of being ridiculed.

The go-to presenter among Rachel's colleagues was a well-spoken, friendly young gentleman in his thirties. Public speaking seemed to come naturally to him. Even though Rachel usually liked being behind the scenes and in her comfort zone, she was jealous. He just seemed so effortlessly good at it. I suggested she ask him to mentor her or at least give her some advice. When she did, Rachel was surprised to learn how much he actually practiced before each presentation to pull off that effortless impression.

We further explored the relevant and interesting things about our perceptions of others. It's easy to believe others are the product of overnight success. But we don't see how much work goes on behind the scenes. We don't see the starts and stops, the failures, and the do-overs. We overlook all the effort, but it's that effort that makes a good speaker a great one. For Rachel to go from fear of presenting to accomplishing it, she'd have to make the effort to practice, not just this time, but the next, and the next.

Bearing all that in mind, we talked through how she could improve her skills by practice and didn't have to become an excellent orator overnight to give this one presentation, just like she didn't become such a great writer and researcher overnight. Rachel just had to take action and move from a fixed mindset to a growth mindset – which she did.

By cultivating a growth mindset, she gave herself the tools to nourish her Happier Being. She slowly learned that she could build her presentation skill, that it was okay to practice something she wasn't as naturally good at, and that she could even feel joy in facing new challenges and developing new skills. Rachel also felt a great sense of pride. It wasn't easy stepping out of her comfort zone into inevitable difficulties and eventual disappointments. Still, she did it – and that was the key to developing a growth mindset in this area of her life.

One of the more surprising things that she found herself admitting in our next session was that she always thought she could be really good at public speaking, if she only tried. She often felt she could have spoken on different matters better than her brother, who was given the stage at home. Later in life, she continued with that which was familiar and adopted a fixed mindset about her public speaking ability. But deep down, she longed to overcome the fear so she could materialize the speaking abilities she felt she possessed. Utilizing a growth mindset helped her express just that.

As Marianne Williamson says, "Our deepest fear is not that we are inadequate. Our deepest fear is that we are powerful beyond measure. It is our light, not our darkness that most frightens us."

Be open to your light and your power, even if it scares you a bit. Use the empowerment and joy that comes with moving the needle toward your goals. This is really your Inner Giggle guiding you to become not only more successful in life but also increase your well-being. Remember, you are forming your newest identity as a lifelong learner. So be open to circumstances in the present, and Happier Being will be your gift!

Recap

- People with a fixed mindset believe that they were born with a set amount of intelligence or talent that will always land them in the same place (fixed).
- People with a growth mindset believe that what they were born with is just the starting point – and with diligence, patience, and effort, their potential is vast (growth).
- Whereas people with a fixed mindset tie their self-worth to outcomes, people with a growth mindset tie themselves to the process. Fixed mindsets tend to stay in their comfort zone, avoiding failure at all costs, while growth mindsets embrace failure as a learning experience, a steppingstone, and remain malleable to life's many challenges. Most people have experienced both types of mindsets, just in different aspects of their lives.
- Due to neuroplasticity of the brain, your repeated actions and habits forge new pathways and strengthen neural connections. This makes changing your mindset from fixed to growth easier over time. Your brain's neuroplasticity is a daily gift to you, so use it.
- People suffer from a focus gap – not a talent gap – and when focus turns into effort, great things happen. If you give yourself the time, invest in your work, and listen to your Inner Giggle, you have a tremendous chance of success waiting for you.
- Remember to acknowledge your progress and results. Reward your hard work before inherent skill. Practice matters. Talent is an added bonus.

Bonus information and mental training exercises relating to this chapter can be found here: happierbeing.com/exercises

Connection+:
Recognizing a Deeper Love

Watch Your Heart Happiness Thrive

Our Happier Being yearns for connection and belonging. As Thich Nhat Hanh said, "We are here to awaken from the illusion of our separateness."[30] Yet many obstacles can get in the way of that deep desire. Take loneliness, for example, which is increasing worldwide despite all the connectivity that technology brings. In my clinical practice, I'm now seeing more clients suffering from loneliness than ever before.

Data collected in the US and worldwide reflects what I've seen in my practice. According to a 2019 report by Cigna, a large health insurance provider, about sixty-one percent of Americans reported being lonely – an increase of seven percent from the previous year. The report also showed that about twenty-four percent of Americans rank their mental health as fair or poor. It's no surprise then that we are seeing more organizations, hospital systems, insurers, and well-known figures speaking openly about mental health issues. Words and concepts such as "well-being," "self-love," and "social connections" have become commonplace, and for good reason – we are lonelier than ever before. So what's causing the unfortunate and steady increase of loneliness?

According to Cigna's report,[31] the main contributors to loneliness are lack of social support or meaningful social interaction. The other contributors are negative feelings about personal relationships, poor physical and mental health, and a lack of balance in day-to-day activities. The report explains that those who generally have a higher annual household income, say $125K or more, are lonelier than lower household income, say $25K or less. Additionally, the report shows younger generations are lonelier than older generations – with Gen Z at seventy-nine percent, Millennials at seventy percent, and Baby Boomers at fifty percent.

These numbers are generally in line with the BBC Loneliness Experiment,[32] a large-scale global study published in 2020. The study concluded that loneliness is highest among young people, followed by middle-aged people, and lastly older people. It also found that men (as opposed to women) and those living in "individualistic" societies were shown to be lonelier. Moreover, this study found that loneliness significantly affects the brain. It doesn't just make us feel sad, it can actually cause physiological changes. One study in the BBC loneliness experiment on social distancing during the coronavirus pandemic showed this phenomenon.[33] The study showed that the neural underpinnings associated with isolation are similar to those of physical hunger – so when we say we're starving for contact, we're not far off from what's happening to our brains physiologically.

At the time of writing this book, there have already been concerning surveys showing that loneliness is on the rise due to COVID-19. Over the years to come, I have no doubt that we'll gain more data on how social distancing has affected loneliness across the globe. There is no underestimating the pandemic's devastating effect on the well-being of so many. For this reason, the topic of loneliness and the importance of social connections have to be at the forefront of our Happier Being journey.

Journal

How did social distancing during the Covid-19 pandemic affect your well-being? Have you been taking social connections for granted? Are you still?

The Missing Ingredient – Other People Matter

Loneliness is really your brain's way of signaling that your body is missing something important – that your balance is off. And the truth is, if you are lonely or isolated for too long, you can develop a long list of health problems. Think about it. Why do you have physical reactions to mental pain, such as heartbreak, for example? Why does your mood change once you're around close friends and family?

Being connected is a powerful augmentation to your practices in order to get many of the results you want in life. As Michelle Tillis Lederman explains in her book, *The Connector's Advantage,* whatever you are working on or hope to accomplish will come about faster, easier, and usually better with the support of your connections. For example, you are more likely to get a job if you were referred by your social connections. Or you are more likely to find and accept a good referral when you received it from a friend. The closer connections you have, the higher the chances of success in your endeavors. Connecting with others is good for you, period. Thus, figuring out your beliefs about your ability to socially connect is paramount to your well-being.

Apart from personality differences that might make you more or less natural at making connections than someone else, there are external circumstances that affect your ability to connect. For instance, I believe that the opportunity to create strong social connections and close relationships is on a downward trend. The remote-work status has increased tremendously for many, and with that the amount of daily, face-to-face interactions has decreased. The gig economy and the use of tech, namely texting and emailing perpetuates the lack of sharing space and time. Further, competing in the gig or contract work economy may mean working overtime or on weekends. Although these jobs provide flexibility, many people don't have days off that match up with those of their friends, making it difficult to stay in touch or make plans to meet. Others find it hard to maintain their familial connections due to work relocation taking them away from their family.

There is also a trend toward socializing online and texting instead of talking, resulting in fewer opportunities to have in-person social interactions. We all know the overall time spent behind screens has its own detrimental effect when overused. My take: use technology to your advantage. I myself am incredibly grateful that the internet has allowed me the opportunity to meet and connect with others, personally and professionally. In many ways it's beneficial to connect online, but it has to be used wisely! Overusing technology can affect our relationship-building skills and has far-reaching consequences on the fabric of our social interactions.

We need to find ways to create strong social connections and close relationships, via the internet and in person. For many of us who spend time in front of screens, I believe it's also important to prioritize the latter, especially with significant others. We must accept that those close relationships take work to create and more work to maintain. Investing in your circle of connectors is vital to your well-being. As Christopher Peterson[34] simply and sweetly said: "Other people matter." When you don't feel as if you have strong connections, you feel less belonging, and you experience more loneliness. That is a painful price to pay for being disconnected.

In our first session, Liz came to me wanting a game plan. She was a determined woman from an affluent family and had a history of abuse. She exhibited confidence, used humor, and put up thick walls when it came to emotions and close connections. She was well-liked by her peers but thought she didn't relate well to them and often felt lonely. She felt different and disconnected, and it stifled her ability to feel happy — she noticed that she was becoming more isolated. As we worked together, Liz's main goal, in her own straightforward and exasperated words was: "I don't want to feel lonely anymore, period."

We worked together to determine why she felt deeply lonely, and how this related to her negative childhood experiences. Putting language to any former negative bonding experience or even social trauma was a good place to start, not only for loneliness, but also for overall well-being. Liz quickly realized how deeply and unconsciously her childhood trauma had been in the background of all her relationships. Her old, isolating pattern had made her feel safer back then, but she was still operating from it in the present despite it no longer being useful. Liz needed to learn how to form secure attachments with others, even if she initially felt emotionally unsafe.

We explored how her patterns pushed her toward a "me versus them" attitude and contributed to her loneliness. I asked Liz to pay attention to her core beliefs around that mentality. She acknowledged that she scanned the environment to find evidence that she was different from the rest. I asked her to pay attention to this theme and notice the thoughts that caused loneliness to percolate. Then, together, in our safe environment, she would fill in the gaps of what was happening in reality, not just how she perceived the situation in between her own ears.

Liz practiced statements that allowed her to hold the two opposing sides of a scenario at the same time. "It is possible," she acknowledged, "that I am not as 'different' as I feel I am, even if I still experience myself differently at times." She also noted, "As a matter of fact, the other day, Peter expressed how easy I am to talk to."

This practice would, in time, help Liz acknowledge that there were others out there like her – because there was. The more Liz spent time investigating how different she felt, the more she started noticing how others are plagued with the same fear of not being able to fit in. As she shifted her focus, her hippocampus created new neurons that created new memories. (As a refresher on this topic, you can refer to neuroplasticity in Chapter Four).

Liz began feeling less isolated, and we worked together on building that feeling by reintroducing supportive, loving things into her life. Slowly, Liz was drawn back into more social settings, even small ones. She began feeling the joy of positive daily interactions with strangers – at the supermarket, the doctor's office, or even in the elevator. The warm exchanges with others made Liz feel good and gave her small doses of positivity in her daily affairs. They increased her ratio of positive emotions and tipped the balance away from feeling isolated, depressed, or anxious about her ability to connect. Slowly, other doors opened in her emotional life, and Liz became more confident and motivated. Liz was ready for the next step.

Because Liz enjoyed gardening, I encouraged her to join a gardening group to begin forming more meaningful social connections. From there, it was time for Liz to address the scarier, deeper layers of social connection – the kind of connection that could leave her feeling very vulnerable. I had Liz pick one person she could trust and be honest about how she felt with them. This would be someone she could reveal her authentic self to, that would act as a sounding board for her negative emotions. Liz now understood that if she was to have a deeper connection and a fulfilling bond, she would have to be willing to open up – revealing parts of herself that perhaps she considered less desirable.

She was, of course, not in love with this idea; it made her nervous. But slowly, we peeled off more emotional layers from her emotionally isolated life in the past and connected it to how it played out with others in the present. Eventually, Liz became more confident in taking social risks. The more Liz engaged in deeper social connections, the more she realized that those she trusted did not let her down, and the less vulnerable she felt. With more trust, the less lonely she became. And the less lonely she became, the more joy she experienced in her social life.

Social Connections

By now, I trust you are on board with the fact that being happier is not an indulgence reserved for after you accomplish your goals, but rather an important ingredient in reaching them. This poses the question: How then can you start increasing your levels of happiness today?

The immediate way to increase happiness levels is by leveraging your social connections. The strongest, most consistent finding in psychology research across the board demonstrates time and time again that those who have strong social ties are less depressed. Becoming more genuinely connected will increase your happiness level. As Dr. Peterson also said, you don't need many, but you have to have one person you feel connected to that you can call at 3 a.m. for anything at all. Do you have someone like that?

Think about getting happier like it's a team sport. In other words, start strength training your social connection muscles. You must put in your best effort to be fit enough to belong on the team. But you also have to find the best teammates. To become happier, you need the people you socialize with and who are closest to you to be your support system. Putting your best foot forward to connect with your team while they cheer you on will provide you with a winning formula to feeling happy. And, like in team sports, it's not only about winning the game or, in this case, becoming a happier player. The total experience of belonging to the team is in and of itself a way for you to feel happier. Your team can get you out of a daily funk or even long-standing, low-grade depression. So, if "Happier Being" is the main goal of the game, then just feeling connected to the "team" will already set you up for a win-win.

All this "team" discussion reminds me of a particular team I was once a part of – a psychiatric emergency team. Perhaps this next story is a bit of an extreme example, highlighting the importance of human connection even when one finds themselves disconnected from normative society. Nonetheless, it powerfully illustrates how connection – brief as it may be – has the power to heal.

Some of the most painful moments working as a psychologist are when you face mental illness at its more intense. This is the case when family members, friends, or neighbors have reached a point when they need someone to come and assess their loved ones and decide if hospitalization due to their mental state is warranted.

As part of my role in a mental health clinic years ago, I was on what's called a Psychiatric Emergency Team (PET). The PET unit is called upon in such cases to perform an assessment and consists of mental health professionals, often accompanied by police. The scenarios of when a PET unit is sent out vary, but in general, a person has to reach a state of being a danger to themselves or others.

I encountered many different types of mental illness as part of the PET unit, and I know that severe mental illness can distort the mind and shatter the heart. If psychosis breaks out, the inability to know what is real or not real is extremely frightening and distressing to the sufferers. It's a difficult experience to observe and can become challenging to contain. Imagine trying to communicate with someone who is paranoid that others are out to get them, or looking into the empty eyes of a suicidal person whose soul has momentarily exited. It is challenging and heartbreaking, to say the least, but also a profound moment of human care and connection.

Once we got through to the person in crisis, the PET unit and I would perform a psychological assessment to the best of our ability to determine if voluntary or involuntary hospitalization was necessary. If the person was coherent and willing to cooperate, they would be escorted to the hospital and placed on a voluntary hold. But if they were not, they would be committed involuntarily. In the involuntary case, the person had to be taken against their will (but for their own well-being).

After they were released from the hospital, they could choose where to continue treatment. Although they could choose any other clinic, many of them decided to return to our clinic, with the same staff who were on the PET unit (including myself) that hospitalized them. This meant I got the chance to continue therapy with them and ask them about their decision to do so.

Remarkably, many of them expressed that despite the chaos of their mental breakdown and involuntary hospitalization, they still felt cared for during their crisis. It didn't matter that the clinic staff were technically strangers to them or that the PET unit took them against their will. Post-hospitalization, they had improved enough to accept that the deed was done for them and not to them. The human care and connection had registered to them even under such duress. Instead of being angry and eager to place blame on me and the PET unit, they were thankful – thankful for the people who'd reached out a hand at the lowest, darkest point of their lives and lifted them up out of quicksand when they couldn't do it themselves.

Never doubt the power of connection. Connection that serves as a positive support system has the ability to greatly improve the quality of your life. Unfortunately, many of us lack the positive relationships or supportive connections we need to become our happier selves. But while you can't change the family you were born into, you can choose who you spend time with as an adult. Remind yourself daily that connecting with the right social support is of the utmost significance if you want to become happier. Make plans to incorporate it into your routine. Think about all that's possible when people work together. We are, after all, social beings who flourish with connection. Since social connection is so important to your well-being, I encourage you to prioritize it. Invest in relationships and build your best connections. This will help you move away from lingering loneliness, and in turn, nourish your inner self.

Journal

What are the underlying psychological reasons – the social connection stories you tell yourself – that keep you from deeper kinship? Once you gain insights into why you have these stories and how they make you lonelier, finding a secure and nourishing attachment with another person is easier to achieve. Think about Liz's story and write down some ways you might be able to start increasing your social connections.

Concluding this section, I'll leave you with a quote by Baltasar Gracian from *The Art of Worldly Wisdom*, "There is no desert like living without friends. Friendship multiplies the good of life and divides the evil. It is the sole remedy against misfortune, the very ventilation of the soul."

A Quick Side Note: Connection as a Physical Health Booster

Being connected is good not only for your mood but also for your physical health. Extensive research from the medical community supports the numerous positive effects that social connections have on your health and well-being. For example, it was demonstrated that those living in isolation are more likely to suffer from the aftermath of viral infections and inflammation. As a matter of fact, some researchers go as far as to say that social isolation is a stronger predictor of death from chronic diseases than lack of physical activity, alcohol use, or smoking. They give the example that social isolation can be as damaging as 15 cigarettes a day. As evident in many health-related support group data findings, members who join a support group can decrease some of their chronic condition markers faster than they could by just taking medications.

Comparison Is the Thief of Joy

You need to invest in your Inner Giggle by investing in social connections. But what's around you, your environment, is vital too. Let's start with easier remedies: things that are in your control, that you can do less of.

One thing that might be causing you to feel lonelier is in the palm of your hand – your cell phone. You've probably heard that comparison is the thief of joy. I'd like to add that comparison doesn't only steal away joy; it can also cause bad moods, and, if you get stuck there too long, it might lead to depression as well. One of the more accessible and easiest platforms on which to compare yourself to others is social media. Let me be clear, I think that social media is an amazing tool if used carefully. But social media usage affects different people differently, and therefore you must be watchful.

People spend hours on social media – how much depends on which survey you read. This is especially true for younger generations, but all ages are susceptible to the effects of comparison, via social media or otherwise. When you post something on social media, your addictive brain prods you to check how many "likes" or comments you got. In a way, this "internal texting," if you will, is the most demanding type of communication you engage in. Moreover, every time you cave in to this internal pressure to check your social media accounts, you get sucked into checking your friends' posts.

For some users, consistent engagement with social media is detrimental to their well-being. It goes like this: The stimuli with the reward circuit in your brain, detects the potential for pleasure (the number of reactions or comments). Checking social media then releases the neurotransmitter dopamine. Soon you find yourself spending more time scrolling through your feed or semi-stalking your Facebook friends than you anticipated. And though you are very aware that most people post the positive highlights of their life and rarely share disappointment, hurt, or rejection, you can still fall prey to the deception of skewed positive posts. Consequently, you end up feeling a host of negative feelings as you compare your current status to their posted one.

For other users, the same behavior of checking their feed isn't as detrimental to their mood. If you are in this group of people, then you not only afford others joy but perhaps even absorb it on some emotional level. And that is absolutely great for you as luckily, it is a great group to belong to. The Dalai Lama alludes to the fact that if you can be happy when others are happy, you can always be happy, because after all, there is always someone somewhere around the globe who is happy.

That being said, many of us are not in this group. We are in the group who compares, and as a result form self-judgments. When we see our peers experiencing joy or success and we are not, we feel "lesser than" and bad about ourselves instead of only happy for them. On the flip side, as Dr. Lyubomirsky[35] concludes in her studies, when we see our peers' downfalls or failures this can even lead some to feel relieved as opposed to sympathetic. But this relief does not make us feel good about ourselves. The detrimental effects of checking social media and comparison can impact even one's true nature of being a good friend. Clearly, that's not the way to connect with others, and certainly not with your authentic, happy self. You are disappointing your Happier Being.

More on finding ways to overcome the tendency to compare later in the chapter. But for now, I want you to practice directing your comparison inward. In other words, when you find yourself comparing, bring your attention back to yourself, and compare yourself to how you are today, as opposed to yesterday or the year before, on whatever measurement that matters to you. Focus on aspects of your life in which you can find increments of joy, indicating your dedication to stay on course with your path. As fitness coaches like to say, look in the mirror, that is your competition.

Stop and think. Do you find yourself relating to the negative loop of checking social media and comparing yourself to others? Where do you fall on the continuum of socially comparing? Do you tend to celebrate the success of those around you, or do you rejoice in their failure? Be honest with yourself – it's okay if you're more aligned with the latter. The important thing is that you recognize this so you can move toward change.

Your Abundant Being Creates Your World!

We worked on mindset in Chapter Four, and it is crucial to address your heart mindset here as well. Open your heart to the idea that there is "enough" of everything out there, including many ways to win, enough great relationships or professional success, enough friendships, or plenty of travel destinations and enough time to do it. Therefore, if your relatives are doing things which you wish you could do – say traveling – that doesn't mean they are taking away your chances to do the same thing. Or if your close friend who was divorced for many years finally found her new love connection, resulting in you both spending less time together, still celebrate it for her. Acknowledge the reality that someone else living the good life does not prevent you from living a good life. Remember oftentimes social comparison has nothing but a detrimental effect on your Happier Being. Shifting your focus to an abundance mindset instead will help nourish your Inner Giggle metrics.

I'd like to pause for a second here to make the point that, in general, we do learn by comparison. Hot or cold, short or tall, rich or poor. There is no escape from comparison when it comes to human nature, and comparison per se is not a bad thing at all; quite the contrary. It can act as a safety feature, knowing which risk is too big or too small, all comparatively to your standards and different scenarios. But here we are discussing social comparison from a scarcity mentality that leads to the inevitable conclusion that because others have – whatever that might be – you, therefore, do not get to have it. And here lies the emotional price you pay for such a mindset. It leaves you feeling envious, or worse yet, separated from the rest who do have.

Scarcity Mindset Out, Abundance Mindset In

What if, for half a day, you decided to relate to "those who have" with the opposite of envy or jealousy? Don't abandon your prior way of feeling; for now, just explore another perception. Sneak in a compassionate, happy thought for them. Consider how it would feel to experience your day from this abundance lens. Can you sense the relief that comes with it? Do you realize how much energy you use when you feel resentful, upset, or that things are unfair? Without that energetic expense, do you feel the shift in your muscle tension, in your breathing?

In his book, *The Secrets of the Millionaire Mind*, Harv Eker,[36] a Canadian author and businessman, writes that you should "bless that which you want." I think this is a powerful view to aspire to, with the understanding that you can still allow some envy, but to be pleased for others' fortune too. After all, why not allow positive envy which can inspire you and feel happy for others who have what you'd like to have? Bless their gifts with an open heart, immersing yourself in the comfortable feeling of an abundance outlook. This idea of an abundance mindset will also increase your own self-worth and allow you to experience yourself as enough. What a welcome experience that will be!

So, in the context of connecting with others, what's stopping you from experiencing yourself as enough? If you have internalized core beliefs about your emotional abilities or values that have damaged your self-concept, like Liz (whom you met earlier in the chapter), your life experiences of rejection or shame may have created beliefs like, "I'm not like anybody else. Something is inherently wrong with me. I'm not lovable. I'm not good enough." These core beliefs were formed early in your life but affect your emotional life in the present. The question now becomes what can you do?

You can start off by becoming cognizant of any resistance to change you may have. Though you crave more social connections, your style of interaction with others – be it isolating, avoiding, wanting not to appear needy, or even the inability to accept compliments – are all psychological-emotional defense mechanisms you developed to protect yourself. These are the early childhood adaptations that served you well enough around that time due to familial or social circumstances. But these same defense mechanisms might work against you as you try to change. They create resistance to you venturing into new social territories.

In short, your past adaptations are causing your maladaptive symptoms in the present. They maintain your loneliness and reinforce your feelings of inadequacy in social contexts. For example, if you used to isolate or present yourself as needing no one, you did so to fend off the likelihood of social rejection or ridicule. But that self-isolation also kept you from feeling a part of a community, or feeling what it's like to risk being vulnerable, or even loved without feeling devastated. Your mind is perpetuating your experience of not feeling socially good enough in the past into your present. I urge you to fight this distorted notion with the insights you gain into your past behavior, and how it does not serve you today. Overcome your inner resistance to change your social interactions, and your social life will flourish.

Surround Yourself with Those Who Nourish Your Happier Being

Here's a fascinating and relevant fact that will help keep you moving toward making more meaningful social connection. Research has shown that sharing positive events with people close to you can increase personal and relationship well-being.[37] This is due to the phenomenon of mirror neurons.[38] A standard mirror reflects the choice you made to cut your own bangs (ouch!) or the fun new outfit you picked out for a special event. Our brain's system of neurons does something similar, reflecting others around us. Yes, mirror neuron theory hypothesizes that emotions can, essentially, be contagious.

Mirror neuron theory means it's actually vitally important to surround yourselves with what you want to experience for yourself: happy people willing to share that positivity with you and boost your Inner Giggle! It also means that it is equally important to let go of those who poison your spirit. If connection is currency, don't hold onto those who put you at a negative emotional balance.[39] This is worth repeating:

Some of these people might be casual acquaintances. Others might be friends, or even family members. One way to determine if someone is sucking your energy away is if, after you hang out with them, you feel more emotionally depleted than when you're alone. That's your cue. They cause some emotional deficit. They make you feel alienated, ashamed, unaccepted – they are not your people.

Empower yourself to let them go. Having a smaller number of friends will not make you lonelier. It is the type of meaningful friendship you are looking for that will nourish your soul. Moreover, it will nourish your overall potential for success in your life.[40] According to research, those you customarily spend time with can account for as much as ninety percent of your success in life. So be responsible for whom you spend your time with. Actively construct your social connections. Don't determine whom you hang out with based on old patterns, physical proximity, or inertia.

As business philosopher, author, and motivational speaker Jim Rohn says, "You are the average of the five people you spend the most time with."

Journal

Figure out who are the people that nourish you, those you admire, and those who drain your energy. Decide how much time you should spend with either. Invest in your strongest, most nourishing social associations. Can you take this moment to ensure you spend more time with them? Give them a phone call or set up a time to meet, right now!

Reticular Activating System to the Rescue

The Reticular Activating System (RAS) is a part of the brainstem that performs many crucial roles in your survival. This region of the brain is so critical that trauma to it can result in a coma. The RAS receives 400 billion bits of information every second – and it deletes and destroys any bit of information you don't focus on or give significance to.

A countless number of messages are thrown at you every minute of your day. Logically, it is impossible to attend to them all. But your RAS handles it easily, by labeling and sorting them. It intentionally blinds information you've proven to care less about and brings awareness to that which is familiar and important to you. A great example would be noticing more pregnant women out there if you're trying to get pregnant or already pregnant. Or, if you're out shopping for a particular car, your RAS allows you to filter your awareness so that you begin to see the same car all around you. It's not that the number of pregnant women or this type of car increased, it's that you made this stimulus more familiar and important, and your RAS is responding to that which triggers it and brings it to your attention.

Guess what? The same mechanism comes into play regarding your longstanding beliefs and emotional states. Your RAS zooms in on the more familiar experiences, the thoughts repeated many times before, and labels them significant. Equally important, it deletes any signals to the contrary. Take, for example, a significant trigger that can inhibit you from forming strong connections at work, like the thought, "I am not enough." Your RAS is on the lookout for any evidence out there that substantiates this thought, and rejects any evidence that signals otherwise. It's no surprise that any thoughts or actions that prove you are enough go largely unnoticed. For example, if you received positive feedback at work but it wasn't the highest praise, you quickly assess it as though you were "not enough." Not smart enough, not creative enough, not liked enough. The personal, negative narrative you're creating influences your mental map, as your RAS has learned to scan for this evidence quickly – but perhaps (given that you received positive feedback) you are even more than enough!

This is why it's so important to create new beliefs – and to spend more time with those new beliefs than you do with the old ones. The RAS is why it's crucial to focus on what you want to grow. If you want to grow your self-worth, for example, if you want to lessen the painful old pattern that you are not enough, you have to start entertaining the idea that you are enough. Big leap? Perhaps, but if you can pace yourself and maintain realistic expectations, your changed focus will pay off.

You can't change this built-in habit of scanning to prove you are not enough overnight. But you can allow your heart and mind to accommodate the goal of finding new evidence that proves otherwise. This new aim refocuses your attention on it, invites you to rehearse it, and primes your RAS to follow and help you along. The more you venture to find it, the more you signal to your RAS that this is an important topic to filter in for your consideration. The repetition of aiming to the new goal of self-acceptance will increase the likelihood that you will find the self-confirming details needed to reinforce it. Your RAS will filter in more of what you signaled as relevant, and before long, you'll start seeing more tidbits of data out there that are self-affirming, that you are enough, in real-time. That is when the transformation of being enough takes off.

The RAS shows why "you have to see it to believe it," – and it also explains why you have to *want* to believe it to see it. It's a two-way street. We'll talk shortly about tools to boost your feelings of belongingness and increase your positive emotions in general. For now, if you feel a bit lost about where to begin, I want you to start by calibrating your "not-enoughness" emotions. Start with what seems easiest to perform and hardest to believe, simply by making "I am enough" statements.

Does that sound ridiculous? Do you feel it's not for you? I can relate. I have not always been big on affirmations, and yet there is great data that attests to their efficacy. Using "I am enough" statements can help reactivate what your mind already knew when you were born: that you were born perfect, whole, enough. It will help your RAS scan for information that confirms what you focus on and reject anything irrelevant.

Journal

Have you ever looked at a baby and thought, "Gosh, this baby is not enough"? Of course not. That baby is more than enough – and so are you. Find one of your baby photos and take a look. Are you looking cute enough? Lovable enough? Write this "I am enough" statement, read it, say it – and repeat. Have these words – "I am enough" – visible on your mirror, your screensaver, in your calendar reminders. Use those words as a trigger to the evidence of your "enoughness" all day long. Catalog it into your abundance mindset.

Resist the temptation to do just the opposite, which comes so easily to you. After all, this theme of not being enough keeps you from forming meaningful relationships with yourself and others.

Increase Your Positive
to Negative Emotions Ratio

In her book *Positivity,* Dr. Barbara Frederickson[41] explains why positive mindsets – such as joy, hope, and gratitude – are more than just "feeling good." They help optimize your brain and body to perform at their best. That said, it's important to note that it's not bad to have negative emotions. First, it means you're still alive and breathing. Second, you are a human who interacts in the real world, where there are plenty of reasons to experience negative emotions. No matter how privileged you may be, there will still be annoying people around you, you will still face disappointments, and, as life goes on, some suffering will occur. It's good to experience and express all your emotions as they come. In fact, T. Kashdan and R. Biswas-Diener wrote an excellent book[42] about the need to access our full range of emotions. Feeling anger, it turns out, can fuel your creativity. Guilt can motivate you to change. Even self-doubt, despite its painfulness, can still enhance your performance. As Golda Meir famously said, "Those who do not know how to weep with their whole heart don't know how to laugh either."

Emotions like anger, guilt, and self-doubt mirror back to you what needs to be taken care of in your life. Thus, ignoring or suppressing all negative emotions is not ideal. Figuring out what's required to solve those issues is the goal. Having a reservoir of inner strength to do so is what you are here to learn to do. Interestingly enough, increasing your overall ratio of positive emotions to negative ones is what aids greatly in building this reservoir and dealing with the upsets and challenges of life. That's why, for now, we are focusing on the benefits of positive emotions to your well-being.

Dr. Fredrickson developed the "Broaden and Build Theory,"[43] which examines how positive emotions have both short-term positive outcomes (broaden effect) and long-term positive outcomes (build effect). While negative emotions cause our thoughts to narrow and focus on the specifics of a problem (which has its place and relevance to our survival), positive emotions cause our thoughts to expand or broaden and build bigger storages of potential practical behaviors.

The Broaden and Build Theory argues that positive emotions stretch your thought processes by allowing your focus to expand and consider new options, novel ideas, or thoughts. That, in turn, provides you with more potential actions. This greater awareness of novelty choices, over time, enlarges your built-in skills and resources.

This can happen, for example, when someone feels curious about a particular subject or person. They may have the desire to dig deeper and learn more. They may take creative action to get more information, find new ways to approach and connect, etc. Thus, curiosity as a positive emotion doesn't only change the content of your thoughts (from being bored to being interested) it also changes the range and boundaries of your mind (gaining new insights about a person or a subject) and impacts your actions and well-being.[44]

How does it look in your daily life? If you feel tickled by something when with a friend, you will seek out more ways of sharing laughter together longer. Once you experience more joy, you will look for more play with that friend or in your life. Play will reinforce more joy and more potential for creation. If you experience more gratitude for that creation, you might look for new avenues to be more giving to others, as gratitude manifests that.

There is one emotion that will provide you the experience of all the other emotions described above (and more): love. Love, according to Dr. Fredrickson, exists in more ways than we may realize, and we'll get into Dr. Frederickson's unique definition of "love 2.0" shortly. Still, all positive emotions can create more motivation, opportunities, and reinforcement of the cycle of positive emotions you experience. We all like a positive cycle that just keeps going and going!

Experiencing More Positives

Experiencing positive emotions more often will help you organize new information, prolong the time it stays stored, and decrease the time it takes to retrieve that same information later on. Getting yourself to increase your ratio of positive versus negative emotions is undoubtedly crucial to your problem-solving ability. And that is one heck of a benefit of feeling good!

The more positive emotions you're able to add, the more positive change you will experience, and the more hopefulness you'll gain. This equation also works in reverse: hopefulness leads to positive experiences, which lead to positive emotions. It feels good, and it is good for you. Small changes, big differences.

Journal

Which positive emotions would you like to experience more of in order to broaden and build your repertoire? What positive emotions, for example, will widen your path for more social connections? Explore new ideas to experience more range of emotions that will add to your day-to-day life. Write them down, and get creative. Broaden and build your Happier Being!

The following are some suggestions on how to increase your positive emotions:

Increase Your Positivity Ratio

The optimal ratio for flourishing, according to research, is 3:1. For every negative emotion experience, you should seek out three positive ones.[45] Now, life of course does not follow a mathematical formula, and indeed the ratio itself is not necessarily the thing to focus on. It's an important self-assessment and feedback tool but not the end-all and be-all. Any increase in positive emotions will provide benefits. Notice which activities you engage in on the days your ratio is higher, and do more of that. Get creative with increasing this positive emotion ratio. Find ways to add laughter, enjoy art, dive into meaningful explorations, go to peaceful locations (the ocean for me), etc. Do whatever works to tilt the ratio of positive emotions in your favor.

Random Acts of Kindness

When I think of random acts of kindness, I think of a story I heard about a restaurant in Chicago called Karma Kitchen. Karma Kitchen lets you eat for free, but it asks that after you enjoy your meal, you pay whatever you can, from your heart, so the next person can have food to enjoy. That kind of giving can pay it forward for someone else, who might be in a rough patch, to put some food in their belly.[46]

Think of random acts of kindness you can do. How easy is it to pay for a drink for the person behind you in line? A random act of kindness is giving a bit of your best self to others – even strangers – without expectation of payback. That kind of giving is not only an amazing way to express the best parts of human nature but also establishes the need to love, as opposed to being loved, as the giver's intention. The recipient of your kindness feels acknowledged, even if momentarily, even in a small way. And as a psychologist, I can attest that at the root of so many of the complaints of emotional suffering is the need to be acknowledged. So what an amazing gift you are giving that random person with your random act of kindness!

The Giver of Kindness Gets Rewarded Too

The wonderful thing about random acts of kindness is that there are not only benefits to the receiver but also to the giver. Here are a few of the positive effects associated with random acts of kindness for the giver[47]:

- A warm sense of awe when the giver thinks about profound acts of love or virtue. In fact, whether you are the recipient or the giver or merely just a witness, you can feel the benefits of an increase in love, self-esteem, and optimism and a decrease in overall aches and pains. How's that for elevating your positive emotion ratio? Kindness is the gift that keeps on giving.
- Kindness can increase the feeling of strength and energy for the giver; it can also make them feel calmer and less depressed.
- There is even evidence to show that being a giving person protects your heart. Literally, it decreases your risk of heart disease.[48] Therefore, it will come as no surprise that those who are fifty-five years or older and volunteer have a much lower risk of dying early.
- Anxiety is also positively influenced by acts of kindness, as demonstrated by a study[49] of a group of highly anxious individuals who agreed to perform kind acts for four weeks. After one month, they saw a significant increase in positive moods and relationship satisfaction, and a decrease in social avoidance.

What a concept: do good to feel good. A sure way to increase your positive emotions!

I encourage you to put these tips into practice in a way that fits your world, and notice how it boosts your morale and nourishes your Happier Being. I know that as a child, I used to give up my seat while riding the bus to anyone who seemed old to me (back then, "old" might even have been a twenty-year-old, ha). It was something my parents taught me and always made me feel good. I assumed it felt good doing something I was expected to do, that I thought I was feeling good because I was obeying my mother (for something that made sense to me, for once). I vividly recall how the whole interaction was just great. The receiver was thankful and smiley, and I for sure had this warm cozy wave in my stomach that something important was accomplished. Little did I know, I was practicing random acts of kindness, as best as a child could have.

Show Your Happier Being Some Love

In Barbara Fredrickson's second book, *Love 2.0*,[50] she continues her research on positive emotions, this time focusing on love. She tells us that we must pivot away from what we usually think of when the word "love" comes up (like intimate relationships). Instead, she offers a new perspective, "Love 2.0," which consists of micro-moments of shared positive emotions between people. These moments of love can happen anywhere on any scale. Maybe you catch a stranger's eye, share a smile, and share a micro-moment of positivity resonance. In essence, love, according to this perspective, is connection. It's the cozy sensation you feel when you share a bear hug with someone – an emotional unveiling that you both experience. It's a reminder that love exists all around you, as long as two or more people – even strangers – connect over a shared positive emotion. These encounters result in biobehavioral synchrony in the body, translated into feelings of oneness. To experience this love connection, both sides have a motive to invest in each other's well-being, which results in mutual care.

I find this exploration of expanding our definition of love fascinating. In my opinion, it adds to the more conventional definition and circles back to many philosophies that discuss how humans experience themselves as separate from others – and erroneously so. It protects us from that wretched feeling of being lonely. If you can express more love and feel more love for others, as fleeting and as brief it might be, then you have nourished and deepened your sense of belonging.

If you define love as such, it influences everything you feel, think, do, and become. When you experience love as something that expands your heart, mind, and soul, you not only set yourself up to be better connected with the people in your life but you also position yourself to experience more health, happiness, and wisdom.

Obstacles to Increasing Self-love

Life and Western culture place plenty of obstacles in the way of experiencing positive emotions and self-love. For example, our culture perpetuates the myth that being in a relationship is the only way to be happy; the fallacy that you need to be a people-pleaser at work in order to get ahead; and the norm of being much harsher on yourself than you ever would be to a coworker or friend. These are just a few of the cultural norms that set you up and steer you away from self-love. That's why it's so important to break away from the social conditioning that holds you back from expressing and experiencing your Happier Being. Your goal is to be authentic to your inner self and still experience joy.

Luckily, there are ways to tackle these obstacles.

Mastering Love – Love Starts Within

Feeling safe and connected to your own self is an integral part of the self-love prerequisite – and necessary for the success of any relationship. Alas, it's easy to forget that love begins with yourself, from self-compassion to respecting your own needs. These are critical parts of keeping your Inner Giggle healthy and thriving.

To experience self-love, you need to start by defining what it looks like to honor your unique expression of self-love. Your goal is to define it in any way that is best for you, and match this with actions that demonstrate acceptance of its importance to you. It won't be easy to always follow through with respecting and actively choosing the behavior which will shield your self-love. Still, while in the process of growing it, you must do it with self-acceptance. Acceptance of the current you, and your starting point – with the constant emphasis and development of self-compassion.[51]

Every one of my clients has told me about something they felt ashamed of: being overly crabby with their kids, overeating in secrecy, disliking their mother-in-law, having sexual fantasies in their dreams they could not explain. The list goes on, but the point is that everyone has something they're not proud of and feel bad about.

Besides issues or episodes of life frowned on by conventional society, like infidelity, many people struggle with an aspect of their own internal compass, that, for whatever reason, got knocked off course. They tell themselves stories and convict themselves of things that any court of law would find wildly exaggerated or ridiculous. They've found reasons to severely dislike parts of themselves because they are afraid of being found out and rejected by their tribe. Consequently, they start shutting down parts of themselves that they do not appreciate, the parts they fear, if exposed to the outside world, would reveal them as not smart enough, pretty enough, worthy enough of others' company and care, etc. Slowly but surely, they try to disown these parts of themselves that they dislike and they start discounting their own significance. They quiet their voice, let go of aspiration, abandon self-compassion, and become depressed.

So, how can you break that cycle?

Become Comfortable with All of You – Express Your Truth

Experiencing yourself as enough is, in part, about speaking your truth, as well as showing up and acting from it. How would people who feel strong in their worth act? They'd demand from themselves the same consideration they'd give to others.

Let me explain. We are socially conditioned to be nice, to be kind, and compromise. Our parents, teachers, and authority figures tell us to be "good," "well-behaved," "share with others," and to "do as you're told." However, this social conditioning might affect your Inner Giggle and self-worth when taken to the extreme. It might leave you feeling like you can't say no, like you can't set healthy boundaries. This is why it's extremely important to grow out of focusing on pleasing others other than when you want to. You have to start recognizing where you may be denying yourself in your attempt to please other people instead. It could be getting in the way of living your truth.

Journal

Identify where your desire to be overly nice in order to please others comes from. Did you grow up with negative connotations regarding expressing your needs? Was it scary to voice your opinion, fearing ridicule? Were you punished? Are you feeling like a mean and egocentric person if you assert yourself? There is a lot of room in between being a martyr and a ruthless, selfish person.

Luckily, there are many ways to honor your truth, find your balance, and learn to express yourself without the fear of being rejected, unwelcomed, or unloved. After all, if you are putting on a facade, if you are lying, if you express what others want to hear, then the one they are welcoming is not really you. And that, I can tell you for sure, does not satisfy the need to be loved. So express your feelings. Find assertive ways to communicate so you do not have to hold in that which is not yours to carry, namely, the anxious or depressive feelings bottled up inside you as a result of not letting them go.

As you work on expressing yourself, listen for those thoughts holding back your feelings. Become aware of how they wrongly reinforce your feelings of being different, not belonging, and not deserving to speak your truth. I have heard many variations of self-silencing. From never really learning how to express one's feelings – thoughts like: "no one was interested in hearing," "what if I am wrong," "others' needs came first" – to learning to bottle up because it was safer, or because of that ensured closeness. Whichever story applies to you, it is time to write a new chapter.

Challenge your thoughts around why it's not worth it to speak up and stand your ground. The emotional price you pay for your silence is high. Give yourself a discount! Express a little more, pay a little less.

It's all too easy to endure negative emotions instead of modulating them. You habitually did not try to make much sense of these emotions. Instead, your focus became the need to feel emotionally safe again. Thus, you started to disown any parts of you that made you feel otherwise. Ironically, disconnecting from the parts of you that made you feel depressed or anxious contributed to these same exact feelings. You can keep telling yourself that you are not depressed, but your body keeps track of this denial, especially if not dealt with.

That being said, you now have the tools to start recognizing where you may be self-silencing in an attempt to please others. You also have the tools to change it.

Cozy up to Your Anxiety: Get Comfortable Being Anxious

The first rule for any psychological growth, be it your thoughts or feelings, is being more consciously aware. Your goal is to become aware of all the cards you've been dealt and how best to use them. Gaining insight into all your cards is a huge advantage for the best chance of changing anything for the better. The good news is that you're not only a player but also the dealer.

Let's focus on anxiety for now. One of the hallmarks of anxiety is avoidance. Stated simply, the more you avoid what makes you anxious, the more you reinforce it. Public speaking is a good example. If you are anxious about public speaking and you avoid it, the anxiety surrounding this topic will not go away. More likely, it will intensify until you approach it head-on. Thankfully, with public speaking, you have a choice, as you are not obligated to do it to live a stress-free life.

However, free-floating anxiety from your unmodulated emotions is not like public speaking, where you can just decide to avoid it and expect your life will not be so negatively affected by it. Conversely, free-floating anxiety about being more authentic, with yourself and around others, well, that travels with you all the time, and everywhere you go. It makes sense then that becoming more comfortable with being anxious in everyday life and learning how to better modulate it is a necessity for better living.

Furthermore, by cozying up to anxiety you become more socially courageous. By taking the emotional lid off more often, you may be surprised to find that others have felt like you. And just like you, they did not dare to voice it. By sharing more of you and your anxiety, you will have a chance to be rewarded for your efforts by contributing truth to your encounters. Recall growth mindset? Here it is in action. You can take any small steps to be your authentic self and see your self-esteem grow, despite your anxiety. You will experience yourself as you wish to feel, and that is the whole point.

Journal

Since anxiety is held not only in between your ears but everywhere else in your body, start taking stock of when, where, with whom, and how often you experience it. A major theme that runs through this book is allowing more space between your stimuli and your response – it's the same case for anxiety. The best way to start it is to connect to your breath. That will initiate the process of calming your anxiety down. Gradually, one breath at a time, pay attention when you experience anxiety without the fear of falling apart. Notice yourself feeling paradoxically more comfortable when you allow the space to acknowledge it. You are being more courageous and authentic when you allow yourself to note and accept your anxiety, as opposed to pushing it away. Become the observer of your anxiety as it is a great first step to modulating it.

Envision the Relationships You Want to Manifest with Yourself

Picture yourself in your mind's eye as someone who has high self-worth. Anything you want and/or would like to feel, sense, visualize it. See yourself expressing your absolute best in the realm of self-love. For example, enter the room with your chin held high, your shoulders rolled back, and your voice projected strongly. Feel how your heart is syncing smoothly with your thoughts, assured in its beautiful rhythm, while hearing you are speaking your truth from this same heart! Visualize in your body how wonderful and cozy it feels to have someone who adores you put their arms around you. Smile, absorb. Become aware that you are wonderful. You are enough, especially when you bring all of you out to play!

A Quick Side Note: Make Smiling a Habit

If you want to work on your love mindset, overtly express your Inner Giggle with a smile. Here are a few fun facts.[52]

- One smile can generate the same brain stimulation as 2,000 chocolate bars.
- Smiling increases endorphins and reduces stress, even blood pressure.
- Smiling makes you more attractive and seem more competent.
- Smiling is built into us. Even blind babies smile at the sound of a human voice.
- Smiling is contagious. If you need to get a dose of smiles, try spending time around children (they smile up to 400 times a day!)

Increasing Connection and Love

The hippocampus is the part of your brain where, from birth on, new neurons get together and form new memories. Your hippocampus loves repetition. Introduce it to repetitive lovable thoughts, so it can thicken the neural pathways leading to greater self-acceptance. Use the following exercises to facilitate the change towards your desired emotional state, perceived value, and connectedness with others.

Confirmation Bias Debunked

Scan mentally and create a list of the people in your life. Those you encounter routinely but barely know (e.g. at the food truck at work) to those you already interact with daily (e.g. your roommates). Can you entertain the idea of creating new opportunities to bond more strongly with them? Can you form new experiences of feeling more included while with them?

Find ways to combat your oldest confirmation bias – that subjectively perceived social distortion that keeps you from connecting deeper. Your confirmation bias is always looking for reasons to be rejected, unloved, unpopular, or simply socially awkward. Therefore, it always finds it. Take over. Look for the opposite.

Write yourself a love letter

Perhaps you don't let people truly know you because somehow you learned that it was not safe. Maybe you've disconnected from your childhood self, and somewhere along the way, forgotten how wonderful you are. Write yourself a love letter from your adult self to your childhood self. Whatever comes to mind, even if it's about being sad about what did not work out but grateful for how some things turned out fine today. What do you want your young self to know?

Go on a date

Often there are sad consequences to not expressing and taking care of your emotional and social needs. Take couple-hood as an example. If you downplay your needs with your partner, there comes a time when you realize you have not only numbed your emotions, but are also no longer sure what you would enjoy most if your wishes were to be taken into consideration. Same happens with your own self-love. If you have neglected it for a while, it's hard to know how to implement self-care.

Go on a date with yourself. What's the ideal way to spend it? Listening? Seeing? Feeling? Where do you want to spend that time? What would be the ideal time of the day? How long will it take? What else would you need to make it as cozy an experience for yourself as it can be?

Rules of Engagement

Write down any insights into your inner narrative as it pertains to how you see yourself socially. What are some internal stories you tell yourself that keep you from deeper kinship? What are the familiar themes that run through your heart? If you want to add new chapters, you have to make the familiar pattern of loneliness – unfamiliar! Get creative and fill those pages with new and improved plots depicting your own personal happiness. Write over what was familiar but dysfunctional thus far, and make room for your new rules of engagement. The best place to start is to ask yourself: How can I be more open and accepting of myself and others? If you adapt this attitude, you will find it easier to connect with others. Show up socially strong, and enjoy.

• • •

You are now starting to master the Inner Giggle of your mind and emotions. However, it only goes so far. If you want to truly optimize, to help with a dysregulated body, you have to attend to your energy. We'll take that on next.

Recap

- Current data shows that despite our digital and physical capacity to be connected with others faster than ever before, we are lonelier than ever before.
- This loneliness gap is caused by a lack of genuine, strong, social connections and felt most prominently by younger generations.
- To be happier, healthier, and more successful at home and at work, you need to invest in your social connections. Those who have strong social ties are less depressed.
- Developing strong social connections means practicing the following: avoiding the detrimental side of social media (comparison), utilizing an abundance vs. scarcity mindset (being pleased for others' fortunes too), spending time with people who emotionally energize you, and creating new beliefs about your ability to have good relationships (your Reticular Activating System to the rescue).
- The key to continually maintaining strong relationships (with self and others) has to do with increasing your positive to negative emotions ratio (adding joy to your life, performing random acts of kindness, and expanding your definition of love as micro-moments of positivity resonance or connection [*Love 2.0* – Barbara Fredrickson]).
- Obstacles to strong connections start with internal roadblocks but can be recovered by learning to express your feelings, cozying up to your social anxiety (becoming more courageous), and visualizing the relationship you want to manifest.
- Remember the importance of repetitive, lovable thoughts on your hippocampus – the part of your brain that forms new memories. This will lead to greater self-acceptance (by thickening the neuron pathways), and better, stronger social connections and relationships over time.

Bonus information and mental training exercises relating to this chapter can be found here: happierbeing.com/exercises

SIX

The Physical Components to Happiness

Your Physiology at Play: Epigenetics, Neurotransmitters, the Immune System, and the Vagus Nerve

Your biology is important in cultivating your Happier Being and understanding its connection to your energy and how you feel every day. This chapter will explain the unquestionable correlation between your lifestyle choices and your health, mood, and overall well-being. It is my assertion that to optimize your happiness levels, you must take a holistic approach focusing on bettering all the aspects – body and mind – that are in your control. As you will soon read, you have lots of ways to optimize your health and boost your well-being in the process.

Going Beyond Your Genes with Epigenetics

It was once believed that our health is genetically pre-determined, and that we had no choice about or control over the hereditary diseases or conditions our genes made us vulnerable to. But recent science has proven that genes are not as "set" as we may have thought. In fact, we actually have a good deal of control over how our DNA and genes are expressed.

I'd like you to think about that last sentence for a minute; this is extremely powerful stuff. It means you are not cursed by whatever high probability of disease your genetics appear to have predicted for you. You are not doomed to get an illness just because it runs in your family. You're not destined to develop diabetes, obesity, high cholesterol, autoimmunity, allergies, etc.

This is not to say health problems are all your fault. I am personally (and painfully) aware that we can follow the best health practices out there and still get sick, still struggle with diseases that were handed down by inherited genes, or get very ill due to environmental factors that are beyond our control. Nevertheless, knowing that you have more control over your genes than previously believed can empower you to address your habits. Within your genetic tendencies, you can still optimize your chances for well-being. You have greater control over your statistical percentages, your health outcomes, than you were probably ever told. This is the phenomenon of epigenetics.

"Epi" is a prefix taken from Greek, and it means above. "Genetics" is the study of genes. Thus, epigenetics stands for studying what's "above the genes" – and what's above (or actually around) the genes is *energy*. This energy signals to your DNA when/how it should be expressed, and as it turns out, every single cell can be expressed in over 30,000 different ways!

Think of your genes as the rough draft you were given when you were born, something that has been passed down to you by your ancestors but that can also change and be expressed differently. The old scientific debate about nature vs. nurture has ceded to the realization that it's about nature *and* nurture and always has been, right down to the way your genes express themselves.

This is important because even being born with a specific set of unfavorable genes doesn't mean those genes will be expressed in a certain way – or even expressed at all. Your genes are influenced by both inner and outer energetic frequencies that communicate with your DNA. Most importantly, you have influence over those frequencies and the ability to help turn certain genes on or off. Epigenetics tells us that you can influence phenotypic expression (observable characteristics resulting from the interaction of genotype with the environment) – and that can impact your health tremendously.

All of your genes have a purpose and function in your body; they're not inherently good or bad. I would add that it's important to see them in that way – allowing your mind to be kind to your body, despite any inherited conditions you might have. Once you learn how much more in control you are of your genetic expression, you can start focusing on keeping certain genes from manifesting themselves in ways that could lead to potentially negative health outcomes. Largely, you can do so by optimizing your Inner Giggle energy boosters (eating, sleeping, and moving habits).

Mark Sisson explains in his book *The Primal Blueprint*[53] that your body is just trying to keep you healthy in the short term and that it's actually moving toward efficiency, health, and happiness by its own design. The problem, as it turns out, is not necessarily in your genetic make-up (or "good vs. bad" genes), but in your health choices that point certain genes in one direction or another. We know some of the processes that make bodies thrive, such as exercising, being out in the sun, sleeping long enough hours, and eating real, quality food. But many of us are still mostly indoors at our desks, going to sleep late, and eating processed foods.

I hope it's become clearer to you why epigenetics is an important concept to understand, especially for those dealing with inherited conditions. The power to optimize your well-being, despite your genetic predisposition, is much more in your control than you've probably realized. Creating healthful practices will help you optimize your genetic expression. As you will read, it doesn't take much to make that switch, the genetic switch if you will, for better health and overall well-being. (Note that even if you already struggle with a physical stressor or an illness of any sort, practicing your Inner Giggle energy boosters will contribute to your healing process. More on that later in the book.)

After epigenetics, the next physiological feature that's critical to cover is your neurotransmitters: your body's critical chemical messengers.

The Basics of Neurotransmitters

Neurotransmitters are chemical messengers that transmit information to and from your neurons (nerve cells) via nerve synapses (the small gaps between neurons). That information is communicated throughout the nervous system and affects your body functions. In short, neurotransmitters are essentially your brain's language/communicator, sending instructions from one brain cell to the next and then causing changes throughout the body – all to keep you protected and healthy.

All neurotransmitters have a biological purpose. Some make you feel excited, while others make you feel anxious, and so on. That being said, each and every one of them has evolved to help you function more optimally in your environment. For example, you may have already heard of the term "happy chemicals"[54] – the brain chemical signals that make you feel good. I'd like to introduce some of them to you, and to help you remember them, I offer the following acronym DOSE: Dopamine, Oxytocin, Serotonin, and Endorphins.

Here are your four happy chemicals broken down by function:

Dopamine – elicits feelings of joy in the pursuit of new experiences (the motivation) and achievements, which often come with seeking and fulfilling rewards. Unfortunately, the chemical plays a major role in addiction, too, which is relevant to food intake (to be further discussed in Chapter Seven).

Oxytocin – elicits feelings of comfort, safety, trust through social support and touch (often referred to as "the love drug" or "cuddle hormone" because of its release during sex and in partnerships, friendships, and parenting interactions.

Serotonin – elicits feelings of social importance, respect, pride. Often seen as a mood stabilizer (among its other functions for your well-being, like sleep).

Endorphins – elicits feelings of euphoria that mask physical pain, or at least reduce it (often released during exercise, belly breathing, stretching, and, my favorite, laughing!)

Given this breakdown, I bet it's become clearer why you should be working on increasing your daily DOSE.

Ways to Increase Your Daily DOSE

You can intentionally get this quartet of happy chemicals flowing by practicing "small wins." Remember how I mentioned the importance of rewarding yourself along the way when it comes to habit formation (see Chapter Two)? Setting and meeting your intermittent goals result in the anticipation that something good is happening, and will trigger your brain's reward center more often, releasing dopamine.

When it comes to increasing your flow of oxytocin, think human connection, and in particular, touch! Known for his academic work in human connection, Dr. Paul Zak tells us that we should be hugging much more than we probably are per day (his recommendation is eight times!) to increase our oxytocin levels. Additionally, having a healthy sex life is important for your oxytocin levels, as it's released by both men and women during orgasm. There's a reason it's called the "love drug," and why many people find pleasure in close relationships, intimacy, and sex.[55]

As for increasing your flow of serotonin, think about belonging and significance. Recall the importance of social connections and statistics on the current state of loneliness and depression. Perhaps it's no surprise that many of our modern-day antidepressants are focused on the production of serotonin. In order to build up this "happy chemical" in your brain, you can take a few moments to recognize what you've accomplished so far in life (intellectually, financially, etc.), and feel your sense of belonging to a certain group of people (through religion, organization, family, friends, hobbies etc.) – whatever it may be. Add practicing gratitude to it all. It works wonders.

Lastly, if you want to increase endorphins, think of ways to incorporate more humor into your life. It will be easier to diminish your anxiety levels and/or pain perception (and who wouldn't want that!) when you find more ways to laugh. You'll also want to focus on getting your body moving as much as possible (see Chapter Nine on Moving), which is what endorphins are typically known for.[56]

Immune System: Powering Up Your Body's Defenses and Optimal Health

As you may already know, the immune system helps protect and fight against infection and keeps your body strong. The system itself is a fascinating and intricate network of cells, tissues, and organs that keep a "germ record," as I like to call it, of every bacterium that enters the body. This way, it can recognize, attack, and attempt to destroy unwanted, reentering microbes in an effort to keep you healthy.

Needless to say, your immune system is complex – recent science has proven just how much. For example, it turns out that we have actual neurons in our gut, leading many health professionals to call it our "second brain" (the phrase "I had a gut feeling" seems clearer now, doesn't it). And this second brain is extremely powerful. Why? It turns out most of your immune system – an estimated eighty percent! – is actually located in your gut.

The Gastrointestinal Tract and Your Microbiome

Your digestive system carries about a hundred trillion different microbes, including about 1,000 different species represented by about 5,000 different strains. Some of these bacteria are helpful and others are harmful – but the balance between them is both unique to each of us and very important. When your gut microbiota is balanced, you have a wide array and diversity of healthy gut flora, and your immune system strengthens.[57]

Unfortunately, our lifestyles have shifted dramatically over the years, and this has had a deleterious effect on our gut. We spend more time in sterile, indoor environments – away from the sun, dirt, and even interactions with others (pets included) that contribute to our microbiome (the totality of existing microorganisms in the gastrointestinal tract, such as good or bad bacteria, fungi, viruses, etc.). We've been conditioned to believe that all bacteria are bad, so we clean and sanitize and are often prescribed antibiotics—which unfortunately can have the negative side effect of killing good gut bacteria.

Taking all the above into consideration, the question is: what about further challenges to the immune system when it comes to a devastating pandemic like COVID-19? The need to sanitize and stay largely indoors skyrockets – and rightfully so. How do we still follow the recommended guidelines to overcome challenges of this magnitude without hurting our gut? It's about balance.

An imbalanced gut weakens, and the immune system suffers. When you're in contact with unhealthy microbes and/or are continually trying to fight them off, you won't have enough healthy microbes to fight, and your immune system will continually be taxed – leaving you to have a hard time recovering. Therefore, your job is to replenish your gut with good bacteria, adding biodiversity and keeping your immune system strong. Luckily, your Inner Giggle energy boosters can help you do just that – starting with perhaps growing, picking, cutting, preparing, and eating healthy food (see Chapter Seven).

The Vagus Nerve and Our Immune System: The Gut-Brain Connection

The vagus nerve is arguably one of the most important nerves in your body and is responsible for our body's homeostasis, the harmony of our automatic physiological life processes. The vagus nerve is part of the autonomic nervous system – the part of our nervous system that's "automatic," working without us consciously doing anything, like pupil dilation and constriction, respiration, digestion, or thermoregulation. The autonomic nervous system is broken down into the sympathetic nervous system (fight-or-flight response, your go-go-go mode) and the parasympathetic nervous system (rest and digest response, or your brakes mode).

Mental and physical healing can only occur when your body is in a parasympathetic state, but most of us spend our day in the sympathetic, or fight-or-flight, state. We are constantly running on alert mode as if we have awoken every day just to keep on surviving, resulting in a dysregulated autonomic nervous system that does not let us fully play out our body's essential functions. Thus, we're left with poor vagus nerve functioning.

Now, being busy during the day and keeping our productivity high is not the problem. The issue is the way we react to the daily stressors and added stressors that seem to keep many of us in flight-or-fight response, with our sympathetic nervous system switched on for too long. Without nourishing your body enough to allow the parasympathetic (rest and digest) periods to offset the overly active ones, you will remain in anxious survival mode, instead of the balanced living – or, better yet, flourishing - mode.

Poor vagus nerve functioning dysregulates normal body function, which is a primary reason why people not only get sick but stay sick for a longer period when stressed. Good health manifests when your relaxation response is activated, not your stress response – and this is what you want to strive for. No one wants to get stuck in survival mode. It's exhausting, to say the least!

Vagal Functioning & Chronic Physical Stress and/or Conditions

Those who are dealing with chronic physical stress or illness find that their bodies simply *are* in survival mode – and this is a major hurdle when it comes to recovery (see also Chapter Ten.) If you are managing a chronic condition, you're not choosing to be overly stressed – in other words, you are not choosing to be in a sympathetic nervous system state. But you often are all the same, due to the chronic stress and duress your mind and body are under every day. When you're not able to rest, detoxify, or digest throughout the day due to your chronic physical stress, your energy suffers. This is why it's so key to do your best to strengthen your vagus nerve functioning by using your energy fundamentals when you are physically hurting.

The vagus nerve is also a key component in the connection and communication between your gut and the brain, or the "gut-brain axis," as it's often called. The vagus nerve can send signals in both directions, from the brain to the gut/body (fifteen to twenty percent of information is transmitted this direction) and the gut/body to the brain (eighty to eighty-five percent of information is transmitted in this direction). A simpler way of saying this is that our mind and gut communicate via nerve fibers bi-directionally.

This means that your gut microbiome can activate the vagus nerve and mediate effects on the brain. Subsequently, the brain can send signals via the vagus nerve, resulting in physical changes in the gut – for better or worse. For example, animal studies have shown that stress inhibits the signals sent through the vagus nerve and causes gastrointestinal problems. Poor vagal functioning due to stress can also lead to the suppression of stomach acid, leaky gut, bad nutrient absorption, and other issues.

Additionally, poor vagal functioning is linked with inflammatory issues and chronic inflammation. When the vagus nerve cannot send signals to shut down the inflammatory response, high levels of pro-inflammatory cytokines increase, as does your sympathetic nervous system activity. This, in turn, increases stress hormones, which when pumped into the body over a sustained period can lead to a host of issues and malfunctions. It's no surprise that chronic inflammation is implicated in almost all well-known and debilitating diseases.

This explains why many people with chronic physical stress and/or conditions have poor vagal tone, as their bodies have a hard time switching from sympathetic (fight-or-flight) mode to parasympathetic (rest and digest) mode, where healing occurs. For many years the immune system has been at the forefront of chronic conditions. Still, more and more research points to underlying vagus nerve dysfunction as a culprit – an important and interconnected piece of the puzzle when it comes to healing and well-being.[58]

The vagus nerve is truly a master communicator, connecting your mind's needs with bodily actions and vice versa. For more optimal health, you want strong vagal tone/functioning, which can, of course, be improved with healthful eating, quality sleep, and light movement (your Inner Giggle energy boosters!). The key is to focus on getting yourself into rest and digest mode, instead of fight-or-flight mode, so that real regeneration and healing can occur and a more optimal, happier being can be achieved.

• • •

I trust you can see just how important your biology and physiology are to your Happier Being. Your physical health is indisputably connected to your mental health and happiness – and learning to optimize both is the goal. I'd like to leave you with a story about a client of mine, Leon, who was able to do just that.

Leon, exasperated, shifted positions on the couch in my office. "I'm really not sure I have the energy to get through another week of work come Monday," he said, "and your suggestion to me after getting more sleep is to exercise more?

I think it will deplete me, not lift my spirits. Besides, last time I joined the gym it was a total waste of money."

I explained to Leon that he had never experienced the direct connection between elevating his physical energy and his mood. He wasn't into fitness or sports growing up, but he did love riding his bike. So I suggested he start out riding along his neighborhood lake, and riding with other friends like when he was younger (instead of the gym, like in a spin class). Leon seemed to enjoy that idea more and agreed to join an outdoor cycling group. As he left my office he jokingly said, "I always liked the saying, 'It's like riding a bicycle.' Just never thought I'd find my older self on one again!"

Reluctant as he was, initially, Leon began to slowly enjoy his bike rides. He noticed muscles firing in his body that he'd forgotten about, and feeling them slightly sore, or as he commented, "doing what they're actually supposed to do," brought a smile to his face. This, along with having a bit more energy and no more sniffles (making him question if his immune system had strengthened) felt really good. Plus, he learned to enjoy the growing comradery when others helped him out or even teased him slightly (he was the newbie, after all). Overall, Leon felt he was doing okay.

After several more sessions, he shared that he felt stronger with every ride, and he'd even started joining his friends for more challenging rides. I explained to him that on a biological level, this was neuroplasticity at play (the more times he went out, the easier it became for his brain to make the decision to be challenged, and the execution became easier as a skill). Plus, the physical exercise gave him his daily DOSE (dopamine, oxytocin, serotonin, and endorphins) of "happy chemicals" that boosted his mood. It added a nourishing cycle of goodness to his well-being.

It was clear to Leon that he was not only getting physically stronger but also emotionally stronger. What once was a complication or incident at work that would shatter his week or "get to him" now felt easier to handle. He felt calmer, less stressed, and more focused (his vagus nerve functioning strengthened, keeping him in a parasympathetic "rest and digest" state more often). He also became more open to challenging projects. As he said to me in one session, "It's like my spirit is more solid." To his great surprise, he was smiling more and burning out less by the end of the week. Not to mention, he was looking forward to the weekends when he got to cycle some more.

Leon's increased energy was infectious in other areas of his life too. He felt more motivated to cook and grew more careful about his diet. He *retired earlier to bed, as he was physically more tired, and his sleep became more rejuvenating. Plus, his competitive self wanted to make sure he was optimizing his sleep to maximize his rides. Leon also got more optimistic about finding a new apartment and expressed more gratitude in general about the small stuff in life.*

The compound effect of boosting his biological functioning by means of fundamental energy habits was impressive. Leon's Happier Being kicked into high gear. He derived so much meaning and pleasure from his new habits — all due his willingness to get back on the bicycle.

Recap

- Your physical makeup (biology and physiology) is important in cultivating your Inner Giggle and understanding its connection to your energy and mood.
- The four physical components at play I've focused on based on recent research are your epigenetics, neurotransmitters, immune system, and vagus nerve functioning. Each of these can function and/or be expressed more optimally through healthy habits.
- Your epigenetics prove that you can be born with a specific set of unfavorable genes but not necessarily express those genes. In fact, you're much more in control of your genetic expression than previously thought.
- Neurotransmitters are chemical messengers (your brain's communicators) that carry instructions throughout your nervous system from one cell to the next, affecting your bodily functioning, your mood, and your actions.
- The most important neurotransmitters to remember (and work on amplifying) are often referred to as your "happy chemicals" and include what I've termed DOSE, or dopamine, oxytocin, serotonin, and endorphins.
- The immune system, particularly your gut's microbiome, needs to have biodiversity (or a healthy balance between "good" and "bad" bacteria) in order to keep your immune system strong, and your mind and body healthy.

- The vagus nerve functions as a key connector and communicator between your gut and the brain, or the "gut-brain axis." Having strong vagal tone (which is an indicator of the strength of your vagus nerve) will help keep your nervous system in the parasympathetic mode (rest and digest), where healing happens, as opposed to the sympathetic mode (fight-or-flight), which leads to a host of health issues.

In the following chapters, you'll learn how to change the way you eat, sleep, and move in order to become a healthier, more resilient person. There will be bumps when practicing your energy-boosting habits – remember, it's a marathon, not a sprint. But if you learn to enjoy the process, the identity you are building, the person you are becoming – you will experience your Inner Giggle more often.

With that, I'd like to make it clear that all of my recommendations for the following chapters are just that – recommendations. I am not a specialist or practitioner in these fields, and I'm not in a position to prescribe a course of action to you individually. But I intend to give you the most updated research and information. With that said, it's important that you consult your physician before making any changes to your fundamental energy habits (eating, sleeping, and moving).

SEVEN

Fundamental Eating Practices for Well-being

Nourish Your Happier Being with These Eating Principles

By now, you've probably made assumptions about what foods might be better or worse for you. I'd like to reiterate that there is no "one-diet-fits-all" and that the word "diet" itself actually means what you usually consume – your diet. Nevertheless, we are accustomed to using that word to convey that we are restricting some foods.

How many diet plans have you seen come and go over the years? Too many to count? They're unable to meet your nutritional needs and don't address the core issues of weight management. They don't take into account your personal diet story, your psychological and emotional eating practices, or your mind-body connection, and they for sure don't address your overall happiness level. There is also the reality that these diet plans are hard to follow. You have to get used to both eating less and eating more healthfully at the same time. However, when your fat cells start shrinking, they deposit toxins that burden your body even further – making "dieting" an exhausting process. When your body gets exhausted, of course, your emotions do too. This is not a good state to be in when trying to make better eating choices.

I don't want to convince you that one way of eating is "better" than another. I only wish to give you the most updated knowledge on food and human behavior, and help you stay away from what I call "nutritional noise" – all the hoopla around restrictive diets, fads, trends, etc. I trust that once you know some of the newest nutritional research and begin following fundamental eating practices, you will feel empowered to make the right food choices for yourself and not pass judgment on whatever you choose to consume.

Eating for Your Physiology

As you learned in Chapter Six, your physiology matters, and when you begin to make healthier choices for yourself, you'll begin to become healthier, more resilient, and happier – harnessing your Inner Giggle more often to become a Happier Being, and that is the ultimate goal. Remember to consult with your doctor before any dietary changes (for example, it can be important to know your own unique DNA makeup/mutations, as that might require variations to some of the general nutritional suggestions beyond the scope of this chapter). With that in mind, let's start with how nourishment can increase your physiological health.[59]

Gene Expression: Nutriepigenomics

Nutriepigenomics is a field of science that examines how nutrition changes the way certain genes are expressed. Research demonstrates the strong connection between sound nutrition and your ability to change gene expression, promote good health, improve chronic physical stress, and reduce susceptibility to disease. For example, polyphenols (found in fruits, veggies, and yummy chocolate) can turn on genes that promote resilience against stress and depression by modulating inflammatory responses and synaptic plasticity in the brains of those with depression. Blueberries are high in antioxidant properties, and antioxidants help lower free radicals in the body, which at high levels lead to inflammation and a host of problems. They can also work to reduce DNA damage and protect humans against carcinogens and aging.[60]

Changing what and how you eat can make a big difference in your well-being and your physical and emotional health.

Research has also looked at nutrition and DNA methylation, a process involved in switching a gene on or off. One study has linked the Western diet to harmful changes in DNA methylation in mice, changes that could negatively impact their offspring even before they're born.[61] Plant flavones, or certain plant molecules, have also been connected to changes in DNA methylation. They have also been linked to a reduction in cancer rates.

The point is that we all know eating well is important but we may not have realized just how deep the connection is between food and health. On a molecular level, what we eat can literally "save" us by turning off genes that could have future negative consequences for our health. The good news is that what we eat is largely within our control. We have an opportunity to capitalize on it and express our Happier Being to its fullest.

Boosting Your Neurotransmitters

You already learned that you want to increase your daily DOSE of the big four: dopamine, oxytocin, serotonin, and endorphins. As it turns out, you can increase these hormones through your diet. For example, fermented foods containing probiotics such as kimchi and sauerkraut can influence the release of DOSE. Spicy foods can trigger endorphin release, and almonds, eggs, beans, and low-fat meats, among others, can trigger dopamine release. Also, the cocoa in chocolate not only interacts with neurotransmitters such as dopamine but also serotonin and endorphins, elevating your overall mood.[62]

Additionally, anti-inflammatory foods (like those high in omega-3 fatty acids and antioxidants) can stimulate the release of a hormone called leptin. Leptin, which is released by your body's fat cells, lets your brain know that you're satiated. This inhibits hunger and signals that it's time to stop eating and get your body moving. Ideally, this keeps us from overeating and becoming unhealthy.

But it doesn't always work. Sometimes, leptin gets released by the fat cells but doesn't signal satiety. Why? The answer is that leptin is often blocked in the brain by insulin.[63] And how do people's insulin levels rise? By eating too much sugar and refined foods.

This is no joke. If you want to experience more energy and get healthier (and thinner in the process), you need to decrease or cut out processed sugar and all refined flour/foods (that act like sugar in your body) from your diet. If you don't, it truly becomes a vicious cycle – one that's probably become clearer and clearer as you read:

Junk Food → Increased Insulin → Blocked Leptin → Unsatiated Feelings → Overeating → No Trigger to Move → Body Conserves Energy as Fat → Reduced Physical Function → Decrease in Energy / Happiness.

It's not enough to simply decrease the amount of sugar and processed foods you're consuming. You'll also want to increase anti-inflammatory foods that produce leptin, like wild-caught salmon, almonds, and avocados (all high omega-3 fatty acids).

The Nucleus Accumbens and the Importance of Food Choices

Once we know that eating the right foods can increase or decrease our daily DOSE and, in turn, our positive energy, productivity, and the overall way we show up in the world, it should be a no-brainer to follow a nutritious diet, right? But it's not that easy. Most of us crave unhealthy foods, particularly sugar, quite strongly. Why?

Quite simply, our brains are wired to be attracted to sugar. Hundreds of years ago, when humans looked for food, they found mainly vegetables, nuts, seeds, and, only occasionally, a sugary dense food source like honey. Honey was rare, scarce, and sought after – and when someone was lucky enough to find it, they'd have to eat as much as possible for as long as possible before it went bad. Fast-forward hundreds of years to the present day. There's plenty of honey to go around, but when your mind sees sweets, it still says, "Binge on that!"

This isn't your fault. Remember, nobody is born with more willpower than others; this sugar craving is hardwired in. The problem is that today, sugar is available everywhere and anytime; it is at your disposal 24/7. And thanks to big food companies, the refining process makes sugary foods even more addictive, resulting in the fact that most people's sugar intake is higher than they realize. It's no wonder that many people identify as addictive eaters, myself included. Once you start, it can feel impossible to stop.

Chemically speaking, this is largely due to a part of your brain called the nucleus accumbens (NAc), often referred to as the addiction center. The NAc is responsible for feelings of cravings and reward.[64] Remember dopamine, the neurotransmitter responsible for the addiction mechanism? When you eat sugar and refined foods, your brain gets an enormous influx of dopamine – in fact, too much. Your body recognizes the overload and literally shrinks the dopamine receptors that are supposed to allow you to feel pleasure. You are taking away the "giggle" part of your inner gigglability, so to speak, and instead, you have to eat more and more unhealthy foods to feel an ounce of "good" again.

But I'm here to tell you that the cycle can be broken, oh yes indeed! When you stop eating poorly, your dopamine receptors regenerate, your "bad cravings" subside, and you're able to feel better naturally. This is key when it comes to eating and food: you want to eat as naturally as possible and avoid addictive foods. For example, have you ever heard anyone say: "When I eat kale, I'm out of control!" "I just can't stop eating this lettuce." "Don't put that broccoli in front of me, I'm too tempted." The answer, I'm willing to bet, is no! And that's because, like I said, natural food is not addictive.

Even sugar in its natural form is less addictive. Sugar comes from a plant (a cane or a beet), but when it's refined, processed into a powder, it's degraded into something harmful. The same process happens to cocoa leaves used to make cocaine or poppy plants to make heroine. So, who's to say sugar is not as "addictive" as drugs? As it turns out, countless studies have shown that sugar has the same effect on your brain as drugs, lighting up your NAc under a brain scan like it's the 4th of July (in a bad way). That's why it's so important to stay away from processed/refined sugar (my #1 fundamental food practice) and move toward more natural foods overall.

I'd like to share with you the successful story of my client, Alicia, and her triumph over her eating practices, despite the undeniable involvement of her addictive brain when it comes to food. Her story will further demonstrate how the vicious eating cycle connects to her personal story of emotional overeating:

Alicia walked in, slumped on my couch, and said: "Well, I'm exhausted. Not sure how it happens, but after every weekend I just feel wiped out." She smiled. We both did. As this was months into our sessions together, Alicia knew I'd challenge her major source of energy regime over the weekend: her eating habits.

Alicia was, by her own self-characterization, an emotional eater. For a long time, she self-deprecated over this. Through our work together, it became clearer that as a young child, she had experienced inappropriate sexual tension from those close to her, resulting in her feeling unsafe, and wanting to protect herself and her body with weight. Since she understood from a very young age that being overweight was not "attractive," she actively pursued overeating to divert attention as well as shield herself from any further hurt. Alicia, without even knowing it at the time, used weight as her defense mechanism (similar to how a child with an abusive parent may also gain weight to be physically bigger, feel stronger, and thus more protected).

Alicia knew what I was going to tell her next, so she beat me to it. Slightly defeated, she said, "I know I need to make my eating habits a priority, but I make progress, and then it keeps falling through, as does my energy. I'm starting to feel like this is an unreachable goal."

I, of course, disagreed.

We discussed, not for the first time, how some abuse survivors use their weight as a destructive force in their lives. They sabotage every attempt to get to a healthy body size as soon as they might reach it. They appear invested in their fitness, get the personal trainer, and hire the diet coach, but once they get close to their ideal weight, they sabotage it.

As Alicia had seen time and time again, her unresolved underlying emotions always won over the logic of any diet or fitness regime she tried to uphold. If she wanted to get ahead of her emotional eating, she would have to continue to dive deeper into the painful layers of her past in order to reframe her reality.

There were two important facts that I proceeded to share with her. One: "You're safe now. And although I believe there is a correlation between the way we behave as adults and the way we were treated as kids, the fact remains that, today, you are not your childhood. Once you get an even better handle on your emotions — naming them to taming them — you will not be consumed by food."

Two: "Food is a major source of energy itself. Everything you put in your mouth has its own energy and gets broken down by your body's energy. But eating food goes deeper than that. Food, and food quality, affect all levels of functioning, both physical and psychological. What you eat becomes you, and your food intake will make you stronger by its nourishment, not by keeping your bigger size."

I saw Alicia's expression change slightly, like something new had clicked, something hopeful, and she began to open up more and more to the new and improved take on eating. As our sessions continued to unfold, she made better connections between her overeating patterns, her emotions, and how what she ate affected her energy, her self-esteem, and her mood.

It wasn't long before she was able to see that her weekend eating habits caused her energy, concentration, and productivity to drop the next day. She learned to identify the subsequent downward spiral of not enjoying herself as much at work, not feeling like she fully contributes, and wanting to reach out for comforting food. She also learned more about the ins and outs of a healthy diet (cutting back on sugar, late night snacking, etc.). And then, together, we worked on creating her own unique eating habits, and laid out what she'd need to do to prioritize eating well so she could increase her energy and happiness levels.

Soon after that, Alicia attained what many emotional overeaters long for: the ability to feel good about her food before she ate, while she ate, and after she ate. It happened because eating became more than just an act of momentary satisfaction or satisfying taste buds. It was about the value of real meals, real nourishment, and the energy that arose as a result. The more she practiced clean, healthy eating habits, the more motivated she became to sustain the balanced, positive energy she was experiencing.

To sum up: if you want to live a fuller life, you have to feed your body the food it needs to support your desires. Add the good stuff; let go of the bad. If you struggle with eating well, or know you're an emotional eater, maybe it's time to make this your keystone habit (see Chapter 2). This is the habit that, followed on a regular basis, will keep you energized to achieve your goals.

Everyone has a food story, with its history and its trajectory, but it's time to make that story work to your advantage and improve your overall well-being. In short, I want you to get hungry for the Inner Giggle experiences that lead to Happier Being!

Increasing Your Defenses

One of the keys to increasing your biodiversity and immune system functioning is plain and simple: eat real, fresh, food grown naturally in clean soil. Nowadays, we're consuming more unhealthy, sugary, processed food than we ever have. These products not only lack any form of healthy biodiversity but they also strip our healthy gut flora. That's why you must repopulate your gut with good bacteria from food, including fresh produce. I'll even go a step further and say that the more organic and local food and the fewer chemicals (pesticides, etc.), the better. Biodiversity helps you maintain a healthy gut microbiome, increased immunity, and all-around higher functioning.

In recent years it's also become apparent that food for immunity is a medical necessity. Since the rise of antibiotic resistance, or "superbugs," many people, even in modern Western cultures, are turning to food for both preventative and healing medicine (herbs, oils, etc.). Along with the flu being more harmful each year and the coronavirus dismantling our lives, we see the rise of superfoods — nutrient-dense foods that help us fight off foreign pathogens and increase our immune functioning.

Superfoods contribute to a strong gut microbiome, among other benefits. They include dark cruciferous vegetables, generally leafy greens, antioxidant-filled berries, foods with high omega-3 fatty acids such as nuts, seeds and avocados, and fermented foods such as kombucha and sauerkraut. Nutrition guru Dr. Joel Fuhrman[65] describes these nutritional recommendations and claims: the goal is to achieve "super immunity" when the body's immune system is working to its fullest potential. With the right raw materials and nutritional factors, you can double or triple your immune system's protective power.

Improving Vagus Nerve Tone

Stressors to your system increase the likelihood of poor vagal functioning, leading to problems with regulating your gut and immune system. Stressors that keep your body in a sympathetic state (fight-or-flight mode) instead of a parasympathetic state (rest and digest mode) include the demands of life – work, family, relationships, and chronic conditions. In addition, many if not most of us are exposed to harmful electromagnetic fields (EMFs) emitted by Wi-Fi routers, computers, phones, and other appliances in daily use. There are also environmental toxins in our air, water, and food that decrease vagus nerve function. But of all these factors, I would argue that the most important – and certainly the most within your control – are your food choices. Particularly – surprise, surprise – your sugar intake.

Your body's response to poor eating habits is essentially the same as it would be to other toxins. Frequently your liver cannot detoxify correctly. The liver has about 500 different functions and is a master organizer, so to speak. It does its best to make sure unwanted elements stay out of your body. This communication, from your liver (body) to your brain, transpires via the vagus nerve. That is why you must not overload the liver with toxins that force it to over-exert. It might hinder critical messages your organs are trying to send to your brain and vice versa. Essentially, the command center is glitching, leading to a decrease in your functioning, energy, and overall ability to be a happier being who eats well.

We see these glitches a lot with heightened consumption of sugar and blood glucose levels in the body. Dr. Navaz Habib, who works on vagus nerve dysfunction, explains it nicely. He states that when our blood sugar gets high, our liver signals to our brain that we need to get glucose into our cells, which lets the pancreas know it's time to produce insulin – all through the vagus nerve. But if our cells can't take on all the glucose, we can't break it down well, can't get our blood sugar level down, and, over time, develop insulin resistance. This is why dietary levels of blood sugar are so important.[66]

In order to be healthier and therefore happier, you must try and reduce stressors such as refined sugar and other processed foods. Instead, choose to consume foods that will help you optimize your vagus nerve functioning. You may do this by adding more fiber (from greens), zinc, omega-3 fatty acids (from seafood), and probiotics (especially Lactobacillus and Bifidobacterium). So, if you happen to be reading this now while drinking or eating something full of sugar, please stop! As a major inflammatory and damaging stressor, the detrimental effect sugar has on your body is devastating.

The Ever-evolving Diet

Now, what's sometimes frustrating about nutrition research is that it's always changing, which can get confusing. For example, in the past, we were told that egg yolks were high in cholesterol and bad for us. But recent studies show that the egg yolks may actually be healthy, and with that, there are new suggestions and guidelines of how many eggs we should be eating. Similarly, research has proven the importance of adding "good" fats to your diet, especially for those with autoimmune conditions – but for decades, all fats were viewed gloomily (recall all the low-fat diets?). The same has happened regarding red meat, which – after being shunned for some time – is now making a resurgence (paleo, keto, and even carnivore diets).

Sometimes, the more you learn about food, the more complex eating can become or feel. For example, drinking cow's milk has proven to increase calcium levels. Still, it's also been linked to young girls beginning menstruation at younger ages because of the number of growth hormones unfortunately present in regular cow's milk.

Hence, I would urge you to treat your diet as "evolving," like other aspects of relationships in your life, which you know won't look exactly the same five or ten years from now. Regardless, you can embrace the most up-to-date knowledge available and then make your own decisions regarding what feels right, or what nourishes your mind and body most. For example, I once put together a summit where I interviewed nineteen different experts on their well-being practices. Two of the experts followed different diets, vegan and paleo. One cured herself and others of a chronic illness following the vegan diet, and the other built an empire of cuisine centering on paleo cooking. Both swore by their diet's positive effects on their body, but what they ate was almost completely different.

I myself began life as an omnivore, but at a young age became a vegetarian and, decades later, a pescatarian because I needed additional sources of protein. I also became gluten-free and largely dairy-free when I was diagnosed with Lyme Disease to lower my inflammation markers. I've focused on eating what's right for my unique body, nourishing my mind and spirit in the process, and have continuously chosen what works for me when it comes to new nutritional research on optimizing my energy. The point is, you don't have to drop all your old ways of healthful eating and adopt all-new ones. Choose what works for you according to what's out there, where you are in your life, what your unique body needs.

With that in mind, I want to give you what I call my "fundamental eating practices" – the basic nutritional guidelines and food practices that all diets, health professionals, and nutritional research have proven to be critical to health time and time again. The aim of these fundamental eating practices is to move you away from nutrient-poor, disease-causing foods to nutrient-dense, disease-fighting foods. It's not a restrictive diet plan that feels impossible to follow, but a guide to sustained healthful eating – one that frees you from the clutches of modern processing and supports you in eating well without having to think about it too much. And if you recall towards the beginning of this book: automating your habits is key. The more you automate, the more you can move to a true lifestyle change, not a temporary "diet."

I hope you realize that my aim is not to prescribe you exactly what to eat, but to help you understand what you're eating, how you're eating, and its direct correlation to your level of health and happiness. You don't need a nutritionist to advise you that potato chips are not real food and that they don't nourish your body – you just need to start making some habit changes. These fundamental eating practices will help you do so.

Eating for Your Happier Being

So, to kick things off, we'll start with my number one food rule:

If you only do one thing, avoid processed sugar.
The absolute number one principle is to avoid refined sugar. If the cocaine = sugar comparison wasn't enough for you to view sugar as a toxin, maybe some

of the following facts will. Sugar and its derivatives have been scientifically linked to many chronic diseases, including diabetes, obesity, heart disease, and cancer. It also accelerates aging, inflammation, and even tumor growth.

On top of the harmful physical effects, sugar also has detrimental psychological effects. For example, sugar actually shrinks areas of the brain responsible for mood (causing higher rates of depression) and causes memory loss due to wearing on the hippocampus. This is because sugar intake, in particular highly processed sugar, decreases your metabolic functioning, leaving you more prone to a range of psychological and health issues.[67]

Now, you may be thinking that you don't have a bad sugar problem, that you're in the clear. But are you really? Do you know how much sugar you actually consume?[68] The answer is probably no. It's estimated that the average American consumes approximately 152 pounds of processed sugar per year (up from five pounds per year in 1700)! This is because sugar isn't present in desserts only; it's hiding in other foods that many people have been told are better for them. For example, most "healthy" drinks other than water have exorbitant amounts of sugar (fruit juices, vitamin drinks, iced teas, coffee drinks – don't even get me started on the Frappuccino). And foods at your coffee shop advertised as "low calorie," like yogurt parfaits, still have tons of sugar in them. Same with items like sports drinks or power bars, which actually power you down, not up. Even things like pickled and smoked foods (like salmon) that you would never expect to be sweetened sometimes have added unnecessary sugar![69]

These hidden sugars take a toll on us every day, a toll that might change the course of our life entirely. In America, we must change what's become known as the "SAD" diet (Standard American Diet) and turn it into a HAPPY one – one without sugar. This is why it's so important to pay attention to your sugar intake. When in doubt, read the ingredients. If the second ingredient is sugar, it's pretty much candy, and you want to avoid it.

To sum up the number one fundamental eating practice: Eat as little processed/refined sugar as possible. Instead, increase fresh foods and produce. The fresher the foods and produce on your plate, the healthier you'll generally be. If you only choose to make one change to your diet to be healthier and happier, decreasing sugar should undoubtedly be it.

A Personal Side Note: If you – like many of my clients – are curious to know if I avoid sugar 100 percent of the time, the short answer is: no. You may have noticed that I recommend decreasing rather than eliminating sugar intake, even if the ultimate practice according to research might suggest avoiding it all together. But I, the human that I am, recognize the gap we all experience between what is the best practice, and what is *our* best practice every day. I hold the knowledge to empower me to focus on optimizing my eating habits, which inspires me to make better decisions. I aspire to identify myself as someone who minimizes her refined sugar intake, but I acknowledge the deflating power of unrealistic perfectionism. If you are a vegetarian, it's a clear-cut practice of what you eat or not. Unfortunately, sugar, as explained above, is not that easy to cut out of your diet. Nevertheless, it is doable to decrease it significantly. Be intentional and kind to yourself while working on this most important habit of decreasing sugar intake, and you are on your way to increasing your well-being.

Stop counting calories and start counting quality.

Calorie counting is not a path to optimal health, despite what you may have learned. Yes, if you burn more calories than you consume, you will lose weight, but it should not come at the expense of your internal health and well-being. Calorie counting for weight loss can lead to depriving your body of nutrients – often while you try to accomplish the difficult task of burning more calories than you're consuming daily. For example, it would take a 160-pound person jogging on a treadmill for approximately two and a half to three hours to burn 1500 calories (three average-sized meals per day with no snacks in between).[70] Now, unless you're a gym rat, this is going to be difficult, and you're not likely to see the weight loss results you hoped for. That's why I believe that the focus should be on consuming quality food, not the number of calories. There is a way to improve your well-being, happiness, and as an outcome, become slimmer in the process – and this is achieved by eating healthy, quality food and not worrying as much about the calories. So, if you're going to count anything, count grams of sugar; they're more harmful to your overall health.

Make sure you're eating as many "good carbs" as possible, as opposed to simple and refined carbs.

Good carbs are often referred to as complex or whole carbs. Complex and whole carbs give you a range of nutrients, fiber, and sustained energy over longer periods (this includes vegetables, some fruits, legumes, whole grains, etc.). Simple and refined carbs, on the other hand, like sweetened drinks and "whitened" foods, cause spikes in blood sugar levels, accompanied by quick crashes and desire for more "bad carbs."[71]

A note about grains and gluten. Yes, they can be inflammatory (so if you're celiac or have an inflammatory condition, you should cut them out), but many whole grains have gluten and are still healthy enough. Additionally, many gluten substitutes (like cornstarch) are not "healthier" than their counterparts. Just be conscientious of the quality and quantity of ingredients. As author Michael Pollan writes in his book *Food Rules*,[72] you should refrain from eating anything your grandmother wouldn't recognize as food – you know, the ones with all those unknown ingredients you can't pronounce. The author also warns people not to buy food that won't eventually rot. These practices will help you avoid eating these harmful simple/refined carbs, as well as the #1 culprit: refined sugar.

Don't be afraid of healthy fats in moderation.

Healthy fats, or lipids, are fats that are generally high in omega-3 fatty acids, as well as some omega-6 fatty acids. These types of fatty acids generally come from monounsaturated and polyunsaturated fats found in foods such as salmon, sardines, walnuts, flax, chia seeds, and others. You want to avoid trans fats (which don't decompose) and saturated fats found in foods like fried/processed foods, dairy items, and fatty cuts of meat, among others.

What's great about healthy fats is that the omegas (especially omega-3 fatty acids) work to power up different bodily processes, such as lubricating the joints and improving mobility and energy – even brain functioning. In Lisa Mosconi's book, *Brain Food*, she makes the connection between Dan Buettner's "Blue Zones" (the areas of the world where people live longer) and their naturally high "good fat" diets. It's not surprising that many of the original Blue Zones were coastal and in the Mediterranean, with high omega-3 consumption from fish, olive oil, etc. Remember, an avocado a day keeps the bad cholesterol at bay (my personal favorite monounsaturated and polyunsaturated fat source!)

Don't keep unhealthy food in the house.

Research has shown that you eat up to seventy-five percent more food when it's in your field of view! If you buy and bring unhealthy food into the house, at some point, no matter what, it will get eaten. Remember, our brains are hardwired to seek out sugar, and today's availability has made many of us addicted. The key is to remove the temptation by not bringing junk food into the home in the first place. If you bring it into the house and try and get "willpower"[73] involved, you'll end up with decision fatigue, making it that much harder to form a new healthy eating habit. As mentioned previously, here's a good question to contemplate: if you were an alcoholic, would you bring alcohol home and test your ability to resist it daily?

Many of your food choices come down to time and effort, so become an intentional shopper. If you are already at home and cravings arise, you are less likely to go out and buy the temptations you left behind.

As an additional note: if you have a food item in the house that was bought for your kids or partner but is addictive to you, do your best to keep it as physically far away from you as possible, either by making it less visible in containers, or by buying the flavor you like least, if possible. It's a fact that if you're an addictive eater, seeing food around will make you eat more, and that's even more true when it's an addictive food item. Additionally, if you're still having cravings, compromise and eat something else. For example, if the addictive item is sweet, try to have some fruit instead to curb the addictive craving.

Plan and prepare your meals.

Most of us have busy day-to-day lives. We work nine-to-five jobs, and then many of us come home to families, kids, chores (the list can go on and on). As a result, you may find yourself with little time to cook or prepare healthy meals (or at least that's what you rationalize to yourself). The good news is that this can, of course, be avoided by prioritizing planning and building it into your schedule. If you shop for groceries on Saturday and prepare your meals for the week on Sunday, you don't have to worry about the time crunch during the workweek – making things as convenient as possible for you, which is key. This is an extremely effective practice that will help you form healthy eating habits. Many people will eat healthier simply because the food is ready to eat. So, if you're a busy bee, get busy meal prepping!

Prioritize adequate portions.

Once your meals are planned and prepped, don't fall into the excuse of having a storage conflict. Treat yourself to the right portion size and the number of containers you actually need – don't overpack or under pack your lunch box; no excuses, please! You might think, OK, give me a break. Do I really need to plan ahead to that degree? Yes. I have heard clients come up with the most creative excuses for how they ended up packing too little (so they had to buy food out) or too much (so they overate). Make sure you prepare, and then get your portions right for you.

Additionally, when you're eating meals at home, arrange your dishes from smallest to largest in the cupboard. You're more likely to grab the plate you see first, and when the smaller or medium-sized plate is easier to reach, you use it more often. Do you even need those large-sized plates available on a daily basis? Probably not. Remember that outer order contributes to inner calm (in all areas of life, not just food)!

As a final note on adequate portions: happiness does *not* come from having more, *nor* from having less, but from wanting what you do have. The same rule applies to food and your portions.

Remember to eat slowly, doing your best not to feel "stuffed."

Eating slowly is a healthy and important practice. When you eat slowly, you chew more before swallowing, which results in releasing the enzymes you need to help you break down food better, digest well, and increase energy. Eating slowly is also important because you're giving your body time to let you know that you're full and thus not overeat. The body needs approximately twenty minutes to signal to the brain that it's full, so when you shovel down food in five minutes, you can't really tell if you're satiated or not. Lastly, your stomach literally expands when you eat too much; it's uncomfortable. When the stomach expands, you will eat more on future occasions – not a great way to keep yourself healthy.[74]

Eating slowly and stopping eating before you're full is actually ingrained into the food customs of many different cultures. In Japan, for example, you're supposed to eat until you are "eighty percent full" or what is called: *Hara Hachi bun me.* Are there any food customs in your culture or family of origin to help you slow down the dining process?

Create food rituals; have your "tea break."

Food rituals are daily eating or drinking practices that are supposed to help prime your brain for the day's next task. By actually pausing for five minutes to connect with the pleasure of enjoying something nourishing, you create positive food rituals. I suggest forming a quick and easy food ritual that you enjoy, associating it with as many senses as possible. For me, having a tea break – drinking tea at a certain hour of the day to clear my mind and re-energize – is such a welcoming ritual. I take the time to prepare the tea, smell it, and use different mugs that bring about positive memories of where I purchased them or who gave them to me. These warm, few minutes nourish my body and soul.

As an added note, learning to make the ordinary special is imperative for our success in life, and eating practices are no different. When we do it for our kids, for example, we might cut their toast with cookie cutters to create fun shapes for their enjoyment. You deserve smiley-shaped food too! So, create your unique, positive reinforcing food ritual, and enjoy. Nourish your Inner Giggle with creativity. It optimizes the benefits of your meals.

Journal

Now that you have all of my recommended fundamental eating practices, I urge you to create your own short-list for healthful eating, your "Golden Food Rules." This will function as your unique eating guide or "rules to eat by." Remember, you are not ruled by food. You are ruled by your own terms of eating! Here is a sample of what your Golden Food Rules could look like: I don't eat sugar. I eat when hungry and stop when full. I eat with joy and practice mindful eating. I manage my portions and hydrate with water. I'm kind to myself when it comes to food and remind myself that cravings are never emergencies. I read food labels. I buy healthy foods.

As demonstrated above, make sure you write in the present tense and in an affirmative way – as though you've been practicing the habits for some time already (e.g. I eat only while sitting at the table). You should also replace any words like "try to," "hope to," "wish for," etc., which automatically lower your self-accountability, conveying the theoretical option to your brain as if it's wishful thinking and not an action step. Consolidate your Golden Food Rules by presenting them as the ways you are choosing to do things now.

Your Golden Food Rules list is there to put you in a state of certainty regarding your dos and don'ts for healthful eating. Having a structure to follow might seem controlling, but ironically provides you with great freedom. It strengthens your food confidence and decreases your anxiety about food choices. Less decision-making regarding when or how much to eat frees up your time, energy, and willpower reserves.

With your Golden Food Rules written down, and knowledge of the fundamental eating practices in your back pocket, you're now more available to fully participate in other parts of your day, guarding your appetite to be truer to its nature, and becoming a happier, healthier person in the process. Congrats – you're eating for the optimal you: your Happier Being!

With that, let's move on to our next Inner Giggle energy booster: sleeping.

EIGHT

Fundamental Sleeping Practices for Well-being

Set Yourself up for Success with Calming Habits and Rejuvenating Sleep

When you sleep, your cells switch into repair and rejuvenation mode (recall the parasympathetic nervous system from the previous chapters), allowing you to function optimally during your waking hours. For some, like famous investor and business tycoon Warren Buffet, quality sleep has become their keystone habit (the one habit they choose to do every day no matter what). Buffet famously said, "When forced to choose, I will not trade even a night's sleep for the chance of extra profits." But whether or not it's your keystone habit, you've probably felt the consequences of sleeping poorly. I would urge you to start taking your sleep more seriously.

When you're sleep-deprived, your biological and psychological functions are depleted, you run on reserves, and you allow your body to overwork itself. In doing so, you leave yourself exposed to a variety of mental and physical health problems – in addition to a worsening mood and, of course, lack of energy.

Sleep gets interrupted by a myriad of ways (stress, anxiety, noise, light, physical pain, illness, or just good old menopause, among other causes).

Nevertheless, a better understanding of sleep will equip you with the tools to boost it. So, how do you sleep? Why is it so important? How do you get better sleep? Let's look into these topics now and then dive into my fundamental sleeping practices.

Our Sleep Cycle and Its Stages

Understanding the basics of your sleep cycle will help you begin to understand how your body moves in and out of sleeping and waking, and start to get you thinking of ways in which you might enhance your sleep for better well-being.

Your sleep cycle consists of non-REM and REM sleep. (REM stands for Rapid Eye Movement.) To adequately cycle through, most adults need approximately seven to nine hours of sleep per night (which we'll get more into the importance of soon). Non-REM and REM can be broken down into the following stages:

Non-REM

Non-REM sleep has approximately four different stages, divided into two categories. Stages 1 and 2 are considered light sleep (should take up about sixty percent of your total sleep) and stages 3 and 4 are considered deep sleep (should take up about twenty percent of your total sleep).

- Stage 1: Transition between awake and asleep, slowing down of breath and heart rate and beginning of muscles' calming and relaxing (light sleep)
- Stage 2: Further slowing down of breath and heart rate, calming brain activity, muscle relaxation, and dropping body temperature (light sleep)
- Stage 3: Nourishing and rejuvenating part of sleep, slowing brain waves, linked to waking up feeling refreshed (deep sleep)
- Stage 4: Further nourishing and rejuvenating part of sleep – vitals, brain waves, and body temperature are at their lowest point (deep sleep)

REM

REM is the last stage of sleep.

- Stage 5: REM is considered your dream state. It is a form of deep sleep, like stages 3 and 4, and should account for about the last twenty percent of your total sleep. REM is rejuvenating, as you experience temporary arm and leg pseudo paralysis, but it is also the period when your vitals, brain activity, and breath start moving towards waking.[75]

The Importance of Sleep: Are You Getting Enough?

As the sleep stage descriptions above detail, nourishing, rejuvenating sleep happens during stages 3 through 5, also known as deep sleep stages. It fits that deep sleep is really where the bulk of one's healing occurs, and unsurprisingly, rejuvenating sleep is an essential ingredient to a healthy foundation for optimizing your Happier Being.

Sleeping for Physiological Health

Sleep is not a passive activity, despite how it seems. Deep sleep helps your body develop growth hormones, balance your hormones, store memories, improve cognition, detoxify your body, lower inflammation, repair and heal your muscles, and bolster your immune system. It also helps you function more optimally during your waking hours. Getting consistently good sleep can increase productivity and concentration, help regulate your appetite, and improve your overall mood (lowering symptoms of depression and anxiety). And these are just some of the reasons that quality sleep is so highly encouraged – because when it comes down to it, the better sleep you get, the more you'll be able to optimize your energy and function as a Happier Being.

Improving Healthy Gene Expression

Unsurprisingly, sleep also influences gene expression. One study out of Surrey Sleep Research Centre at the University of Surrey looked at how genes were expressed in men and women who got about eight and a half hours of sleep per night instead of about six hours or less per night over the course of one week. What they found was remarkable, with changes in over 700 different genes.

The results of this research showed that those who were more sleep-deprived showed more negative epigenetic changes linked to genes responsible for cardiovascular disease, chronic inflammation, decreased immune functioning, and metabolic disturbances, among others. What this study proved is that even slight differences in sleep duration and/or disruption can not only make you tired but also have epigenetic effects that could lead to serious health problems down the line.[76]

Additionally, these changes are being linked to compromised neuroplasticity and neurodegeneration involving certain genes, potentially due to insufficient sleep. Of course, more research needs to be done, but it's clear just how important sleeping is for our genes, gene expression, and overall health and well-being.

Sleeping to Boost Your DOSE

Neurotransmitters are both deeply involved in and affected by sleep. Dopamine and serotonin (two chemical messengers you now know) each have receptors in the pineal gland – a small gland in the brain that helps regulate your sleep-wake cycle. Serotonin is known to induce sleep and keep you up – I'll spare you the details as to how and why. But what's important to remember is that your body needs serotonin to produce melatonin, which helps you feel sleepy.[77] On the flip side of this process is dopamine. When dopamine attaches to receptors in the pineal gland, your body begins to wake up because dopamine halts the production and release of melatonin by norepinephrine (another neurotransmitter). Frequently, those who suffer from sleep deprivation and/or restless leg syndrome have abnormalities regarding dopamine and/or dopamine receptors in the brain.

Of course, dopamine and serotonin are not the only chemicals involved in the sleep-wake cycle. GABA and adenosine, inhibitory neurotransmitters, make you feel sleepy and help you fall asleep. Caffeine (usually consumed in the morning) blocks adenosine, making you less sleepy and more alert. Several other chemical messengers help regulate and sustain wakefulness during the day, like epinephrine, histamine, hypocretin (orexin) (plus cortisol, though it's not a neurotransmitter per se).

With that said, not all brain chemicals and neurotransmitters help induce sleep or wakefulness. Some also help you recharge and remember things you did while you were awake. For example, acetylcholine helps your brain store information during the day and sets it as you sleep. This, along with a host of other brain benefits associated with sleep and high-functioning neurotransmitters/receptors (like cognition, mood, etc.), make clearer the biological importance of quality sleep on your health and your memory functions.[78]

Building Your Self-defenses

The microbiome is also extremely important for quality sleep because intestinal health has a connection with brain function. Depletion of microbes in the gut eliminates serotonin (hello, neurotransmitter!) in the gut as well, affecting your brain's serotonin level, which helps regulate your sleep-wake cycle. To keep and create serotonin, as well as dopamine (another friendly neurotransmitter) in the brain, and to maintain a normal sleep pattern, you need to have a healthy and balanced microbiome. For those with sleep problems/disorders and even fatigue or brain fog, focusing on the gut and boosting your immune system can be key.[79]

In the same way that boosting your immune system can help you sleep, sleep also boosts your immune system – building your body's resilience.

Recent research has proven that good sleep can boost your body's T-cells (specialized immune cells), which work to fight against intracellular pathogens such as cells infected with a virus.[80] Similarly, sleep induces the production of cytokines, which can increase inflammation. Although too many cytokines can be harmful, there's a difference between waking and sleeping inflammation. The inflammation produced during sleep can actually help you fight off infection and speed recovery. In other words, sleep reinforces the immune system's inflammation response during sleep in order to repair your cells, even when no illness is present. It is as if during sleep, when other functions of the body slow down, your immune system has more energy to take care of healing.

When your sleep cycle ends, the inflammation calms down, since your immune system self-regulates through its circadian rhythm (your body's twenty-four-hour internal clock).[81]

Protect Your Parasympathetic Nervous System

When your vagus nerve is in tip-top shape, you're more likely to get better rest. This, as we know, is because the vagus nerve is a critical part of the parasympathetic nervous system, where healing occurs. And when the vagus nerve is functioning well, we're able to shift faster from fight-or-flight mode to rest and digest mode, allowing us to relax more quickly after being in a heightened or stressful state all day.

There are several ways to improve your vagal tone or strength of your vagus nerve that we'll get into next (in the moving section), but when trying to get some shut-eye, the most helpful method is generally breathing. Deep, slow belly (or diaphragmatic) breathing can improve your vagal tone, helping slow your heart rate as well as lower your blood pressure before bed. Your vagal tone can also be improved by humming. Yes, you read that right. Things like humming, singing, chanting, and gargling create vibrations and can also help strengthen the vagus nerve for more restful sleep, among other positive effects. I recommend trying to incorporate these as new meanwhile habits in your routine.[82] (Meanwhile habits, as mentioned earlier, are habits you can do as a quick add-on to things you plan to do – but in order to do these, you find yourself waiting for something to happen first. For example, while waiting for the hot water to reach your sink before washing your face, gargle for that minute with the cold water. Or while waiting for the train to arrive, sing to the other passengers' content. Ok, maybe save this one for the shower? Your call).

Get Enough Sleep!

Although many of us have been told how important sleep is, most of us don't get enough – leaving us prone to unhealthy cravings, forgetfulness, irritability, brain fog, and a host of potential medical problems. In fact, about sixty percent of adults in the US report having sleep problems a few nights a week or more. Sixty-nine percent of children report having one or more sleep problems during the week as well. That kind of sleepiness can be costly. According to the American Psychological Association, it's estimated that sleep disorders, sleep deprivation, and sleepiness in the US results in millions in direct cost and billions in indirect and related costs. Beyond costs, sleep deprivation can have devastating life consequences. Take drowsy driving, for example. According to reports by the National Highway Traffic Safety Administration in the US, 91,000 of police-reported crashes involved drowsy drivers, which led to about 50,000 people injured and 800 deaths in 2017 alone. And even this is a large underestimate by experts of the total damage per year.

There's a reason driving while sleep-deprived is compared to drunk driving. In fact, twenty-four hours without sleep brings your body into a similar state it would be in at a blood alcohol level (BAC) of 0.1 percent. For reference, someone is considered legally drunk when their BAC is just 0.08 percent or above!

It's clear that the detriments of sleep deprivation can be harsh, and for most people, they accumulate somewhat slowly and compound over time – reducing quality of life. One of my clients, Tamika, who attended one of my workshops on stress reduction, was a serious businesswoman with a "never-quit" attitude, but her inability to prioritize sleep cost her Happier Being.

When I first met Tamika before the group workshop started, I noticed that she was a confident, natural leader who took great pride in her work. So it was no surprise that Tamika took the floor first. As she presented her struggles to the group, it became clear that upholding the persona of a serious businesswoman meant she made no time for fun and games. She didn't socialize much in the break room or even engage in small talk because she wanted to maintain the identity of a respected worker: someone to look up to, someone reliable. She spent every night working extra hours even after she got home. To Tamika, pleasure was only to be had once the work was done. In fact, the notion of balancing work stress with some leisure time or self-care practices — even at the end of the formal workday — was something she viewed as "not for me. I don't quit until the work is done."

Then I addressed the group: "It is impossible to attain the so-called 'good life' and hope to lower your stress levels if you've invested all your available energy in your work. You must find some balance to nourish your energy, or the ability to balance your stress levels will remain off. From what I have heard so far, sleep seems to be the last thing on the 'to take care of' list. But I am here to challenge that perception."

An attitude of no pain no gain, as Tamika described, will motivate you to keep your high working standards, but it is black or white thinking. In Tamika's case, it kept her working unrealistic hours in the fear that if she strayed from it, she wouldn't be validated as a serious, successful businesswoman by her colleagues — or even by herself. But the devastating negative effect of such stress on her well-being was becoming clearer to her.

What Tamika failed to do is use her Inner Giggle as a guiding compass. Yes, being dedicated, responsible, and determined about her career goals was commendable. She seemed to derive deep meaning from it (the "Inner" part of her Inner Giggle). I get that. No need to change that. But what about her "Giggle"? What about the pleasure? The stress and depressed mood that brought her to the group workshop had to be addressed.

Tamika was forgetting her energy fundamentals — most notably her sleep. Her unrealistic expectations of being able to work non-stop to maintain a specific, serious persona deprived her of it. And her lack of energy was depleting her further, adding to the cycle of stress and depression. Her serious work ethic was becoming a serious detriment to her life. And yes, it's okay, perhaps even good at times, to have a "never quit" attitude — but only to a point. You have to take breaks, emotionally and physically. You have to practice your energy fundamentals. You have to allow for rejuvenation. You have to get good sleep, and you have to remember that sleeping is not quitting.

It was validating for Tamika to hear that many other group members realized that their lack of sleep, or even good enough sleep, was certainly

A few weeks after the workshop had ended, I received an email from Tamika. She told me that she had a fun thing happen on her walk back home one day. As she walked by the neighbors' children, she noticed they had a mischievous look in their eyes. "We're having a water fight in the yard; do you want to join?" Tamika was about to say something when BLAM! One of the kids had thrown a water balloon at her! They ran for it, and to her surprise she smiled and ran after them, grabbed some water balloons from their bucket, and participated in their game. She took the plunge, and she had a blast.

She explained that for those few moments, it felt so good to just let her guard down. As if she washed off all the stress of what she thought being a successful, serious businesswoman looked like, with the water dripping off her wet blazer. She felt what it was like to really enjoy the moment, and experienced her Giggle in the present moment, instead of foolishly reserving it solely for the future. And above all, she added, "Since my sleeping practices improved, not only did I have the right mindset not to pass on the fun, I had the energy to run around with the kids!"

The next day at work in the break room she told her colleagues about the water balloon fight!

• • •

I trust that it's clear by now how sleep deprivation can cause a lot of mental and physical strain/harm. Tamika rediscovered her Inner Giggle, reclaimed her livelihood, and became a Happier Being, just by prioritizing sleep. So how do you get better sleep at night? Let's look at the fundamental sleeping practices for better, longer, deeper sleep:

If You Only Did One Thing:
Get Seven to Nine Hours of Sleep Per Night.

According to the American Psychological Association, most healthy adults spend about sixteen hours awake each day, meaning they need about eight hours of sleep per night. Although there is some wiggle room, the widely accepted range for adequate sleep according to the National Sleep Foundation is seven to nine hours per night. Most people will not function optimally or consistently below seven hours (despite what they tell you). Sleep expert, neuroscientist, and UC Berkeley professor Matthew Walker[83] puts it this way: "It is far, far more likely that you will be struck by lightning (the lifetime odds being 1 in 12,000) than being truly capable of surviving on insufficient sleep thanks to a rare gene."

There's a reason why so many athletes cherish/prioritize sleep – like Lebron James, who's known to get twelve hours a night, or Tom Brady, whose bedtime is 8:30 p.m. This is because they want to be at their best every day. Although some people can function with less sleep, and others need a bit more (everyone's physiology is different, and the amount of sleep you need depends largely on your activity level), the seven to nine-hour standard is critical. After all, it's hard to tap into your Happier Being with a foggy brain and little energy, always yearning for some more shut-eye.

One added note: for better sleep, and in order to get those critical seven to nine hours, eliminate or reduce daytime naps. Napping, especially late in the day, can hinder your ability to fall and stay asleep. Now, of course, if you had a sleepless weekend, menopause is interfering, or you're sick or dealing with a chronic condition, your body may need it. But if you must nap, keep your naps short, and try not to nap too late in the afternoon.[84]

Have a set bedtime and wake-up time.

When you set a bedtime and wake-up time based on your optimal number of sleeping hours, you're setting your internal clock up for success. It's important to keep this consistent (even on weekends) so that you don't disturb your circadian rhythm/sleep cycles. This will, in turn, enable you to function more optimally.

As far as what time you should try and get to sleep, research has shown that the most critical hours of sleep for our bodies to heal and repair are from 10 p.m. to 2 a.m. (Some research suggests starting as late as 11 p.m., but most research suggests 10 p.m.). I understand that not everyone will be able to sleep soundly during those hours (maybe you have a newborn at home, work a graveyard shift, etc.), and that's okay. That's why the number one rule is to try and get at least seven hours of sleep. And if you're able to get to bed and fall asleep earlier – your body will thank you.

Now, a note for all you night owls who go to bed or fall asleep later than the average person: Sleep research conducted by Dr. Syed Moin Hassan at Brigham and Women's Hospital says you should not feel shame about your preference of going to sleep late and sleeping in. Some people have what's called a delayed circadian sleep phase that's coded by their genes. Since humans are diurnal, most people follow the same circadian rhythm or internal sleep clock. However, some people's circadian clock sends waking and sleeping signals (hormones like melatonin) much later. Historically, this was particularly useful for humans since those people would stay up late at night to protect the tribe from predators and other potential threats. Today, however, the function is no longer needed, and naturally, late sleepers often suffer from sleep deprivation if they have to get up early for work but can only fall asleep late at night.[85] If you fall into this category (and be real with yourself about whether you do or don't), don't get anxious about your sleeping habits. It's okay to sleep in if your body needs it, especially if you're not getting those seven to nine hours of sleep a night.

Develop nighttime rituals.

Nighttime rituals, or habits, help prime your brain for sleep – signaling that it's time to start winding down, relaxing, and slowing down your system. These rituals may include the same hygiene routine, reading a book, drinking chamomile tea, and so on, at a set time before sleep. When you consistently practice these rituals, your brain remembers and reinforces the effort to shut down for the night. Research headed by Dr. David Lewis, a neuropsychologist, showed that reading before bed can reduce stress in people by as much as sixty-eight percent – quite a big number. And those who read for just six minutes experience slower heart rate and muscle tension. For all these reasons, reading is a great nighttime ritual, allowing you to relax and move your body into a more restful state for sleep.[86]

Meditate.

Meditation is a great way to calm the mind and body for better sleep and let go of any built-up stress or anxiety. It's a great practice before bed (add it to your nighttime rituals!) as well as in the morning before you start your day (where neuropathways to relaxation are created). I urge you to try different types of meditation (breathing, sitting, mindfulness, loving kindness, etc.

Sharon Salzberg's book, *Real Happiness: 28-day program to realize the power of mediation* is a great resource) and see what works best for you.

You can also try a more active type of meditation called progressive muscle relaxation, which involves tensing and relaxing different sets of muscles. In progressive muscle relaxation you are guided to tense your hands, for example, by forming a fist in each hand, then holding this position while you focus on the tension that is being built up. After a few seconds of flexing your fists, you are instructed to let go and to notice the different sensation in your hands now that they are relaxed. This practice can help relieve muscle tension (in general), while giving you that weighted feeling before sleep and allowing you to fall asleep faster.

Each meditative practice affects your nervous system, but it is the accumulated effects of meditation that you need to aim for. It takes some time to experience the full effect, as it reverses the more stressful ways your brain and body were accustomed to. The significant beneficial effect meditation has on your well-being, besides benefiting your sleep, makes it an amazing practice to master. Find the type of meditation that works for you, and stick with it for a while. You will be amazed by its balancing, ripple effect during your days.

Add some movement to your day for better sleep at night.

Exercising in the earlier hours of the day can help keep you awake and alert, as well as strengthen your circadian rhythm for better sleep. Experts say it's best to exercise in the morning instead of late in the day or at night. This is because your cortisol levels (stress hormone) should be highest as you wake and lowest as you go to sleep. You don't want cortisol or body temperature rising before bed. Recent research has also proven that morning exercisers generally get deeper and longer sleep at night. That being said, if you're not a "morning person," don't be discouraged! Even five minutes of walking when you wake up can help reset your cortisol levels and lead to better sleep at night.[87] As a rule of thumb for those who work out later in the day, you should try and complete your workout at least four hours before you go to bed – giving you some time to lower cortisol levels.

Although you shouldn't work out too close to your bedtime, you should still stretch. Light stretching before bed can not only help you fall asleep faster but also improve the quality of your sleep. Stretching elongates the muscles, easing tension and potential cramps. It also forces you to focus on your breathing, practicing mindfulness as your body relaxes. Add stretching to your nightly rituals if possible.

Try to "ground" yourself, literally.

Putting your bare feet on the Earth's surface (like having your toes in the sand or feet in the mud) can positively impact health and sleep. As it turns out, both the Earth and our bodies run on electromagnetic energy, and humans are highly conductive. When you touch your skin to the real ground, you're balancing this electromagnetic energy and getting something author Shawn Stevenson calls "Vitamin G" ('G' standing for Ground) in his book *Sleep Smarter*. We spend so much of our time indoors, disconnected from the earth's surface, that we sometimes need a reminder to ground ourselves, literally.

Avoid caffeine after 2 p.m.

That warm mug of coffee tastes great in the mornings, but you must be cautious of that afternoon "pick me up" cup. This is because caffeine stays in your system for many hours after you consume it. If you want to hit the hay by 10 p.m. or earlier, aim to stop drinking any form of caffeine by 2 p.m.

And if you're naturally high-energy or know that caffeine has quite an effect on you (quickened speech, jitters, stomach upset, etc.), consider tea instead of coffee for your second cup of caffeine – or try to ditch afternoon caffeine altogether.

Don't eat dinner or drink alcohol too late.

You may not think of digestion as an exertion of energy – but for a body that's trying to fall asleep, it definitely is! It's much harder for you to fall and stay asleep when your body is trying to break down food late at night (which makes it harder to decrease heart rate and body temperature). I recommend you have dinner at least three hours before going to bed. Late-night snacking could also be affecting your sleep.

Like eating, your body also needs time to digest alcohol. As a rule of thumb, try to cut off alcohol intake at least three hours before bed. If you tuck in for the night while you're still digesting, it can negatively impact your sleep quality.

Avoid light and noise late at night and while sleeping.
When you're winding down for bed, you want to start decreasing light and sound – calming your senses and priming your brain for sleep. In addition to dimming the lights in whatever room you're in, you want to have a "digital sunset," which means turning off all your screens (TV, cell phone, laptops, etc.) at least ninety minutes before bed. If that's too early, know that any length of time before bed helps, as you are shutting down your brain's exposure to the different lights emitted. The most notable so far, blue light, blocks the production of melatonin. You can use specialized apps that control light settings in the evening. You can also wear special light-blocking sleep glasses in the evening to help prime your brain for relaxation and better sleep.

Additionally, these devices, when connected to Wi-Fi, emit electromagnetic frequencies (EMFs) that are not only harmful but can negatively affect your sleep. Make sure that when it's time to put your screens away, you either turn them on airplane mode or turn them off completely, avoiding any harmful EMFs in addition to light or sound. If you want, you can even go a step further and keep them out of your room altogether.

Lastly, if you are very sensitive to sound or light, consider wearing earplugs, using white noise apps or machines, and/or adding black-out shades in your room. Little-known fact: your skin can actually pick up light via photoreceptors, which signal to your brain that it's time to produce daytime hormones. Needless to say, that could be a major sleep disruptor!

Set your nightly temperature.
When you start winding down for bed, your mind and body slow. Your body temperature also drops with approaching sleep, signaling your brain that it's time to shut down for the night. Try to keep your room between 65–75 degrees Fahrenheit (18–24 degrees Celsius) at night, so that your body temperature stays low. Too hot or too cold might inhibit your ability to fall or stay asleep.

Pay attention to your blanket. Although this may be intuitive, I feel it's worth sharing. Many people like thicker blankets because of their heaviness or weight. But if you're overheating at night or wake up sweating, obviously, you're not likely to have gotten good sleep. Try weighted blankets instead. They're easy to find online and are well worth the expense if they work.

Either way, experiment with switching blankets according to the weather and your own "internal weather," so to speak.

Enjoy some morning sunlight.

When you wake up, open your blinds and let the light in. Exposing your brain to the best wake-up signal – daylight – will shorten your awakening time. Next, step outside and absorb about thirty minutes of outside light. Getting some morning sun inhibits the release of melatonin (a hormone that helps you sleep, as you now know). Your body and brain wake up faster, and you're better able to regulate your circadian rhythm.

What's important to understand is that our natural rhythm is set by maximum or minimum light exposure throughout the day. Light is often measured using the term lux. To improve your sleep, you need to be exposed to the full range or higher amount of lux during the day, and there's no better way to do this than by getting sunlight. Direct sunlight surpasses office lighting many times over. It's critical to get some morning sun!

Try these additional "last resorts" for sleeping solutions.

If you're still having trouble sleeping after trying to implement these positive sleeping habits for an extended period, you could try supplements like melatonin and magnesium or herbals like passionflower and/or valerian root. You could also get tested for things like sleep apnea. Additionally, if you wake up with a dry mouth, you might be a "mouth breather" – which can cause many sleeping problems.[88]

I would also suggest consulting with your doctor on whether CBN (CBD's cousin) is right for you. Growing research points to CBN (cannabinol) in helping people sleep at night as opposed to CBD (cannabidiol). Both come from the cannabis plant but have different sleep-inducing effects. The bottom line is that CBN seems to be a better sleep enhancer, while CBD a better pain reliever.[89] That said, this research is still very new and still evolving (with more therapeutic chemicals targeted in the cannabis plant, for example CBG – cannabigerol). So again, I advise consulting with your doctor first, and of course using your own informed discretion.

Now that you know some of the most current research out there on how to get better sleep, and the tips to do so, I recommend trying to incorporate a small handful into your routine. Start with only one or two practices that would make the most significant change, and gradually build on them as you solidify each ritual and/or habit. You can slowly try and stack habits (see Chapter Two) to keep improving your sleep. Remember, some people may need to build more fundamental sleeping habits into their routine to get better sleep than others.

Journal

Are you getting enough sleep at night? Take a moment to write down a couple fundamental sleeping practices you think would be most beneficial for you to implement right now. What are some ways you can start implementing them? At what point in the day? How will you remind yourself to practice them regularly? Is there someone in your life you can count on to do them with you – perhaps someone you live with or sleep next to? Having an accountability partner can help form your new habit for better sleep. Write it down, and then act on it!

I trust you are already feeling more refreshed with all the dreamy information regarding your improved sleeping habits. Now let's move onto your next Inner Giggle energy booster: moving.

NINE

Fundamental Moving Practices for Well-being

Energize Your Overall Mood Through Movement

I use the term "moving practices" instead of "exercise" because there is an incredible amount of data to suggest that optimizing your movement throughout the day is more important than optimizing your exercise routine. Though there is still an important, vast body of knowledge around exercising routines and fitness, this is not the focus of this chapter. My intention is to give evidence for the mind-body connection, and in particular, how important moving is for the mind. As you will read, recent research concludes that the benefits do not necessarily require rigorous exercise – but simply moving.

I admit that I have never been a gym rat, but I do enjoy walking, dancing (my favorite), and remaining active in general. Besides these activities being pure fun and joy, I experience how moving is necessary for my overall health and well-being. It is my belief that whichever moving practice you choose, no matter how small the movement is, you still have to experience the pleasurable part of it. Without it, without the Giggle aspect, your motivation to keep moving will diminish. So, like me, you don't have to be training for a "dreadful" marathon to feel good about your moving fundamentals. Think about activities that bring you joy, that will get you moving and keep you moving, and that will nourish your Inner Giggle.

Why Movement Is So Important

Our bodies were designed to move all day, every day. Moving and light exercise improve your blood flow, lymph movement, digestion, and mitochondrial function (your cells' energy production), and also release an array of hormones that make your mind and body feel good. It can also boost your self-esteem, lower stress levels, improve mood and focus, and has many other powerful positive effects.

As it so happens, we don't move nearly as much as we used to. Years ago, the average person would walk several miles each day. They'd also chop wood, tend to animals, and gather food. Today, the average person walks far less, including the distance walking to and from the refrigerator or from the parking garage inside your home. That's a lot less moving! Our brains evolved to rely on the hormones and chemicals produced by movement. While it's true that moving can lift your mood, moving is critical to bring your brain back up to its baseline of functioning.

As a psychologist, I believe this is critical to understand. Movement is as important for your brain as it is for the rest of your body. It's no surprise that having a "sound mind and body" has been promoted by philosophers over thousands of years – and science has now backed it up. Recent research has proven that movement not only benefits cardiovascular health but cerebrovascular health. Movement has been linked to brain neuroplasticity and improved brain communication and cell growth in the hippocampus. This results in better cognitive functioning, learning, memory, and improvements in mental health states like anxiety, depression, insomnia, dementia, and ADHD.[90]

Let's look at the two common mental health conditions: anxiety and depression. When it comes to anxiety, moving regularly can increase neural connections in your brain, aiding in lowering the reaction of your body's sympathetic nervous system (the fight-or-flight response), making you braver, if you will. This is because if you are calmer, you are better focused, and better able to respond to outside stressors. Your anxiety is reduced, and your ability to respond appropriately to the stressor is increased. Movement also increases a protein in the brain, Brain-Derived Neurotrophic Factor (BDNF), which helps nerve fibers grow, thereby boosting your mood and lowering symptoms of depression. There's even research indicating that a ninety-minute walk outside can lead to decreased activity in the area of the brain responsible for controlling depressive rumination.[91]

We'll get into more examples of how movement positively affects aspects of your physiology in a moment, but for now, know that movement truly has a happiness domino effect throughout your day-to-day life. Better mood leads to more motivation and achievement, improved self-image, positive social interactions, and increased experience of your Happier Being.[92]

Turn Gene Expression On and Off

Studies conducted over the past decade show that moving and exercise have been linked to impressive epigenetic changes in people. One study undertaken by Lund University Diabetes Centre demonstrated how exercise and movement can alter DNA methylation (recall, this is the process by which genes are turned on and off) in fat cells. In the study, previously sedentary men around age thirty-five took an aerobics-type class 1.8 times per week, on average, for six months. The results showed epigenetic changes in 7,000 of the men's genes, as well as changes in genes related to type 2 diabetes and obesity. The study, which was the first to map DNA methylation in fat cells, showed how even a little exercise can change your gene expression and the way fat is stored to lower your risk of diseases and improve existing conditions.[93]

Another study by researchers at Keele University linked epigenetic changes to muscle memory – in the literal sense. Without going into too much detail, the study proved that periods of skeletal muscle growth in humans are "remembered" by the genes in the muscle, helping them grow larger later in life. This means that muscle memory isn't just the brain-muscle connection. It goes all the way down to the DNA level. So if you've worked on building muscle in the past, you should have an easier time doing it again in the future! This is a truly promising sign for muscle mass rehabilitation in those who have experienced illness or injury and are now in remission or healthy enough to exercise.[94]

Boosting Your Daily DOSE

Perhaps you've heard of a "runners high"? Chemically speaking, there's truth behind it. Movement emits neurotransmitters such as endorphins, dopamine, norepinephrine (also known as noradrenaline), and serotonin, as well as endocannabinoids (this is the body's own version of cannabis compounds!). Together these chemicals help your body relieve pain and stress by binding to receptors in your brain in areas such as your amygdala and prefrontal cortex. They also improve mood and positive feelings, as previously discussed. There is a reason I always recommend some movement to my clients who suffer from anxiety, depression, chronic physical stress, and more.

> **Moving is a shot of goodness to your brain, and after that, your mood. In a way, we can argue that not exercising is like taking depressants!**

In addition to boosting your mood, the activity of neurotransmitters upon movement has physiological benefits. New research by Drs. Li and Spitzer out of the University of California, San Diego,[95] shows that neurotransmitters and the switches occurring during chemical messaging are also key to boosting motor skill learning. The study compared mice on just a week's worth of exercise (running on a wheel) to those who did not. They found that the mice who exercised had gained motor skills (staying on a rotating rod and crossing a balance beam) faster than the more sedentary group. These findings give more insight into the importance of moving regularly and how you may add more plasticity to your brain. More neuroplasticity leads to increased learning, growth, higher functioning, well-being – and to the ability to tap into your Inner Giggle more often.

Protection Through Movement

Like sleeping, moving influences the strength of your immune system as well as your metabolic health. But unlike sleep, there's a larger debate over how much exercise is "too much." Many scientists believe that intense exercise might lead to overexertion and weaken your immune system, but that moderate exercise can strengthen it. If you've ever felt a bit under the weather after a really hard workout, it may be because, as some studies have found, over-exertion might be harmful. That being said, recent research has proven that athletes and others who regularly work out hard are not prone to increased incidence of infections. Regardless, both sides of the coin agree that light to moderate exercise helps your immune function and moving is better than not moving.[96]

More so, simple, repetitive, and/or bilateral movements – not truly exercise per se – can have very healing and nurturing effects on your immune system. Twirling, rocking back and forth, drumming on your lap, and tapping on your face and head can all send signals from one side of your brain to the other (like a pendulum), which reminds your body that you are protected and safe. Your immune system can relax.[97]

What's important to remember is that exercise, practiced regularly at whatever level that keeps you moving, has a positive effect on your immune system. Habitual movement can improve your immune system's ability to regulate itself, delay dysfunction related to age, and produce beneficial anti-inflammatory effects.[98] In a recent study, researchers concluded that one twenty-minute moderate exercise session seemed to produce an anti-inflammatory cellular response as indicated by the reduction of the cytokine TNF. When our bodies are functioning optimally, and we haven't been recently injured, we want these inflammatory TNF levels to be reduced, since too much inflammation in the body can, as you know, be taxing and harmful to our systems.[99]

Improve Vagus Nerve Functioning

In addition to breathing and vocal vibration exercises for improved vagal tone and better sleep, several other movements help improve your vagus nerve functioning for physical and psychological well-being. Cold exposure (taking a cold shower), yoga, tai chi, massage, meditation, and acupuncture all activate and stimulate the vagus nerve. Improved vagal tone helps with concentration and memory and reduces your risk of conditions such as heart disease, diabetes, stroke, and depression. It also reduces inflammation and improves mood.[100]

This last part, improved mood, is more important than it might sound. Adding positive thoughts to movement and other routines can greatly improve vagal tone. Take, for example, meditation. One study of sixty-five people asked half to think kind thoughts about others and repeat mantras like, "May you feel safe, may you feel happy, may you feel healthy, may you live with ease." The other half, the control group, simply meditated without doing so. The results showed that those who practiced the mantras saw a greater increase in positive emotions such as hope, interest, and joy than the control group. They also felt a greater sense of social connection to others and improved vagal tone whereas the control group did not.

The study, published in the scientific journal *Psychological Science,* proved that strong vagal tone was part of a feedback loop between positive emotions, physical health, and positive social connections. The scientists also found out that simply reflecting on positive social connections and working to improve human bonds also improved vagal tone – truly remarkable![101]

If you're feeling down, depressed, or anxious, remember the importance of positive emotions and connections for your vagal tone. Hop on the phone with a friend and get your vocal cords vibrating for some additional vagus nerve strengthening.

Bottom Line, You Must Move!

Back in my early days as a psychologist, I worked in a clinic with mentally ill patients, including those with schizophrenia. Over time I developed a group called "The Walking Club" with some of my most treatment-resistant schizophrenic patients to help elevate their moods. At first, it wasn't easy. I had to use a token economy (some extra privileges of their choosing) to motivate them to join the club. Some wanted access to more coffee, for example, and some wanted more time with the clinic's piano. I also allowed them to bring their Walkman (yes, back when CDs were still in existence) to allow for the level of social interaction they felt comfortable with. This was a walking group, and that was all that was expected of the participants. Slowly but surely, The Walking Club developed.

Rain or shine, we walked every day before group therapy sessions. When the weather grew colder, we'd walk before opening hours inside a nearby mall. Unsurprisingly, over time I noticed improvements in the patients' mood, exhibited in their ability to participate in and focus on group therapy right after. Many of them started showing up at the clinic for the club earlier than scheduled or came to my room prior, confirming that the walk was still happening each day. It was obvious to them, too, that the effects of the physical effort rippled to their psychological parts, and they were hoping for more. I was proud of their participation and thankful of the possibility that just a little bit of walking showed marked improvements in their overall well-being.

If there's one thing I hope you get out of this story – and this chapter – it's that you must avoid a sedentary lifestyle if your health allows it. When you choose not to move, you're not only robbing yourself of your full capacity but becoming more vulnerable to a host of health issues.

Joan Vernikos Ph.D., is the former Director of NASA's Life Sciences Division. Dr. Vernikos's responsibilities at NASA included figuring out how to optimize the health and well-being of astronauts. In her book, *Sitting Kills, Moving Heals*, she explains that a sedentary lifestyle on Earth is surprisingly similar to that of an astronaut in space. As it turns out, an astronaut's health rapidly deteriorates in zero gravity during spaceflight, similarly to how quickly our health on Earth deteriorates when we choose not to move or exercise. For example, we lose bone density and plasma volume, as well as decrease our aerobic capacity. On the flip side, if astronauts can regain their good health after spaceflight, so can people who suffer from health problems due to a generally sedentary lifestyle. What's more, Dr. Vernikos claims, it doesn't take much. Why? Gravity.

The difference between outer space and Earth is, of course, gravity, and when it comes to movement and exercise, gravity is a game-changer.

Gravitational force means you don't need to exercise intensely to reap the benefits of movement. Simple exercises or activities throughout the day, using gravity as a resistant force, can make you healthier and happier. Dr. Vernikos calls these her "G-Habit" (gravity habit) building tips. They include stretching, moving from standing to sitting, and walking tall (adjusting posture).

Journal

Can you think of any G-Habits that you could put into practice throughout your day? Ways in which you can shift and move your body more? Are there opportune times to take a stretch break while working? What are the barriers getting in the way of you moving regularly? And how can you overcome this? Allow yourself to start small, and slowly you will "gravitate" toward building some moving habits!

Remember, you don't have to run a marathon (though it's great if you do!), lift heavy weights, or push your body to the limit to be healthier. Simple movement is an Inner Giggle energy booster, and making small daily movements can have a major, positive impact on your physical and mental health. So, what are some of these daily movements?

Without further ado I'd like to give you my fundamental moving practices!

Fundamental Movement for Your Inner Giggle

If you only did one thing: walk for at least ten minutes every day.
Walking every day is critical to your overall well-being. It doesn't have to be rigorous or for extended periods. In fact, studies have shown that a brisk walk every day can decrease your chances of premature death (aha, I will use any tidbit of info to get you moving!). Psychologists have also proven, when it comes to elevating mood and reducing symptoms of anxiety and depression, a ten-minute walk can be just as good as a forty-five-minute workout.[102] Moreover, the accumulative effect will have even greater benefits on your mental and physical health. These rewards will serve as the natural reinforcement to move again and, as a result, are likely to increase how many minutes you walk.

I'd like you to think of walking as "oiling" your body and brain's engine: once you get yourself moving, you get your heart pumping and blood circulating – and then all your body's systems (cardiovascular, lymphatic, nervous, digestive) can start functioning and performing better. One study from the *British Journal of Sports Medicine* even found that people who engaged in aerobic exercise at least five days a week were forty-three percent less likely to report upper respiratory symptoms than their less-active counterparts.[103] If you don't do so already, I highly suggest you add at least ten minutes of walking into your daily routine. Your health will thank you.

Practice deep breathing.

Diaphragmatic breathing, also known as "abdominal" or "belly" breathing, has a host of mental and physical health benefits. As the name suggests, this kind of breathing engages the diaphragm, the dome-shaped muscle at the base of your lungs. The diaphragm contracts and moves downward when you inhale, expanding your lungs and letting more oxygen in, and relaxes and moves back upward when you exhale. When you practice breathing from your diaphragm, you not only strengthen it but also help stabilize your blood pressure, lower your heartbeat and cortisol levels, and improve your mental clarity. Many people hold their breath often throughout the day due to their busy lives and forget to take deep, consistent breaths from their bellies instead of their chests. Incorporating some deep, diaphragmatic breathing into your day will help ease stress, anxiety, and feelings of overwhelm.

Add a meditative movement into your week.

Like deep breathing, meditative movement forces you to slow down and reset while also getting in a small workout (double whammy, in my opinion). These movements include, of course, all different types of meditation, as well as practices like yoga, tai chi, and qigong. When you add meditative movement into your routine, you're allowing yourself to shift your patterns of breath, rhythm, and posture. It's no surprise that meditative movements have been consistently linked to a reduction in anxiety, depression, and all-around stress. Try and take one day out of the week to participate in a meditative movement of your choice. I know that slowing down can be hard, but it's worth it in the end. Even once a month to get you started is a good practice.

Take time to visualize internal movement and release tension.
Visualization is a powerful psychological tool, particularly when it comes to mindful movement, healing, and recovery. Studies have shown that visualizing an action activates the same part of your brain as when you actually do the action. That is pretty incredible! It also explains, in part, some of the amazing stories we hear about those with a paralyzed limb suddenly healing from or moving out of paralysis due to visualization.

Take a few moments, perhaps on your lunch break, to stop what you're doing and become aware of your points of tension. Maybe you've been holding your shoulders, clenching your jaw, or even sitting cross-legged too long. Pay close attention to the parts of your body that need release, relax them, and then visualize the oxygen flow going to those areas. See and feel the tension exiting your body.

Make time for a longer commute.
If you live where you can walk, bike, or even run to work, you should build this practice into your schedule if you can. This will help you solidify your daily movement practice and leave you feeling more alert, focused, and energized at the beginning of your day – ready to be productive. It's a scientific fact that your brain works better following exercise, and you can use this knowledge to your advantage. Even if you have to drive or cannot move for extended periods, you can still choose to take the "long commute" once you get back on foot. Park further away from the entrance to your building or use the stairs, when possible, instead of the elevator. You get it. Just make sure moving is built into your day.

Functionalize your office space.
Consider using functional office furniture that will allow you to shift positions often and be less sedentary. Treadmill desks, standing desks, and alternative chairs like yoga balls all help you stand or sit upright. And if you have enough space in your workspace, I suggest buying a foam roller or yoga mat for stretching (which is next on the list). You can also just lie down on the roller to give your back a rest and open up your chest.

Take stretch breaks.
Research shows that the human brain can only absorb information for about forty-five minutes before it begins decreasing its capacity to do

so.[104] So if you want to optimize your attention, focus, and productivity throughout your day, it's important to try and take breaks every hour or so. I recommend movement breaks to clear your head and get into your body at the same time. Frequent stretching, in particular, has benefits like reducing discomfort, fatigue, stress levels, and chances of injury while improving blood and nutrient supply to your muscles and tissues, among other things. All this results in improved energy.

Every movement counts.
This last one is, again, a reminder that moving and exercise should be fun. There are so many activities you can be doing or already doing on a daily or weekly basis that involve moving. You have to appraise them as such, as they are part of your overall movement quota for your day. As a matter of fact, Michelle Segar, one of the leading experts on behavioral change, encourages us in her book *No Sweat: How the Science of Motivation Can Bring You a Lifetime of Fitness* to find opportunities to move as often as we can, because every movement counts. These include, pacing while talking on the phone, walking up and down the stairs in your house, making your bed, playing outside with the kiddos, and even jumping into your neighborhood lake (lucky!). Remember that there should be joy in moving. It's a big Inner Giggle energy booster!

• • •

I hope you feel empowered by knowing just how connected your mind and body are, and feel inspired by the importance of your Inner Giggle energy boosters. I believe that if you use the fundamental eating, sleeping, and moving practices I've laid out for you, you'll start forming healthful habits that positively impact your life and increase your overall well-being.

I encourage you to go back to Chapter Two, the habit formation chapter, and create your own personal path to optimize your energy boosters. I hope that the healthy habit formations tips, together with the energy-boosting fundamental practices, will underscore the importance of the changes you are making. It may also remind you how hard it is to change. That's why there's one last rule I'd like you to remember when it comes to practicing all your fundamental energy boosting habits: be kind to yourself.

Self-compassion is one of my favorite rules for becoming a Happier Being. It applies to any challenge or setback you face in your life (or feel that you may have caused), and it is an essential meditation to contemplate as often as you can.

With that message in mind, let's move on to the final chapter.

TEN

Chronic Physical Stress – The Healing Equation

Why include a whole chapter about chronic physical stress in a book about happiness?

When I set out to write *Happier Being,* I honestly did not intend to share my story of healing and recovering from Lyme Disease. But the more I wrote, the more I realized a couple of important things. First, I can use myself as a genuine example of how health challenges can set you back, and I can lay out how I practiced what I preach to increase my daily dose of happiness. Second, I wrote this book during the COVID-19 pandemic. Since then, the global health crisis has brought many health-related challenges to the forefront of millions of people's lives.

Of course, it's not as if prior to the pandemic there weren't many people who were, unfortunately, dealing with invisible illnesses, chronic diseases, or painful conditions. But undeniably, the pandemic brought the fear of losing our health, our lives, or the life of a loved one to the top of everyone's mind. Tragically, that fear turned into reality for many, and those losses have had heartbreaking ripple effects.

We are all experiencing the immense chronic stress of Covid-19, and I've witnessed people suffer in many different ways. Almost all of us have faced some type of health-related challenge in the process - whether it be mental or physical. We were forced to deal with the unknown, the unpredictable, and with the isolation, pain, loss, depression, and anxiety that came with the pandemic. For this reason, I felt that including a substantial body of knowledge on chronic physical stress would greatly benefit not only those who have been ill or in pain for a while, but those who have been affected either directly or indirectly by recent events.

I hope the following pages will help you navigate your way to Happier Being when it comes to dealing with chronic physical stress.

Positive Psychology to the Rescue

Is it possible to cultivate your Happier Being when, like me, you're dealing with chronic physical stress?

Lyme Disease has put me through the ringer – physically, mentally, emotionally – so I know that chronic conditions can feel like an inescapable cul-de-sac of your existence. As I learned to deal with the disease, I realized that there was no hidden epiphany to healing. With the diagnosis my life had changed, and with that, some of my views. But it wasn't the initial driving force behind my interest in positive psychology[105] and its related topic of happiness and fulfillment.

I spent years, before my diagnosis, working with clients experiencing psychological issues. Some had severe chronic mental illness, and some had chronic pain or illnesses too. The range of their ability to experience positive emotions was astounding. I saw that some of them, regardless of their deeply ingrained emotional pain, could have happier moments. Others could not. And I wondered why that was.

I saw the same thing happen while I was undergoing Lyme Disease treatment in the IV room of my doctor's office. Some people could keep their spirits up (even if they were only putting on a good show for others) and had uplifting stories to share. Others weren't able to muster so much as a single smile (and yes, I'm aware of the underlying physical discomfort and the different emotional states we find ourselves in while getting any treatment). Still, this is part of the point. Despite their circumstances, some people were able to find a way to add some joy, even momentarily or semi-artificially.

These observations drew me more closely toward positive psychology literature – as did my own experience with physical illness. I realized how important it was to work on increasing my joy every single day. I needed to find something to be grateful for when I woke up in the morning, something to giggle about during the day, and something to look forward to and plan for the near future. Just eliminating the sadness of being sick wouldn't solve all that; I had to *add to* my life to make it better – just like my clients did.

Your unique interpretation of happiness becomes so important when you're dealing with Chronic Physical Stress (CPS). You must tailor your healing path accordingly. CPS is the term I coined to include any chronic medical symptoms, pains, diseases, or conditions. Those which are visible to the outside observer, and those which are not. In other words: any unwanted, chronic physical stress.

I don't believe that "everything happens for a reason." But I do believe that once something has happened, you can *find* a reason – in anything – to keep going. So before we get into the rest of the chapter, you should know that I will *not* be writing about CPS as a cliched, "glass half full" lesson. This is a tough chapter, but one I believe truly embodies what it means to become a Happier Being. My hope is that you're able to see through the setback, the undeniable toll, to reach deep down into your Inner Giggle on your way to becoming a Happier Being. This is your most cherished and precious resource, and the strongest version of yourself.

Dealing with CPS and its related symptoms is complicated, and by no means am I suggesting that you forego addressing any symptoms with your physician. My goal here is to give you more psychological tools for happiness, and allow you to experience your Inner Giggle more often, despite it all.

The Healing Equation

At the heart of it, healing is mastering the practice of staying on the path of an upward spiral. Part of this spiral means tuning into your Inner Giggle boosters and optimizing your well-being. Upgrading your fundamental energy practices is a big part of healing. Another equally important part is using positive psychology.

Everyone – but especially those dealing with CPS – should make room for more positive emotions, more joy, and more happiness. The physical body can be such a killjoy, whether because of a chronic condition that messes unpredictably with the quality of your days or a tragic and disabling accident. Even the ailments of ordinary aging take their toll on your appearance or bodily functions (like me not being able to type these words without my reading glasses). We will all experience decline, whether it's CPS or not.

This is why it's so important to be mentally strong – strong enough to experience joy and happiness, even in difficult circumstances (like those in the IV room with me who were able to smile and converse). As I contemplated my own experience with CPS, it got me thinking: What if happiness, with resilience as its counterpart, makes up the psychological immune system of our lives? It does, after all, shield you from would-be invaders like depression, doubt, anger, and resentment.

Does it follow, then, that these two factors – happiness and resilience – are part of the equation for healing? From my personal and professional experience, I believe the answer is *yes*.

Building Resilience: A Key Concept for Healing

Resilience is what keeps us going after major setbacks or life-changing events. Events like this may cause anxiety, depression, and sometimes even Post-Traumatic Stress Disorder (PTSD), but resiliency can help you recover. I won't say that resilience helps us fully bounce back – because life never truly goes back to the way it was after these types of experiences – but it does help to rebuild a new, healthful baseline. This baseline is a new starting point to grow from, and hopefully one that's even more solid than before. Resilience is not about time travel. We can't negotiate with the past, and we can't undo what's been done, but we can find healthy ways to integrate these events into our lives and live side by side with them.

Journal

I want you to imagine holding a stress ball in one hand and a tomato in the other. What would happen if you squeezed both hands? The stress ball would of course dent inward and then spring back into shape, whereas the tomato would squish into a mess. Now imagine the stress ball and tomato as a metaphor for your resiliency. The stress ball equates to rapid recovery after a period of hardship, one way to think of resilience. But the tomato shows us a different path to recovery. When squeezed, the seeds and juice slump out all over, but if those seeds fall into healthy soil underneath, they might grow into strong, new plants in five years' time. That's a different kind of resilience. It's the power to renew, to start again and to grow out of devastation.

Can you think of a very difficult period in your life where the tomato seeds prevailed? If you're dealing with CPS or have dealt with CPS in the past, can you see how resilience is not about the stress ball (quickly bouncing back to the way you were before). Write down any thoughts this may have elicited.

Always remember that your Inner Giggle is like those tomato seeds. Buried deep in the Earth, it can withstand days filled with rain or snow. Having that sense of agency over your growth is crucial to cultivating and maintaining your Inner Giggle, even in times of high stress – mental or physical. Learning from your past resilient experiences enhances your belief in your present abilities. Become aware of your resilient powers!

Building Your Everyday Resilience

First and foremost, it's important to learn to rethink stressors in your life. The way you approach a situation makes a difference in your ability to bounce forward. Research shows that when you think about stressors as a challenge rather than a threat, your mind uses a different region of the brain to process the information. Instead of activating the amygdala to initiate the stress response, you appraise that stress as a challenge, activating another part of your brain, your prefrontal lobe, that provides you with different angles to consider resolving your situation.[106]

If you're dealing with CPS, chronic conditions, or illness, you probably find some days are easier than others. The degree of hardness isn't really under your control. You learn to expect challenge but not fear it. And perhaps the biggest challenge you face is holding your own identity strong. Whichever facet of your identity is called upon at any particular time, it's up to you to hold your identity of an Inner Giggle optimizer strong. How you react to a setback or the stressor is extremely important, not only to your health but also to building resilience to the realities of the condition itself. It places your mind in even greater control when your body is not cooperating.

One way to do so, according to Eric Greitens, is to start by asking yourself who you want to be.[107] Think beyond just this moment and allow a scenario to come into your mind. Focus on your desired identity. How do you want to see yourself? How do you want people to perceive you or remember you? There is no right or wrong answer here. Maybe you want to be brave. Maybe you want to be kind. Maybe you want to be smart.

Once you decide who you want to be, start acting that way. If you want to be happy, start acting in a manner you perceive someone who is happy would act. I don't mean pretend — I mean do the things you assume you'd do if you were happy. This is not the same as "fake it 'til you make it." This is a science-based approach to creating behavioral change and adapting your identity as a result of that. It works like this: if you want to be brave, do the things you'd do if you were brave. You don't have to feel those things yet. But the more you act like you already do, the more those actions will shape how you feel (recall self-perception theory in Chapter Two).

When life calls on your resiliency, have a clear sense of who you're committed to being. Then act like that person to the degree you can, keeping a realistic idea of how much you can do. Venture into your new identity as often as you can. If you want to be the person who faces challenges head-on, you have to be the one who is disciplined in your commitment to not let feelings govern your behavior. That will support the success of creating your identity.

As Greitens explains, too often we put feelings ahead of action, then, from that, try to establish our identity. But that sets you up for being driven by your feelings. If you're feeling tired, anxious, depressed, or scared, you take actions consistent with those feelings, and thus your behaviors and your identity are tied to them. But, as Greitens says, "that's not a winning equation."

The winning equation is actually reversed: IDENTITY → ACTION → FEELINGS.

You see, you need to rely on the identity you choose to direct your behavior. That will influence your actions and leave you feeling better. Having this strong sense of self directly respond to your circumstances is a better way to maintain your overall well-being and strong identity. It allows your identity to be the driving force of your life, creating a more stable, resilient self.

Chip Away at Your New Identity – Be an Inner Giggle Seeker

There's a great story based on Michelangelo's sculpting process of *David,* the famous statue now in the Academia Gallery in Florence, Italy. An admirer asked Michelangelo how he sculpted the statue – how did he craft such a masterpiece of form and beauty? Michelangelo offered this strikingly simple reply: He first fixed his attention on the slab of raw marble. He studied it and then "chipped away all that wasn't David."

If you want to feel different – happier, smarter, calmer – you have to start behaving differently, at least some of the time, than you do now. See yourself becoming that person who is expanding the trait or state you want to experience. Figure what you need to do more of, or less of. What thoughts you best hold onto and focus on and what thoughts you best not.

This is cognitive behavioral therapy (CBT) in a nutshell. It addresses the notion that the way you think is the way you feel. By using this mental training theory, CBT therapists can help clients better deal with their emotions by noticing and changing their thoughts to healthier ones. It helps clients break out of dysfunctional thinking, even when that thinking comes from seemingly rational old patterns. It quiets the anxious mind that tends to exaggerate perceived potential threats. It focuses on present, realistic solutions for the person they're trying to become without losing sight of reality. It strengthens their chosen identity.

So who do you want to be? Do you want to be a happy person? Someone who, despite a chronic condition, still wants to experience their Inner Giggle more often? How would people like that act? Perhaps they would smile at others also getting treatment in the IV room despite their harsh feelings. Perhaps they would embrace, momentarily, another's smiling energy – because they won't be driven to act only according to their feelings. Can you see the power in that?

I urge you to remember that when you're dealing with CPS that has left you feeling seemingly choiceless, you still have the choice to act according to who you want to be and build your resilient identity. I encourage you to activate your superpower – your Inner Giggle – as often as possible to help you along the way, letting you experience meaning and pleasure more often. Expand your experiences outside of your chronic pain.

You'll need this, as chronic conditions are no small feat, and in fact, much more common than you probably realize.

Obstacles to Activating Your Inner Giggle When Dealing with CPS

According to the Centers for Disease Control and Prevention, about six in ten adults in the US live with a chronic disease. And about four in ten adults have two or more. Many of those illnesses are also hard to diagnose. Additionally, about 20.4 percent of US adults live with chronic pain.[108] To me, and I would assume to you as well, these numbers are higher than expected. While chronic illness and chronic pain are distinct and different, people who suffer from either deal with similar psychological difficulties. Let's talk about the kinds of tools you can use to overcome obstacles when dealing with either.

One of these obstacles can be your own suffering – something called meta feelings. Not only are you physically suffering, but you also suffer from feeling bad about having negative feelings, thoughts, disappointment, and anger about your situation. It's another layer to navigate when dealing with CPS. If you get upset in everyday life because you're frustrated with your own body, tired of the pain, that's human. But to feel as if you disappointed yourself by feeling bummed out because you're not able to do something, or feeling bad that you overreacted, is not okay. Of course, the goal is to get to a place where you're controlling your thoughts and feelings better, practicing more acceptance, and looking ahead to what can be done. But there's no denying the adjustments when dealing with a diagnosis and the reality that some negative emotions will be present. Accepting that there will be some days when you'll be handling the pain less than optimally can prevent these negative meta feelings that add to the suffering. Keeping this unconscious process in check is really important for the vibrancy of your Inner Giggle.

There's also an element of grief with chronic pain or illness. Everything changes. You lost some of who you used to be and some of what you used to do. One day, you were a healthy person. The next day, you weren't. And the notion that nothing is guaranteed in life takes on a whole new meaning. The rug that was pulled out from under your feet has now landed you on the floor, and suddenly, you're forced to see your life from a new, less favorable vantage point, even if only for the time being. You realize that the reality you understood before has changed. The present needs to be reevaluated. And this can feel like quite a loss, like the grieving period of one's "prior self" has begun. It pours another layer of emotional pain into the bucket of physical pain. These grieving states may include emotions you have not experienced before. For some it can even result in depression.

Beyond the emotional pain caused by newfound loss, CPS can also cause inflammation, which increases your likelihood of developing depression. So not only might you be depressed by your condition – your condition may actually be physically exacerbating any depression. It's both, and that's why, compounded, it can be so difficult to try and tap into your Inner Giggle.

Lastly, when you are challenged by CPS, there is the added experience of the physical dysfunction warning your whole being that "something is not right." Be it the pain, the immobilization, or the fatigue – it shakes your experience of safety to its core. There is a sense of threat built into your daily life, one that you need to keep evaluating and negotiating with. The lack of satisfying this primal need to feel safe within your own body escalates to higher levels when it comes to CPS – at least in the beginning. That's why mending this escalated sense of anxiety is important. Do your best not to interpret those feelings as alarming. You need to listen to them but not buy into them. They are just your body's way of letting you know it needs more tender love and care – sending you messages of what needs to be attended to. Assure your body and reassure yourself that you are doing just that.

All in all, it's clear that the lack of the grounding you knew before your chronic condition can leave you feeling anxious, outraged, powerless, or hopeless. Also the inevitable social separation from others when you have to stop or cut back on working or socializing can leave you feeling isolated, depressed, deflated, envious, and lonely. Dealing with CPS is undoubtedly a bumpy road filled with many obstacles.

So how do you navigate this? How do you stay resilient, hold onto your purpose, and find ways to add some pleasure for relief, despite the pain?

Keeping Your Inner Giggle Alive

Keeping your Inner Giggle alive despite CPS is directly related to the stories you tell yourself. I'm not trying to belittle the magnitude of anyone's struggle here. Still, when you have a chronic medical condition, the changes you experience in your life can challenge your sense of identity – your very foundation. It poses the anxiety-provoking question: What quality of life is possible for me now?

Over the years, I've found it is always possible to find a way through, even if it feels more as if some days you're not only pushing yourself through, but squeezing yourself to fit through a narrowing door. Here's the key:

> **Any motion in the right direction that will move you forward and improve your quality of life is not just worth it – it's crucial. It's not about bouncing back to the way you were, it's about using resiliency to bounce through to who you want to be.**

Understanding Post-traumatic Growth

There can absolutely be growth after trauma. You can bounce through the struggle. Some psychologists call it post-traumatic growth, others adversarial growth, but the underlying truth remains the same – what doesn't kill you can make you stronger.

Post-traumatic growth is illustrated by the Japanese art of kintsugi and the theory of the Mosaic. Both are worth considering in your journey to accept your new normal. They will give you a more positive and realistic view as you move through and forward after a setback.

Kintsugi (金継ぎ), or "golden joinery" in Japanese, entails repairing broken pottery by mending the areas of breakage with lacquer mixed with powdered gold, silver, or platinum. The repairs of the pieces remain visible to all in the newly joined pottery. As a philosophy, it treats breakage and repair as part of the history of an object rather than something to disguise. The takeaway? Having a setback or trauma is *not* something to feel ashamed of or try to hide. Instead, it should be displayed proudly as part of your life experience. So often we want to throw away the broken pieces of our past and deny they ever happened. But hang on! These broken pieces can add value to your life. By mending the metaphorical object of your past, you prove that out of something broken can come something whole and beautiful again, scars and all. Your resilience and ability to learn from negative experiences are what make you unique and will help you thrive. You can't deny it happened, so you might as well embrace it and learn to live with it as part of who and what you are.

But, what about the kind of trauma that you can't just glue back together with pretty gold lacquer? The kind that really shakes the foundation of your life?

This is where the theory of the mosaic comes in. Say you have a beautiful vase sitting on your coffee table. (Why you put this delicate, breakable thing on your coffee table when so much movement occurs on and around it is a discussion for another time.) One day, inevitably, you accidentally knock the vase over, and it shatters into a thousand pieces on your hardwood floor. Do you attempt then to glue it all back together and recreate the masterpiece? No. Of course not. Instead, you can take the pieces of this vase and create a mosaic. Re-purpose it to create a new work of art. It will still have many of the same characteristics as the previous vase (colors, textures, etc.), but at the same time be new and different (size, shape, use, etc.).

The takeaway? Sometimes, in the face of harsh adversity, life will require serious renovations. And rather than trying to recreate the past, you can get creative, focus on your available resources (including all the pieces, broken or not), and redesign your improved "mosaic self." This new creation is your revamped present, which will motivate you to move on to a new future.

Whether your life's circumstances allow you to choose the route of kintsugi or the route of a mosaic, the most crucial part is the choice you make to grow. To put yourself back together in whatever form works for you, into your most innovative shape yet. This is what post-traumatic growth is all about.

The father of positive psychology, Dr. Martin Seligman, says that the main difference between post-traumatic growth and post-traumatic stress is our perception. In his book *Flourish,* he argues that our beliefs about adversity, rather than the adversity itself, cause the consequent feelings.[109]

I agree and ask you to recall the cognitive behavioral therapy core concept discussed earlier. Simplified, it states that how you think is how you feel. In the context of dealing with CPS with healing as the goal, prioritizing your positive thoughts and focusing on maximizing your Happier Being are key. You will doubtless still experience negative emotions, but you want to begin separating yourself from your challenging experience and addressing, realistically, what's in your control in order to reap more positive emotions.

This is *not* positive thinking in the sense of twisting the reality or the complexity of your suffering. This is a rearrangement of your perspective, refocusing on the parts of your life that are within your control and the components of your life you can still enjoy.

Experiencing Post-traumatic Growth

An important piece of this puzzle of learning to experience post-traumatic growth, despite the stress of CPS, is learning to zoom in on any peaceful moments. Let me explain a bit further.

Every experience we have can be broken down into different aspects. The thoughts you have (with their intentions), the sensations you feel (pains, unfortunately, but also the perception of sounds, touch), and your behavior (the actions you take, and your posture, facial expressions, movement). When you suffer from CPS, aim your attention to expand the momentary good, the peaceful thoughts, senses, and behaviors you experience, in between the bad. Despite what else is going on with you, you can attend to them and nourish that inner joy, even if it's just a tiny bit.

Now I know that on some days, this can feel extremely difficult. You may have days where you can't leave the house or even the bed – but you can still call up your friend and enjoy a good conversation. Connection with the people you love will act like much-needed rainwater to the slightly dry seeds of your Inner Giggle (we'll get more into the impact of others later in the chapter). Maybe you can find the humor in the absurd, unhazardous, or even exhausting scenarios you endure during the day. Like when you're able to make fun of yourself stumbling over the carpet. That brief relief from laughter reminds your spirit that you can still find funny in sadness. You can still have better in worse.

As a matter of fact, I'd like to prescribe it to you as your daily dose of LPD – Laughs Per Day – to keep you moving forward. Savoring moments of relief and lift-me-up energy, and recalling them later, help reinforce joy and resilience. When you zoom in on funny moments and relive them, you integrate those positive influences more deeply into your nervous system. And that contributes to your optimism, your resiliency, and your goal of healing.

This is all possible due to neuroplasticity – the ability of the brain to form and reorganize synaptic connections. Your brain isn't set in its ways, structure, or neural connections. Even if life is totally different now, you can learn to increase positivity with what you have. If you shift your attitude, you can change your brain to help you find more and better creative ways to heal. If you direct your focus to the good, your behavior will change as well.

How can you change your brain to encourage more joy while you suffer from CPS?

Deciding to Change Your Brain

The answer is what neuropsychologist Rick Hanson calls "self-directed neuroplasticity."[110] You already know that neuroplasticity means your brain is constantly changing. At the same time, you should know that this constant change doesn't have to happen completely on its own; on the contrary, you can make intentional changes to rewire your brain and change your circumstances for the better (as in the eating, sleeping, and moving habits previously discussed). To master this, you need to focus your attention on that which you wish to grow. If you always focus on what you wish had gone differently, like not getting sick, not suffering from chronic pains, etc., your brain will receive too many messages relating to your physical discomforts and stay active too long in those areas of the brain. That's no way to nourish your Inner Giggle! But, if you focus your attention on the decent, nice, good things in your day, your brain will grow in those areas.

The hard part is getting a handle on where to direct your attention. These days, your environment can pull your attention and focus in a thousand different directions. Moreover, focusing your attention when you dedicate a lot of your time to dealing with CPS (e.g. researching treatments, following up with doctors, keeping track of your medicine regime, etc.) can be even more challenging. That's why it's so important to add self-directed neuroplasticity to your healing journey. It's a daily reminder that though life may be gloomy now, things can feel better once you add some sweeter moments to your day.

Now, I know what it's like to be self-disciplined and still not be able to accomplish what you set out to do or be. Sometimes, when dealing with CPS, you really are in so much pain that you can't move. The important thing to remember is that it's about having the *mindset* of pushing yourself to do better, to get stronger, fitter, calmer, or whatever elements are important to your recovery. You want to encourage yourself to do as much as possible, so your CPS doesn't rob you of more than it has already. At the same time, you must of course listen to your body. Whatever self-driven steps you take must be monitored with self-compassion.

I recommend you begin to break out of mainly focusing on your chronic condition and establish other constructively energizing habits by looking for what I call "scintillating flashes" and harnessing them.

Harness the Positive Scintillating Flashes

Start with noticing the little victories. Did you get a good night's sleep in some fresh, clean sheets? Did you spend some time stretching? Let those little things make you feel good about yourself and harness their positive effects on your well-being. It's okay if you're only able to enjoy your little victories for a moment – actually, all you need is thirty seconds. Sure, extending it would be awesome, but start with what you can. Then: savor these moments. When you noticed you had a little victory, stay with it a little longer. If you feel yourself rushing, take a moment to slow down and savor something neutral but nourishing. Yes, I'm asking you to stop and smell the roses. Appreciate the sun shining, feel it on your skin, deepen your breath, notice fresh fruit that smells good, pet your dog. You've accomplished a task you hoped to accomplish. Let yourself feel good about it. Absorbing the moment by staying with that positive experience a little longer will help consolidate it into your neural pathways, forming deeper connections in your brain.

Journal

Stop right now, and savor something small around you. Take this feel-good moment, and make it a positive physical experience. Imagine in your mind's eye. If it were to land in your body, where would it go? How strongly can you experience it? Can you assign a color to it? Can it light up your heart? Will it warm up your hands? Will it settle down in your stomach? Does it moisturize your skin? Transform this moment from just a good thing to something more noticeable, to a nourishing physical experience.

The most important thing is to celebrate the little victories in life and savor them. This is harnessing the positive scintillating flashes – acknowledging their significance! It is part of your resiliency tools now, and your Inner Giggle thanks you!

Develop Intentional Gratitude

You can also grow your resilience by developing intense intentional gratitude on the days when you're not doing as well. Surely, days with no pain are worthy of celebration, but so are the days your body is struggling to heal. I might, for instance, intentionally recall the smell of last Sunday's brunch prepared by my daughters, then eating outside in the sun and sharing meaningful conversation. There are moments you've enjoyed and look forward to enjoying again. You can be grateful for them, even on the days when you're struggling.

It's totally understandable that it's easy to overlook life's little blessings when your overall state of being is down. But even though it may feel like inserting brief moments of gratefulness doesn't matter, making an effort to recognize those moments is worth it. There are many scientific studies that speak to the benefits of a repeated gratitude practice – even if done only once every few days, even if done just for couple of minutes. It is not wishy washy; the data shows that gratitude is a mindset that activates the prefrontal cortex and sets brain messages in motion. It can even decrease inflammation in your body!

A Quick Side Note: The Oyster and the Pearl

Think for a moment about an oyster with a pearl in it – a treasured possession you might have first heard about in a children's fable. Perhaps you already know that a pearl develops out of an oyster's response to discomfort and challenge. It's pretty remarkable. This beautiful, shining, hard stone comes to fruition as a result of the stress its oyster endures. So, when you are facing setbacks, remember the pearl in the oyster metaphor. The strength of resilience is another kind of pearl that grows from the struggle of dealing with a chronic and painful physical state. Your response to the challenge has the potential to generate something valuable, something sacred. Your response could reframe your efforts into positives, into healing, into intentional gratitude, and into being proud of any small daily wins you achieve. Anything you're able to muster that contributes to your Happier Being through hard times will be key to creating a shinier pearl. Allow your pearl to glow!

Recognize Negativity Bias, Scan for the Positive

You may have heard of the phenomenon called negativity bias. As early humans, our brains were wired to seek out and prioritize the negative as a way to survive. It was critical to scan our environment for potential threats so that if a predator was in sight, we wouldn't miss it. Even though wild animals no longer roam our streets, we're still on high alert for threats, whether real or anticipated. This is where our fight-or-flight response chimes in. When we encounter a threat, our reaction is typically to flee the scene or set our aim toward battle (fight). When there is a real danger, these responses make sense. But if there are no actual threats to your survival and this alert mode is on too long, you can easily find yourself becoming overly anxious or hypervigilant, or even experience greater chronic pain. As stated before, when it feels like your body is under attack by your CPS, your body is unfortunately often in this primal, exhausting fight-or-flight mode. Frequently, this is activated by your mind's negative scanning or negativity bias tendency (but not always).

When negativity bias sets in, it's easier to neglect and ignore the positive out there. While you can still survive without the positive, you don't want to merely survive. You want to thrive. So learning how to scan for the positive is crucial in your daily life, and in my mind, even more so when times are bad. This isn't just another "be more positive" call to action. I'm asking you to *also* be positive and seek out the positivity that already exists, not fake it or make it up. As psychologist Dr. Hanson so beautifully says, "The mind is like Velcro for negative experiences and Teflon for positive ones."

That's why you need to find any reason to seek out the positive, experience it, and – if you're able – encourage it to stick to you just a little longer, because positivity tends to be naturally fleeting. This is again why utilizing intentional gratitude is so important. It trains your brain to better balance the stressor you find yourself in. It lowers the volume of the negative and ups the power of the positive. A positive outlook puts things into proper perspective when life inevitably throws you that unexpected curveball. It allows you to focus, even momentarily, on the positive that still exists and not allow the negativity bias of your brain to ignore its relevancy and existence. Yes, even during the chaos of troubled times. You have to keep connecting to the inner meaning of your days, to the reasons for healing, and be supported by any little pleasure you can stick to your consciousness. In short, keeping your Inner Giggle front and center in your mind's eye.

Become More Impartial and Apply Uncommitted Thinking

Now, it's not all about positive or negative scanning and thinking. Sometimes remaining impartial to your situation is the way to go. Certainly it's better than overusing the negativity bias. Applying impartial/uncommitted thinking is another tool for boosting your Inner Giggle. Humans are very quick to categorize experiences as good and bad. This is understandable. However, not every moment of your day must be seen as such. There are days when letting go of labeling is relevant and liberating. You don't always have to figure everything out or put a title on how you're feeling. In short, think of uncommitted thinking as the type of thinking that allows you to accept your past diagnosis – with its present consequences – as real, though not the only thing that factors into your future. What determines part of the future is what you do in the present, right now, and then again after that. How you feel right now can be influenced by the smallest things you attend to moment to moment. And the fact is that each moment consists of your pain *plus* your intention.

Therefore, if you're having a tough day due to CPS, shorten the time frame of what you plan to do. Remind yourself that there is sometimes a benefit in doing less while applying some uncommitted thinking. Doing less can be not good, not bad. It just is. Quiet the need to label your day as a good or bad day. At the moment, doing less is more. Embrace that. Embrace just being. Like walking on the beach, being surprised by a furry running dog coming to greet you, or seeing an infant chewing on her toes. What might it cause you to feel, to experience? Perhaps a few seconds of awe? Perhaps it made you smile? Embrace your ability to just shift, momentarily, from your suffering to being happier about being. Happier for noticing any small chance for inner peace.

Develop Your New, Goal-Oriented Timeline and Healthy Foundation

The psychological challenge of CPS is to keep your self-efficacy attitude steady despite the loss of capabilities you experience. The acceptance that it will take some time to build your newest healthy foundation is your goal. In general, you always want to focus on your goals. Having the goals themselves, as we discussed in prior chapters, is a major part of becoming happier. Just knowing that this weekend your kids are coming to visit lifts your spirits today and makes the daily chores more bearable, if not enjoyable. Your mind anticipates something good is about to happen, which sets in motion the reward circuit in your brain. You get a dopamine response before the actual event transpires, experiencing in the present the benefits of what is to happen, which increases your motivation to execute the plan.

However, when you are physically depleted, it's not easy to plan far in advance. Life drains you, and the chaotic feeling of every moment makes it feel irrelevant to look toward the future. Often, long-term goals appear unattainable. But hey, the goal, for now, is to build your newest healthy foundation, one small step at the time. And when your day is overwhelmed with pains, best to shorten your time frame. The goal becomes taking care of your next moment, your next hour, your next day. Of course, you will still have time to go back to your longer-term goals. Optimizing your diet, for example, is still a worthy goal, as is planning for doctors' appointments.

The aim is to be someone who tries to get better right now. As long as you keep this time mindset accessible to yourself and apply it as needed, you are the best you can be. You are a good person. You are a person who is healing, and that is an attainable mission. Make those extremely challenging moments more bearable by bringing your goals closer to you. It is about getting through the next moment and maintaining your composure, your sanity, by focusing on getting through the present. One minute at a time.

Address Any Lingering Fears

When the time is right in your recovery, ask yourself: might defining your fears be as or even more important than defining your goals? Defining your fears will help you define the challenges you face more specifically, a step up from just knowing your diagnosis or your ultimate recovery goal. That can help with reducing any free-floating anxieties, because knowing more specifically what your fears might be (besides the obvious of the diagnosis) will shed light on other important practical issues that might be lingering in your mind. Naming those fears not only structures your healing path more specifically but also lowers the overshadowing sense of madness and turmoil that categorizes the unknown. This is such an important concept that I'd like to explain it just once more.

***Defining your fears will clarify why and how you can
plan to embrace your current reality.***
It will help you be more aware of your perceived losses due to your CPS. That
reality check can help get you more specific about your anxieties and gain
better control over them. Your fears might also reveal to you the values you
find most important, such as family and creativity, to name some examples.
And although you may have lost some practical aspects of your life due to
CPS, you likely have not lost as much as you initially thought – because
your values were not lost. And with your character strengths they could
even get amplified. (More on values and finding out your own character
strengths profile in a moment.)

This brings us to the next point: with your goals closer to you, and
your fears addressed, you are situated to practice acceptance.

Accept That Which You Cannot Change

I know that dealing with CPS was not the path you envisioned for yourself,
but the fact remains that it is the path you are on, and so you're better off
looking for ways to navigate it more gracefully – trust me. This starts with
accepting the reality of cloudy days ahead. Before the onset of your chronic
condition, you may have had structured days and clarity of direction in
your week, or your life for that matter. But now, at least for a while, things
are going to be hazier.

> **There are going to be hours of navigating through the fog,
> where the gap between knowing exactly where you are to where
> you are going will not be as clear as it was before. Accepting this gap,
> this in-between space of the unknown, is crucial – at least for the
> time being. Yes, you did not choose it, but here you are. Accept it.**

The in between-existence space is part of your resiliency because being
resilient with CPS does not necessarily mean pushing through things 24/7.

When you're in pain, it's okay to say "Ow!" Make room for expressing the pain and the lack of clarity that accompanies it. You can't heal if you keep pretending you're not hurting. By not denying the physical and the emotional pain, you accept reality as is. This acceptance of your pain validates that the unwelcome changes in your health status are real and that they are, of course, very difficult. You have the right to feel sad, angry, or other "negative" emotions sometimes. It does not make you weak. It makes you human.

How Can Others Give You a Hand?

Besides accepting the challenge and acknowledging any negative emotions around your CPS, consider letting others in. Sharing your suffering with someone who cares can help tremendously when you allow someone to bear the burden with you – and science backs this up.

Dr. Alex Korb, in his excellent book *The Upward Spiral: Using Neuroscience to Reverse the Course of Depression, One Small Change at a Time,* shares studies which demonstrate the power of other people to support those who experience pain. In one experiment,[111] participants were asked to stick their hands in a bucket of ice water for an extended time. Very painful! Some participants had to endure it alone. Some had a stranger next to them, while others had an actual friend. The results, in short: having someone next to the participant, even a stranger, greatly reduced their pain.

People with CPS can experience the same kinds of benefits – as another study illustrated that people who had their significant others around had a reduction in painful sensations. Further, it was found that even just thinking about a significant other could reduce their pain. Amazingly, talking to someone they didn't know also helped their pain levels; this is in part because pain diminishes when your brain isn't focused on it, and having others around can help release the right chemical to lower the sensations of pain.

Even the discomfort of *anticipating* more pain can be lowered by having others around. Another research study showed that married women who held the hands of their husbands fared better in the face of a small, upcoming electric shock. Under an fMRI machine, they had less activity in the pain region and worrying circuits of their brains (the anterior cingulate cortex and dorsolateral prefrontal cortex, if you're curious). Amazingly, these women also felt less distress when holding their experimenter's hand.

When your body is stressed, it releases a stress hormone called cortisol. It also releases oxytocin (recall your happy chemicals, and the "O" in DOSE), which motivates you to connect with others and feel bonded and cared for. Thus, there is an internal battle, if you will, between experiencing the stress, which sometimes makes you feel isolated, and the need to connect.

I say, empower the connection. The amazing thing about this hormone is that it benefits the giver as well. Those who help others will also have a flood of oxytocin, boosting their overall sense of bonding and creating a more positive mood. So when you feel like you might be isolating yourself too often and have a hard time reaching out, remind yourself of this powerful hormone that acts as a neurotransmitter in the brain and encourages building caring and bonding relationships.

There is one caveat when it comes to reaching out to others: You cannot immerse yourself or others in endless negative talk when you share your pain. The point of bonding with others is to help you navigate and balance your narrative. And though that includes letting others in on your pain, when it comes to sharing, you'll want to be conscious of their ability to "psychologically hold" all the information in a healthy manner for both of you. Taken to an extreme, your sharing can elicit helpless feelings in the listener, which will make the conversation less beneficial for both of you. It's hard for most people to hang in there when the topic shared is continually negative or painful.

On the other hand, sharing with others is meant to decrease the time you are ruminating on your pain. So while you should be true to how you feel and share your pain, it's important not to focus solely on your pain when spending time with others. You risk exhausting a good friend who wants to be supportive, as well as adding a layer of rumination to your suffering. If you sense that your friend is tired of listening, having a hard time with it, or has reached their maximum capacity to be empathic, try not to pile on more negative emotions. Not only is it toxic to your mood but it might directly affect your pain levels.

Reaching out to others is about balancing your narrative and letting the oxytocin flow between you. This means that it should occur in moderation, depending on where you are in your healing path and who it is you share with. Having someone with you or that you can reach out to when dealing with CPS is critical – not just for your spirit but also for your pain levels (as illustrated by Dr. Korb's research). The bottom line is that people help people heal, and you don't need to go it alone. In fact, you really should not!

Digging Deeper: Hope

Why, even when taking into account that people with CPS have different limitation levels, does one person successfully tackle their day-to-day adversities while another person gives up in despair? With all the information I've laid out here and all the resources available out there, why isn't everyone skilled at forming a successful healing mindset?

I believe that though it certainly takes different resources to overcome the misfortune of physical challenge, the one resource you cannot be successful without is hope. Hope encompasses the passion for wanting to be as alive as you can be. It involves finding the strength to dig deep within, connecting with your Inner Giggle to rise above the pains, to become hopeful again. In the deepest levels of your soul, this is where your hope lives. The courage to awaken it again, and intentionally pursuing its daily presence is a significant part of the answer to the question I posed above.

Hope is maintained moment to moment through your intentional choices. It is fueled when you use thoughts and feelings to calm your pain of loss and actively pursue what is possible.

Finding Your "Why"

To enlist more hope in your healing journey, it's important to define your big 'why." Personally, I believe finding your why starts with the expansion of the "Inner" part of your Inner Giggle. It's the expansion of what you derive meaning from now that you've been forced to take a sharp turn on your life journey.

When I was first diagnosed with Lyme Disease, my need to become healthy again became the reason to get out of bed every morning – my fuel and my purpose. It dominated my existence and my conscience. Then I realized I might have to spend many of my days with the effects of chronic Lyme – that there was no defined end date for healing or recovery. I didn't want to start or end my days in unrelenting struggle, so I learned to reframe my circumstances by purposefully reconnecting to my deepest meaning in life. For me, that is being someone who always strives to do better and be better. That has not changed, only intensified.

Now I work to elevate my positive experiences in my life every day – because I can. At the root of it, experiencing the ups and downs, joys and pains (but not just pains) is part of being human. I want to experience the whole darn thing! I insist on feeling that I am truly living. That is the human experience, and in many ways, that is thriving. As a result, I have worked to adjust my mindset to being a Happier Being, a being as an organism, an individual, a human being who is healing. And being as in fully existing. I have refused to be someone who struggles with a chronic condition. *I am, instead, chronically healing.*

As Friedrich Nietzsche so brilliantly said, "He who has a why to live for can bear almost any how." You see, dealing with any form of CPS gives you a tremendous why.

Journal

Pause for a moment. What is your why for healing? I know it's tempting to say something goal-oriented, like traveling, and indeed this is a worthy reason. But I want you to try to think of more intrinsic aspects of the reasons for healing. How does traveling make you feel? Why is it that you want to travel? Is it part of your nature? Do you like the human interaction while traveling to different cultures? The newness feeling that comes with it? The feeling of awe that awakens while seeing new beauty all around? Tasting new foods? Write it down. The specifics behind your why inform the potential steps you can take.

Set yourself up for successful crossing of your psychological bridge.
It takes time to build that psychological bridge between trusting your limits
and figuring out what you need to do to sustain your recovery. Paradoxically,
in accepting this, you can find great freedom. It's a daily balancing act, and
you are its director. The goal is to push yourself to do more but always to
a healthy degree, and that degree is yours to figure out daily. It's my job to
motivate you to do so.

Building your psychological bridge is about trusting yourself to express
those physical or psychological pains when you need to, and then trusting
yourself to move on from them just as well. Trust me when I say I know how
hard it can be to face the health challenges of CPS. Sometimes, you don't
know if it's best to complain, share, cry, try to shake it off, work through
it, or just give in to the grief of it all (which is fine – for a bit). But humans
are tough!

More Practical Tools to
Optimize Your Healing Mindset Habits

Find triumph stories and practice positive broadcasting.
You can be inspired by other people's stories of a struggle with a similar,
if not the same, diagnosis and how they dealt with it and even came
out of it. Seeing it written in story form can help you frame the peak
of your own struggles, like the climax of a movie. Triumph stories are
powerful. Don't forget to share yours, too, if you feel comfortable doing
so. Broadcast any positive news and joy for yourself and for others who
may be looking to you for inspiration or wondering how you get through
it all. Positive broadcasting about the journey does so much good for
yourself and for others.

Psychologist Carl Rogers once said: "What is most personal is most
general." Think about that for a moment. If you have experienced something
as painful as loneliness, for example, due to your pains or illness, it's probable
that others have experienced that very same thing. When appropriate, be
courageous and share those feelings as well as how and what helped you
overcome this hurdle. Open your heart and allow others to peek into your
personal triumph in hopes that your optimism will rub off on them too.

CPS is a training challenge, not just a health challenge.
Shortly after being diagnosed, it can feel like you entered a training session – but that training happens in reverse. In a regular educational program, you're first given material to study, and then you're tested on it. But when given a diagnosis, you're being tested right away. The challenge is on, with no preparation, and you quite naturally fear that this test might never end. However, if you frame it like any training course, you can expect that some parts will be easier to pass than others. Also, no matter what, the training is still relevant (even in reverse order). You still need to acquire skills to get past each hurdle.

Unlike formal training, though, when dealing with CPS there are no assigned chapters to finish, and the learning is done through challenging real-life scenarios. It pushes you to decide between right or wrong (to choose treatment A or treatment B) and then to move along. There is no promised preestablished remedy or cheat sheet of what to follow to ensure your graduation. Your health is complex, and even the best doctors with the best intentions do not hold the absolute, correct answer.

The best remedy is being prepared while training is in session. Your health decisions change according to how you feel and heal. In order to maintain your success, it's important to stay alert and motivated to absorb the new and make any necessary corrections. The need for new skills evolves as your healing progresses. I can assure you that being a thoughtful student of your own challenging class has a positive influence on your future, as these skills will boost your life now as well as later. That's why seeing CPS as a training challenge, not just a health challenge, can be helpful through difficult times.

Work the Step You're In

As I started recovering from Lyme Disease, I wanted so much to go back to hiking. I had to overcome some obstacles: the fear of getting bitten by a tick again, learning how to quiet the nagging comparison of how much "better" I used to be at hiking, and worrying about the amount of pain I might be in afterward. I also had to learn to accept that my fullest hiking potential during tough days with pain and fatigue was not pushing myself to the max or my limits; it was pushing myself only to the next step. From there, my mantra became: "Work the step you're in."

As I began some easy hiking again, I focused on the privilege of being out of bed, of being outside, of enjoying the fresh breeze, of waving hello to a neighbor, of watching an older couple walk by hand in hand, and of really getting to do something that tickled my Inner Giggle. Although some of my pain escalated, my heartbeat increased disproportionately to the climb, and the sun seemed to get hotter by the second, I continued. And as I adjusted the brim of my hat and tilted my head down to avoid direct sunlight, all I could see was a few feet ahead of me and my feet moving step-by-step. I realized that sometimes it was helpful not seeing the very top, not visually experiencing the gap between where I was and where I would've liked to eventually be. All that mattered was that I was already moving towards my goal. I was working the step I was in – literally.

Working the step you're in means keeping focused on just that – the current step. It's not about whether you over- or undershot your goals or reached a certain mark, and it's definitely not about constantly measuring the distance from your goals. It's about reaching the best of your abilities each day, whatever that may be. You will eventually get to the next step, but you have to tackle the moment first, one step at a time. This process will allow you once again to experience that inner joy of resilience at work and your Inner Giggle being activated.

Magic Anyone? Visualize and Verbalize the Results and Healing You're Aiming For

The power of visualization is without a doubt remarkable. I'd like you to see it as a healing wand you can wave over your mind for better outcomes – like real magic. Many sports coaches will attest to the power of visualization as the one factor that distinguishes the superior athlete from the rest. These athletes encourage themselves to stay more emotionally neutral in times of high stress and imagine their desired outcome before it happens. In a sense, they are priming their unconscious brain to expect their desired goal – and it works.

An important part of successful visualization, though, is that like an athlete, you will still need to do the work. Athletes practice the skills they need, then their visualization practice sharpens their skills. Mastering their skills first enables them to use visualization more easily, which readily aids them in times when the game is challenging them even more. Like an athlete, you'll need to keep practicing the Inner Giggle energy boosters, for example, to the best of your ability. So when you direct your mind to visualize yourself reaching a better health status, it aligns with your daily routine. Do not get distracted by the level at which you are able to practice your happiness habits. It is the striving that your mind experiences, while holding your healing mindset intact, that makes all the difference in your progress.

If you feel adventurous about delving into the power of accessing your unconscious, the following journaling exercise can help your mind visualize bringing your desired future status into the present. In a way, it's another form of visualization – but verbal. As you read the statements below, look for those that resonate with you. In order to be effective, they must be grounded with some part of your own personal experience. This is not about practicing positive thinking without context and hoping it will turn things around. This is about practicing a healing mindset, giving your mind the desired message to focus on. That which you focus on grows. Feed your brain the better messages.

Journal

I'd like you to say the following sentence: "My body is a wellness-making machine." Meditate on it. Start coaching your mind to stay centered on its healing capabilities with added phrases such as: "I instruct you to pay attention to your breath, providing oxygen to your cells," or "I compel you to feel your even pulse, your energizing heartbeat, the circulation of nutrients in your blood," etc. Create your own unique sentences that resonate with you, write them down, and say them, out loud or silently. Use your mind's eye to see it, feel it, and relax with it.

Semantics matter when it comes to what your mind hears you say, and what it can help you visualize. Try and stay away from negative phrases like "I feel this is an unbearable illness," or "This is the most devastating setback," or "This stress will kill me." Instead, find softer ways of relating to your current state in your mind's eye with statements like: "I feel uncomfortable," or "I can do this slowly," or "I get to go to the pool" (instead of "I have to go for my aquatic therapy"). When these sentences creep in, refer to your examples of how your body is a wellness-making machine. Remember, not every CPS moment is the worst. Don't relay it to your brain as such. Instead, try visualizing and verbalizing the results and healing you're looking for. Give it a shot!

Adopt a Mindset of Values

Values are the standards, beliefs, and ideals with which you appraise your own and other people's behaviors, actions, or things. Examples of values that seem to be universal across cultures are generosity, justice, and love of learning, to name a few.

When you recognize your values, it shines a bright light on the aspects you're working hard to link your Inner Giggle to. In this context, it helps you find the many reasons you strive to become a healthier being. It reinforces the responsibility of your healing journey into the hands it belongs to – your own. This is one important reason I'd like you to become more cognizant of your values. But there's another reason I want you to study and identify them. And this is because simply writing them down can increase your health and happiness.

Many research studies have shown the positive effects on your well-being from writing about your values. For example, a classic study conducted in the 1990s asked Stanford students to keep a journal over winter break.[112] Some of these students were asked to write about their most important values and how their day's activities related to those values, while others were just asked to write about the good things that happened to them. Unsurprisingly, the first group proved to experience fewer health issues during their break and were in better spirits upon returning to school. They were also more confident in their ability to handle stress at school, especially those who had experienced the most stress over break.

Researchers concluded that when the students wrote about their values, it helped them see the meaning in their lives. When they were then faced with a stressful activity, they no longer saw it as something that had to be "endured" but as a step toward expressing their values. For example, applying for a difficult internship position could reflect how much those students cared about their future (one of their values). Even giving their sibling a ride reflected their commitment to family (a different value). As a result, these students returned to school with a mental and physical state advantage.

Stanford professor Kelly McGonigal's book *The Upside of Stress*[113] further details the positive health effects of value identification. In the short-term, people can experience more feelings of control, pride, strength, and power when it comes to themselves, and connection, empathy, and love when it comes to others. In the long-term, people can experience greater mental and physical health outcomes, perseverance in the face of discrimination, and less self-handicapping overall. Perhaps even more impressive is that for many, it only takes one single, ten-minute "value writing session" to benefit them for the following several months or even years.

Journal

Put it to the test. Your values did not leave you once your CPS arrived. Some might have shifted, intensified, or maybe even changed. Yet, assessing them now will provide you with the empowering knowledge to plan your healing journey. The tool I recommend assessing it with will connect you to your current character strengths (your wonderful assets) and to the values you care about. For example, it will assess your emphasis on your wisdom virtue, your courage virtue, your humanity virtue, and your justice virtue to name a few. Here is the link to the Values in Action[114] questionnaire: https://www.viacharacter.org/. It will help you find out what your unique character strengths profile is.

As this questionnaire suggests, upon completion, take a moment to consider the following questions: Which five values are most important to you? What did you do this week that's related to those values? Please write it out; don't just contemplate it. Writing as a therapeutic modality has been used for many years. Writing about significant personal affairs, in particular, has been shown to have tremendous health benefits.[115]

Grow Your Optimism

Despite what you may believe, you can learn to be more optimistic, even if optimism isn't something that comes easily or naturally to you! In fact, science is on your side here. According to Dr. Martin Seligman, you can learn optimism, and you should.[116] Seligman, the founder of positive psychology whom I've introduced you to previously, spent nearly four decades researching how optimism impacts our lives. His conclusion: optimism is distinctly different from positive thinking. Rather than simply rehearsing happy thoughts, Dr. Seligman believes optimism is a set of cognitive skills.

Things happen to us every day, whether you find a $20 bill on the ground, hit a huge traffic jam when you're running late, or anything in between. No matter how your day unfolds, you always interpret your daily events and create your subjective stories based on those appraisals. The essential point of the optimism equation is how you explain these events to yourself, and what and who you focus on while doing it. This is what Dr. Seligman calls your explanatory style.

According to this theory, there are three main explanatory styles: Permanence, Pervasiveness and Personalization. To evaluate which explanatory style you use more often, below is a simplified summary of the three styles. It is important to note that the assumption is not that you always use one explanatory style (sometimes also referred to as an attributional style). Or more importantly, that you are always perceiving life as a pessimist or an optimist. Nevertheless, breaking down your cognitive appraisal styles into these three categories, brings great clarity to which aspects of your thought process you can improve. Let's examine these explanatory styles now.

- Permanence explanatory style: Do you tend to interpret events as permanent or temporary? Let's say you mess up at work. Are you more likely to think you'll mess up again ("This always happens."), or are you more likely to think the result was a temporary fluke? Seligman tells us that the optimist usually thinks a bad result is a fluke. However, if it's a good thing, the optimist tends to think the result is permanent. A pessimist, on the other hand, tends to believe the reverse, that a good thing will not happen again. That this was a one-time win, which is unlikely to repeat.

- Pervasiveness explanatory style: Do you assume the event that just happened explains everything in your life? That it is prevalent in all aspects of your work? Your relationships? Let's say your boss compliments your project. Are you more likely to think that this reflects your work as a whole, that overall, you do good job, or that it just happened only with this specific project? Seligman tells us that the optimist is more likely to think a good event is universal and extends to their whole work or even whole character. They allow the good event/result to permeate their assessment in the way they perceived the situation. An optimist is also more likely to believe a bad event is isolated to a specific incident. A pessimist, on the other hand, is once again more likely to believe the reverse.

- Personalization explanatory style: When something happens, who do you believe is responsible for it? Are you more likely to place responsibility on yourself or on something outside of your control? According to this explanatory style theory, the optimist is more likely to take responsibility when something good happens and place responsibility on something outside themselves when something bad happens, like bad luck. Once again, a pessimist believes the reverse.

Cultivating an optimistic explanatory style has great benefits. It supports your focus on growing your Inner Giggle. The meaning your attribute to things, and your ability to sustain any pleasure in life is greatly affected by it. It keeps you responsible for the way you think, and therefore for the way you feel and behave. It doesn't mean you have to think positively. Optimism is not about thinking happy thoughts, it's a reactionary cognitive skill that you often use - without your awareness - to assess your circumstances.

This automatic style of appraising your circumstances is active all the time. Best get it under your control. You don't lose the ability to be realistic when a particular gloomy moment calls for it. No, your resilient mindset allows you to see the truth as it is. But keeping an optimistic view when you are focused on getting better is critical. It keeps you accountable to reexamine your automatic ways of thinking that might not only be inaccurate, but certainly don't serve your well-being. As you connect your inner purpose of getting healthier and your inner strengths to persevere despite your circumstance, you have to acknowledge that the way you appraise any situation, has a direct correlation on the way it leaves you feeling. Therefore, the first step in becoming more optimistic is to listen to your own explanatory style – especially in times of stress. Challenge its accuracy daily. Tapping into your explanatory style and confirming that you are optimizing it, is a helpful step in keeping you more optimistic in all your endeavors. It gets you closer to the ultimate goal of living healthier and happier.

• • •

CPS comes with its own set of challenges and hardships, but it does NOT have to rob you of your happiness, or of your life.

> **Part of healing is the refiguring of your wholeness as you are now.**

My belief, and my purpose has been to show you that despite your circumstances you can become a Happier Being. You can, and now, with the tools I've given you, I know that you *will!*

Recap

- CPS – Chronic Physical Stress – is the term I coined for chronic medical symptoms, pains, diseases, or conditions, both those that are visible to the outside observer and those that are not. CPS is any unwanted chronic physical stress.
- One of the keys to healing with CPS is understanding that focusing only on taking away the sadness of being sick or disabled will not necessarily make you as happy as you can become. It's instead about what you add back into your life (i.e., something to be grateful for, to look forward to, new goals, seeking to optimize, etc.) that truly increases your happiness.

- The practice of positive psychology will allow you to be mentally strong, strong enough to experience happiness even through difficult circumstances – because happiness, with resiliency as its counterpart, makes up the immune system of your life.

- Despite resiliency through challenging times being commonly thought of as bouncing back quickly (like a stress ball that reshapes itself once you stop squeezing it), the process is more gradual – like a squashed tomato: the seeds will fall into the Earth's soil and grow into a strong, new plant in time. This plant, which grew out of devastation, now has deep roots that can withstand any type of weather.

- To become more resilient, you need the winning equation: Identity → Action → Feelings (Eric Greitens, *Resilience*). Essentially, you must first see yourself becoming that person (identity first). Then, if you want to feel differently (become happier, healthier, smarter, calmer, etc.), you must act differently. Once you experience yourself behaving so, the accompanied positive feelings reinforce your actions and the desire to keep forming your new and improved identity grows. It feels good to be aligned with who you are being.

- Obstacles to becoming more resilient with CPS include meta feelings (on top of physically suffering you suffer from feeling badly that you feel sad), grief (having lost a part of your capabilities), depression (exacerbated by physical inability and chronic inflammation), and anxiety (causing you to feel unsafe at your core).

- Navigating these obstacles requires working on developing post-traumatic growth. This type of growth entails piecing yourself back together, one step at a time, whichever way you can (e.g. the art of kintsugi or mosaic). It is about expanding the momentary good in between the bad and increasing your Laughs Per Day (LPD). It is about focusing your attention on the positives to develop self-directed neuroplasticity (Dr. Rick Hanson). This way, your brain can experience the positive more often.

- Tactics to change your brain to become more resilient and increase happiness include the following: celebrating tiny victories, becoming intentionally grateful, recognizing your brain's negativity bias (we remember "what went wrong" more often), remaining impartial or applying uncommitted thinking (so you don't drain yourself emotionally), shortening your timeline (not overstretching yourself), addressing any lingering fears (clarifying ways to embrace your current reality), and accepting that which you cannot change (say "ow" – you're human).

- Remember that you don't need to go it alone when dealing with CPS, and in fact, you really shouldn't. People help people heal; therefore, social connection is important. Don't isolate yourself.

- Tools to boost your Healing Mindset with CPS include the following: finding your "why," trusting yourself, seeking out triumph stories, practicing positive broadcasting, keeping the frame of mind that CPS is a life-training challenge (not just a health challenge), working the step you're in, visualizing your desired results, adopting a mindset of values, and growing your optimism.

- Remember, you can optimize your well-being despite your starting point.

Bonus information and mental training exercises relating to this chapter can be found here: happierbeing.com/exercises

A NON-ENDING

Why "non-ending" instead of a "conclusion"?

In practicality, I feel there is no need for a conventional conclusion. The focus of this book is, after all, on introductions: an introduction to the importance of optimizing your precious happier self, and an introduction to a reframe of how to get you energized for all aspects of better living – even when you are challenged with chronic physical stress.

Now that you've been introduced to your Inner Giggle tool for Happier Being, it is your dedication to optimizing it that will elevate you to the next, happier chapter of your life. There will no doubt be hurdles, but the choices you make to optimize your day, every day, will allow you to stay resilient and experience your Happier Being more often. Practice your happiness habits. Train intentionally to achieve your goals. You will watch your being shed its metaphorical skin and allow the stronger, more purposeful *you* to be seen and expressed over time.

Thus, the end note is that there's always another chapter. When you focus on safeguarding your well-being, it becomes a work in progress, not an end result. Your happiness is your commitment to your lifestyle choices. It's the constant process of advancement to a newer, fresher, and more well-equipped you. It happens moment to moment, day by day.

So, lean in to this next chapter of your life, lean in to your unshakable Inner Giggle, and lean in to your new identity as someone who optimizes their Happier Being!

• • •

To be continued …

If you'd still rather have a conclusion, please use the next few lines for your personal "non-end note." After all, it's you who's writing the next chapter of your life …

____

____

____

BIBLIOGRAPHY

Achor, Shawn. *The Happiness Advantage: How a Positive Brain Fuels Success in Work and Life*. New York, NY: Currency, 2010.

Aguilera, Mario. "Exercise Boosts Motor Skill Learning via Changes in Brain's Transmitters." *UC San Diego News Center*, May 4, 2020. https://ucsdnews.ucsd.edu/pressrelease/exercise-boosts-motor-skill-learning-via-changes-in-brains-transmitters.

Alden, Lynn E., and Jennifer L. Trew. "If It Makes You Happy: Engaging in Kind Acts Increases Positive Affect in Socially Anxious Individuals." *Emotion* 13, no. 1 (2013): 64–75. https://doi.org/10.1037/a0027761.

Barreto, Manuela, Christina Victor, Claudia Hammond, Alice Eccles, Matt T. Richins, and Pamela Qualter. "Loneliness Around the World: Age, Gender, and Cultural Differences in Loneliness." *Personality and Individual Differences* 169 (2021): 110066. https://doi.org/10.1016/j.paid.2020.110066.

Baumeister, Roy F. and John Tierney. *Willpower: Rediscovering the Greatest Human Strength*. New York, NY: Penguin Books, 2011.

Bem, Daryl J. "Self-Perception: An Alternative Interpretation of Cognitive Dissonance Phenomena." *Psychological Review* 74, no. 3 (1967): 183-200. https://doi.org/10.1037/h0024835.

Ben-Shahar, Tal. *Choose the Life You Want: The Mindful Way to Happiness*. New York, NY: The Experiment, 2014.

Ben-Shahar, Tal. *The Pursuit of Perfect: How to Stop Chasing Perfection and Start Living a Richer, Happier Life*. New York, NY: McGraw Hill, 2009.

Benson, Herbert. *Relaxation Revolution: The Science and Genetics of Mind Body Healing*. New York: Scribner, 2011.

Bratman, Gregory N., J. Paul Hamilton, Kevin S. Hahn, and James J. Gross. "Nature Experience Reduces Rumination and Subgenual Prefrontal Cortex Activation." *PNAS, Proceedings of the National Academy of Sciences*, June 29, 2015. https://www.pnas.org/content/112/28/8567.abstract.

Breuning, Loretta G. *14 Days to Sustainable Happiness: A Workbook for Every Brain*. Inner Mammal Institute, 2021.

Breuning, Loretta G. *Meet Your Happy Chemicals: Dopamine, Endorphin, Oxytocin, Serotonin*. Inner Mammal Institute, 2012.

Breus, Michael. *Beauty Sleep: Look Younger, Lose Weight, and Feel Great Through Better Sleep*. New York, NY: Plume, 2007.

Breus, Michael. "Is CBN the Next Big Thing in Cannabis Therapy for Sleep, Mood, and Health?" The Sleep Doctor, October 3, 2018. https://thesleepdoctor.

com/2018/10/03/is-cbn-the-next-big-thing-in-cannabis-therapy-for-sleep-mood-and-health/.

Breus, Michael, Deborah F. Bruce, and Arianna Huffington. *The Sleep Doctor's Diet Plan: Lose Weight Through Better Sleep*. Emmaus, PA: Rodale, 2012.

Breus, Michael and Mehemet C. Oz. *The Power of When: Discover Your Chronotype—and the Best Time to Eat Lunch, Ask for a Raise, Have Sex, Write a Novel, Take Your Meds, and More*. New York, NY: Little Brown and Company, 2016.

Brickman, Philip, Dan Coates, and Ronnie Janoff-Bulman. "Lottery Winners and Accident Victims: Is Happiness Relative?" *Journal of Personality and Social Psychology* 36, no. 8 (1978): 917-27. https://doi.org/10.1037/0022-3514.36.8.917.

Brown, Brené. *The Gifts of Imperfection: Let Go of Who you Think You're Supposed to Be and Embrace Who You Are*. Center City, MN: Hazelden, 2010.

Carter, Christine. *Raising Happiness: 10 Simple Steps for More Joyful Kids and Happier Parents*. New York, NY: Ballantine Books, 2011.

"Chronic Diseases in America." Centers for Disease Control and Prevention, 2021. https://www.cdc.gov/chronicdisease/resources/infographic/chronic-diseases.htm.

Cigna. "Loneliness and the Workplace." Fact Sheet. 2020. https://www.cigna.com/static/www-cigna-com/docs/about-us/newsroom/studies-and-reports/combatting-loneliness/cigna-2020-loneliness-factsheet.pdf.

Collins, Marva, and Civia Tamarkin. *Marva Collins' Way: Returning to Excellence in Education*. New York, NY: J.P. Tarcher/Putnam, 1990.

Cousins, Norman. *Anatomy of an Illness: As Perceived by the Patient – Reflections on Healing and Regeneration*. New York, NY: W.W. Norton, 2005.

Covey, Stephen R. *The 7 Habits of Highly Effective People: Powerful Lessons in Personal Change*. London, England: Simon & Schuster, 2013.

Coyle, Daisy. "How Being Happier Makes You Healthier." Healthline. Healthline Media, August 27, 2017. https://www.healthline.com/nutrition/happiness-and-health.

Creswell, David J., William T. Welch, Shelley E. Taylor, David K. Sherman, Tara L. Gruenewald, and Traci Mann. "Affirmation of Personal Values Buffers Neuroendocrine and Psychological Stress Responses." *Psychological Science* 16, no. 11 (2005): 846-51. https://doi.org/10.1111/j.1467-9280.2005.01624.x.

Csikszentmihalyi, Mihaly. *The Evolving Self: A Psychology for the Third Millennium*. New York, NY: Harper Perennial, 1994.

Csikszentmihalyi, Mihaly. *Flow: The Classic Work on How to Achieve Happiness*. London, England: Rider, 2002.

Dahlhamer, James, Jacqueline Lucas, Carla Zelaya, Richard Nahin, Sean Mackey, Lynn DeBar, Robert Kerns, Michael Von Korff, Linda Porter, and Charles

Helmick. "Prevalence of Chronic Pain and High-Impact Chronic Pain Among Adults – United States, 2016." *MMWR. Morbidity and Mortality Weekly Report* 67, no. 36 (2018): 1001-6. https://doi.org/10.15585/mmwr.mm6736a2.

Davidson, Richard J., and Sharon Begley. *The Emotional Life of Your Brain: How Its Unique Patterns Affect the Way You Think, Feel, and Live -- and How You Can Change Them.* New York, NY: Plume, 2013.

Davis, William. *Wheat Belly (Revised and Expanded Edition): Lose the Wheat, Lose the Weight, and Find Your Path Back to Health.* New York, NY: Rodale Books, 2019.

Dicket, Ron. "In Chicago: Eat Free, Pay with Your Conscience." Karma Kitchen, October 15, 2010. http://www.karmakitchen.org/story.php?sid=105.

Dimitrov, Stoyan, Tanja Lange, Cécile Gouttefangeas, Anja T.R. Jensen, Michael Szczepanski, Jannik Lehnnolz, Surjo Soekadar, Hans-Georg Rammensee, Jan Born, and Luciana Besedovsky. "Gαs-Coupled Receptor Signaling and Sleep Regulate Integrin Activation of Human Antigen-Specific T Cells." *Journal of Experimental Medicine* 216, no. 3 (2019): 517–26. https://doi.org/10.1084/jem.20181169.

Dispenza, Joe. *Breaking the Habit of Being Yourself: How to Lose Your Mind and Create a New One.* Carlsbad, CA: Hay House, 2013.

DuBois, Christina M., Oriana Vesga Lopez, Eleanor E. Beale, Brian C. Healy, Julia K. Boehm, and Jeff C. Huffman. "Relationships between Positive Psychological Constructs and Health Outcomes in Patients with Cardiovascular Disease: A Systematic Review." *International Journal of Cardiology* 195 (2015): 265–80. https://doi.org/10.1016/j.ijcard.2015.05.121.

Ducharme, Nicola McFadzean. *Lyme Brain: The Impact of Lyme Disease on Your Brain and How to Reclaim Your SMARTS!* BioMed Publishing Group, 2016.

Duhigg, Charles. *The Power of Habit: Why We Do What We Do in Life and Business.* New York, NY: Random House, 2014.

Durant, Will J., and Ariel Durant. *The Story of Civilization* (Vols. 1-11). New York, NY: Simon & Schuster, 1935-1975.

Dweck, Carol S. *Mindset: The New Psychology of Success.* New York, NY: Ballantine Books, 2007.

Eker, T. Harv. *Secrets of the Millionaire Mind: Mastering the Inner Game of Wealth.* New York, NY: Harper Business, 2005.

Exline, Julie J., Adrienne Morok Lisan, and Elianna R. Lisan. "Reflecting on Acts of Kindness toward the Self: Emotions, Generosity, and the Role of Social Norms." *The Journal of Positive Psychology* 7, no. 1 (2012): 45-56. https://doi.org/10.108 0/17439760.2011.626790.

Feiler, Bruce. *The Secrets of Happy Families: Improve Your Mornings, Rethink Family Dinner, Fight Smarter, Go Out and Play, and Much More.* New York, NY: HarperCollins Publishers, 2013.

Fogg, B.J. *Tiny Habits: The Small Changes That Change Everything.* Boston, MA: Mariner Books, 2020.

Frankl, Victor E. *Man's Search for Meaning: An Introduction to Logotherapy.* New York, NY: Simon & Schuster, 1984.

Fredrickson, Barbara L. "Cultivating Positive Emotions to Optimize Health and Well-Being." *Prevention & Treatment* 3, no.1 (2000). https://doi.org/10.1037/1522-3736.3.1.31a.

Frederickson, Barbara L. *Love 2.0.: Finding Happiness and Health in Moments of Connection.* New York, NY: Plume, 2013.

Fredrickson, Barbara L. *Positivity: Top-Notch Research Reveals the 3-to-1 Ratio That Will Change Your Life.* New York, NY. Harmony/Rodale, 2009.

Fredrickson, Barbara L. "The Role of Positive Emotions in Positive Psychology: The Broaden-and-Build Theory of Positive Emotions." *American Psychologist* 56, no. 3 (2001): 218-26. https://doi.org/10.1037/0003-066X.56.3.218.

Fredrickson, Barbara L., Roberta A. Mancuso, Christine Branigan, and Michele M. Tugade. "The Undoing Effect of Positive Emotions." *Motivation and Emotion* 24, no. 4 (2000): 237-58. https://doi.org/10.1023/a:1010796329158.

Fuhrman, Joel. *Eat for Life: The Breakthrough Nutrient-Rich Program for Longevity, Disease Reversal, and Sustained Weight Loss.* New York, NY: HarperOne, 2020.

Fuhrman, Joel. *Super-Immunity: The Essential Nutrition Guide for Boosting Your Body's Defenses to Live Longer, Stronger, and Disease Free.* New York: NY: HarperOne, 2012.

Gable, Shelly L., and Harry T. Reis. "Good News! Capitalizing on Positive Events in an Interpersonal Context." *Advances in Experimental Social Psychology*, 2010, 195-257. https://doi.org/10.1016/s0065-2601(10)42004-3.

Gable, Shelly L., Gian C. Gonzaga, and Amy Strachman. "Will You Be There for Me When Things Go Right? Supportive Responses to Positive Event Disclosures." *Journal of Personality and Social Psychology* 91, no. 5 (2006): 904-17. https://doi.org/10.1037/0022-3514.91.5.904.

Gable, Shelly L., Harry T. Reis, Emily A. Impett, and Evan R. Asher. "What Do You Do When Things Go Right? the Intrapersonal and Interpersonal Benefits of Sharing Positive Events." *Journal of Personality and Social Psychology*, 87, no. 2 (2004): 228-45. https://doi.org/10.1037/0022-3514.87.2.228.

Gauthier, Claudine J., Muriel Lefort, Saïd Mekary Laurence Desjardins-Crépeau, Arnold Skimminge, Pernille Iversen, Cécile Madjar, et al. "Hearts and Minds: Linking Vascular Rigidity and Aerobic Fitness with Cognitive Aging." *Neurobiology of Aging* 36, no. 1 (2015): 304–14. https://doi.org/10.1016/j.neurobiolaging.2014.08.018.

Godin, Seth. *The Practice: Shipping Creative Work.* New York, NY: Portfolio, 2020.

Goldsmith, Kelly, David Gal, Rajagopal Raghunathan, and Lauren Cheatham "The Pursuit of Happiness: Can It Make You Happy?" *SSRN Electronic Journal*, 2012. Revised October 30, 2018. https://doi.org/10.2139/ssrn.1979829.

Goleman, Daniel. *Focus: The Hidden Driver of Excellence*. New York, NY. Harper, 2015.

Gollwitzer, Peter M., and Paschal Sheeran. "Implementation Intentions and Goal Achievement: A Meta-analysis of Effects and Processes." *Advances in Experimental Social Psychology*, 2006, 69-119. https://doi.org/10.1016/s0065-2601(06)38002-1.

Goodman, Eric. *True to Form: How to Use Foundation Training for Sustained Pain Relief and Everyday Fitness*. New York, NY: HarperWave, 2018.

Graham, Tyler G., and Drew Ramsey. *The Happiness Diet: A Nutritional Prescription for a Sharp Brain, Balanced Mood, and Lean, Energized Body*. Emmaus, PA: Rodale, 2012.

Greitens, Eric. *Resilience: Hard-Won Wisdom for Living a Better Life*. Boston, MA: Houghton Mifflin Harcourt, 2015.

Gutman, Ron. "The Hidden Power of Smiling." Filmed March 2011 in Long Beach, California. TED video. 07:10. https://www.ted.com/talks/ron_gutman_the_hidden_power_of_smiling?language=en.

Habib, Navaz. *Activate Your Vagus Nerve: Unleash Your Body's Natural Ability to Heal*. Berkeley, CA: Ulysses Press, 2019.

Haidt, Jonathan. *The Happiness Hypothesis: Finding Modern Truth in Ancient Wisdom*. New York, NY: Basic Books, 2006.

Hanson, Rick. *Hardwiring Happiness: The New Brain Science of Contentment, Calm, and Confidence*. New York, NY: Harmony Books, 2016.

Hanson, Rick, and Forrest Hanson. *Resilient: How to Grow an Unshakable Core of Calm, Strength, and Happiness*. New York, NY: Harmony Books, 2018.

Hanson, Rick, and Richard Mendius. *Buddha's Brain: The Practical Neuroscience of Happiness, Love, and Wisdom*. Oakland, CA: New Harbinger Publications, 2009.

Hardy, Darren. *The Compound Effect: Jumpstart Your Income, Your Life, Your Success*. New York, NY: Hachette Go, an Imprint of Hachette Books, 2020.

Harvard Health Publishing. "Can gut bacteria improve your health?" Harvard Health, October 14, 2016. https://www.health.harvard.edu/staying-healthy/can-gut-bacteria-improve-your-health#:~:text=About%20100%20trillion%20bacteria,%20both,known%20as%20the%20gut%20microbiota.

Harvard Health Publishing. "Learning diaphragmatic breathing." Harvard Health, March 10, 2016. https://www.health.harvard.edu/lung-health-and-disease/learning-diaphragmatic-breathing.

Healthline. "Five Ways Reading Can Improve Health and Well-Being." HuffPost,

October 13, 2017. https://www.huffpost.com/entry/five-ways-reading-can-imp_b_12456962.

Hefferon, Kate. *Positive Psychology and the Body: The Somatopsychic Side to Flourishing.* Maidenhead, Berkshire, UK: Open University Press, June 1, 2013.

Hofmann, Stefan G., Paul Grossman, and Devon E. Hinton. "Loving-Kindness and Compassion Meditation: Potential for Psychological Interventions." *Clinical Psychology Review* 31, no. 7 (2011): 1126-32. https://doi.org/10.1016/j.cpr.2011.07.003.

Huizen, Jennifer. "How Gut Microbes Contribute to Good Sleep." *Medical News Today.* MediLexicon International, Ltd., December 24, 2020. https://www.medicalnewstoday.com/articles/how-gut-microbes-contribute-to-good-sleep.

Hyman, Mark. *The Blood Sugar Solution: The UltraHealthy Program for Losing Weight, Preventing Disease, and Feeling Great Now!* New York, NY: Little, Brown and Company, 2014.

Hyman, Mark. *Food Fix: How to Save Our Health, Our Economy, Our Communities, and Our Planet--One Bite at a Time.* New York, NY: Little, Brown Spark, 2020.

Hyman, Mark. *Food: What the Heck Should I Eat.* New York, NY: Little, Brown Spark, 2019.

Hyman, Mark. *The UltraMind Solution: Fix Your Broken Brain by Healing Your Body First.* New York, NY: Simon & Schuster, 2010.

Hyman, Mark. *The UltraMind Solution: The Simple Way to Defeat Depression, Overcome Anxiety, and Sharpen Your Mind.* New York, NY: Scribner, 2009.

Hyman, Mark, and Mark Liponis. *UltraPrevention: The 6-Week Plan That Will Make You Healthier for Life.* New York, NY: Simon & Schuster, 2003.

Joseph, Stephen. *What Doesn't Kill Us: The New Psychology of Post-traumatic Growth.* New York, NY: Basic Books, 2012.

Kanherkar, Riya R., Naina Bhatia-Dey, & Antonei B. Csoka. "Epigenetics across the Human Lifespan." *Frontiers in Cell and Developmental Biology* 2 (2014). https://doi.org/10.3389/fcell.2014.00049.

Karma Kitchen. "Karma Kitchen: Growing in Generosity". https://www.karmakitchen.org/.

Kashdan, Todd, and Robert Biswas-Diener. *The Power of Negative Emotion: How Anger, Guilt and Self Doubt are Essential to Success and Fulfillment.* London, UK: Oneworld, 2015.

Keysers, Christian. *Empathic Brain: How the Discovery of Mirror Neurons Changes Our Understanding of Human Nature.* The Netherlands: Social Brain Press, 2011.

Kirkpatrick, Bailey. "Epigenetics, Nutrition, and Our Health: How What We Eat Could Affect Tags on Our DNA." What is Epigenetics, May 15, 2018. https://www.whatisepigenetics.com/epigenetics-nutrition-health-eat-affect-tags-dna/.

Klika, Brett, and Chris Jordan. "High-Intensity Circuit Training Using Body Weight: Maximum Results with Minimum Investment" *ACSM'S Health & Fitness Journal* 17, no. 3 (2013): 8-13. https://doi.org/10.1249/fit.0b013e31828cb1e8.

Kok, Bethany E., Kimberly A. Coffey, Michael A. Cohn, Lahnna I. Catalino, Tanya Vacharkulksemsuk, Sara B. Algoe, Mary Brantley, and Barbara L. Fredrickson. "How Positive Emotions Build Physical Health." *Psychological Science* 24, no. 7 (2013): 1123–32. https://doi.org/10.1177/0956797612470827.

Korb, Alex. *The Upward Spiral: Using Neuroscience to Reverse the Course of Depression, One Small Change at a Time.* Oakland, CA: New Harbinger Publications, 2015.

Kornblatt, Sondra. *Restful Insomnia: How to Get the Benefits of Sleep Even When You Can't.* Newburyport, MA: Red Wheel/Weiser/Conari, 2010.

Kwong, Emily, and Syed M. Hassan. "It's Okay to Sleep Late (But Do It for Your Immune System)." Podcast. Short Wave by NPR, March 23, 2020. Podcast, website, 11:46. https://www.npr.org/2020/03/18/817652830/its-okay-to-sleep-late-but-do-it-for-your-immune-system.

Langer, Ellen J. *Mindfulness.* Burlington, VT: Da Capo Lifelong Books; Special edition, 2014.

Lederman, Michelle Tillis. *The Connector's Advantage: 7 Mindsets to Grow Your Influence and Impact.* Page Two Books, 2019.

Lotker, Michelle. "Sunlight, Serotonin and Your Sleep Cycle." PBS North Carolina, December 22, 2020. https://www.pbsnc.org/blogs/science/sunlight-happiness-link/.

Ludwig, Daniel. *Always Hungry? Conquer Cravings, Retrain Your Fat Cells, and Lose Weight Permanently.* New York, NY: Grand Central Life & Style, Hatchett Book Group, 2016.

Lustig, Robert H. *Fat Chance: Beating the Odds Against Sugar, Processed Food, Obesity, and Disease.* New York, NY: Avery, 2013.

Lyubomirsky, Sonja. *The How of Happiness: A New Approach to Getting the Life You Want.* New York, NY: Penguin Books, 2008.

Lyubomirsky, Sonja. *The Myths of Happiness: What Should Make You Happy, but Doesn't, What Shouldn't Make You Happy, but Does.* New York, NY: Penguin Books, 2014.

Maas, James B., Rebecca S. Robbins, Sharon R. Driscoll, Hannah R. Appelbaum, and Samantha L. Platt. *Sleep for Success: Everything You Must Know About Sleep but Are too Tired to Ask.* Bloomington, IN: Author House, 2011.

MacGill, Marcus. "Half of All American Adults Have a Chronic Disease - CDC." *Medical News Today,* July 2, 2014. https://www.medicalnewstoday.com/articles/279084.

Maguire, Eleanor A., David G. Gadian, Ingrid S. Johnsrude, Catriona D. Good, John Ashburner, Richard S. Frackowiak, and Christopher D. Frith. "Navigation-Related Structural Change in the Hippocampi of Taxi Drivers." *Proceedings of the National Academy of Sciences* 97, no. 8 (2000): 4398–4403. https://doi. org/10.1073/pnas.070039597.

Markman, Art. *Smart Change: Five Tools to Create New and Sustainable Habits in Yourself and Others.* New York, NY: TarcherPerigee, 2015.

Mayer, Emeran. *The Mind-Gut Connection: How the Hidden Conversation Within Our Bodies Impacts Our Mood, Our Choices, and Our Overall Health.* New York, NY: HarperWave, 2016.

McGonigal, Kelly. "Five Surprising Ways Exercise Changes Your Brain." *Greater Good Magazine.* Greater Good Science Center, January 6, 2020. https:// greatergood.berkeley.edu/article/item/five_surprising_ways_exercise_changes_ your_brain.

McGonigal, Kelly. "The Science of Willpower: 15 Tips for Making Your New Year's Resolutions Last." Open Culture, December 30, 2016. https://www. openculture.com/2016/12/the-science-of-willpower-2.html.

McGonigal, Kelly. *The Upside of Stress: Why Stress is Good for You, and How to Get Good at It.* New York, NY: Avery, 2016.

McKeown, Patrick. *The Oxygen Advantage: Simple, Scientifically Proven Breathing Techniques to Help You Become Healthier, Slimmer, Faster, and Fitter.* New York, NY: William Morrow, 2016.

Milano, Steve. "500 Calorie Treadmill Workout." LIVESTRONG.COM. Leaf Group. Accessed January 15, 2022. https://www.livestrong.com/article/416346- 500-calorie-treadmill-workout/.

Mosconi, Lisa. *Brain Food: The Surprising Science of Eating for Cognitive Power.* New York, NY: Avery, 2018.

Mukerjee, Snigdha, Yun Zhu, Andrea Zsombok, Franck Mauvais-Jarvis, Jinying Zhao, and Eric Lazartigues. "Perinatal Exposure to Western Diet Programs Autonomic Dysfunction in the Male Offspring." *Cellular and Molecular Neurobiology* 38, no. 1 (2017): 233–42. https://doi.org/10.1007/s10571-017- 0502-4.

Neal, David T., Wendy Wood, and Jeffrey M. Quinn. "Habits—a Repeat Performance." *Current Directions in Psychological Science* 15, no. 4 (2006): 198– 202. https://journals.sagepub.com/doi/10.1111/j.1467-8721.2006.00435.x.

Neff, Kristin. *Self-Compassion: The Proven Power of Being Kind to Yourself.* New York, NY: William Morrow, 2011.

Nieman, David C., and Laurel M. Wentz. "The Compelling Link between Physical Activity and the Body's Defense System." *Journal of Sport and Health Sciences* 8, no. 3 (2019): 201–17. https://doi.org/10.1016/j.jshs.2018.09.009.

Nieman, David C., Dru A. Henson, Melanie D. Austin, and Wei Sha. "Upper Respiratory Tract Infection is Reduced in Physically Fit and Active Adults."

British Journal of Sports Medicine 45, no. 12 (2010): 987–92. https://doi. org/10.1136/bjsm.2010.077875.

Oettingen, Gabriele. *Rethinking Positive Thinking: Inside the New Science of Motivation*. New York, NY: Current, 2015.

Otto, Michael W., and Jasper A. J. Smits. *Exercise for Mood and Anxiety: Proven Strategies for Overcoming Depression and Enhancing Well-Being*. New York, NY: Oxford University Press, 2011.

Pennebaker, James W. "Writing About Emotional Experiences as a Therapeutic Process." *Psychological Science* 8, no. 3 (1997): 162–66. 1997. https://doi. org/10.1111/j.1467-9280.1997.tb00403.x.

Pennebaker, James W., and Janel D. Seagal. "Forming a Story: The Health Benefits of Narrative." *Journal of Clinical Psychology* 55, no. 10 (1999): 1243–54. https:// doi.org/10.1002/(sici)1097-4679(199910)55:10<1243::aid-jclp6>3.0.co;2-n.

Perlmutter, David, and Kristen Loberg. *Grain Brain: The Surprising Truth about Wheat, Carbs, and Sugar – Your Brain's Silent Killers*. New York, NY: Little, Brown and Company, 2013.

Peterson, Christopher. *A Primer in Positive Psychology*. New York, NY: Oxford University Press, 2006.

Peterson, Christopher, and Martin E. P. Seligman. *Character Strengths and Virtues: A Handbook and Classification*. New York, NY: Oxford University Press, 2004.

Pillay, Srini. "How Simply Moving Benefits Your Mental Health." Harvard Health, March 28, 2016. https://www.health.harvard.edu/blog/how-simply-moving-benefits-your-mental-health-201603289350.

Pollan, Michael. *Food Rules: An Eater's Manual*. New York, NY: Penguin Books, 2009.

Prager, Carol, and Samantha Cassetty. *Sugar Shock: The Hidden Sugar in Your Food and 100+ Smart Swaps to Cut Back*. New York, NY: Hearst Home, 2020.

Pratt, Elizabeth. "How Sleep Strengthens Your Immune System." Healthline. Healthline Media, February 21, 2019. https://www.healthline.com/health-news/how-sleep-bolsters-your-immune-system.

Raghunathan, Raj. *If You're So Smart, Why Aren't You Happy?* New York, NY: Random House, 2016.

Ratey, John J., and Eric Hagerman. *Spark: The Revolutionary New Science of Exercise and the Brain*. New York, NY: Little, Brown Spark, 2013.

Rizzolatti, Giacomo. "The Mirror Neuron System and Its Function in Humans." *Anatomy and Embryology* 210, no. 5-6 (2005): 419–21. https://doi.org/10.1007/ s00429-005-0039-z.

Rogers, Carl R. *On Becoming a Person: A Therapist's View of Psychotherapy*. New York, NY: HarperOne, 1995.

Rönn, Tina, Petr Volkov, Cajsa Davegårdh, Tasnim Dayeh, Elin Hall, Anders H. Olsson, Emma Nilsson, et al. "A Six Months Exercise Intervention Influences the Genome-Wide DNA Methylation Pattern in Human Adipose Tissue." *PLoS Genetics* 9, no. 6 (2013). https://doi.org/10.1371/journal.pgen.1003572.

Salzberg, Sharon. *Real Happiness: A 28-Day Program to Realize the Power of Meditation.* New York, NY: Workman Publishing, 2019.

Sandoiu, Ana. "Just 20 Minutes of Exercise Enough to Reduce Inflammation, Study Finds." Medical News Today. MediLexicon International. January 16, 2017. https://www.medicalnewstoday.com/articles/315255#As-little-as-20-minutes-of-exercise-reduces-inflammation.

Seaborne, Robert A., Juliette Strauss, Matthew Cocks, Sam Shepherd, Thomas D. O'Brien, Ken A. van Someren, Phillip G. Bell, et al. "Human Skeletal Muscle Possesses an Epigenetic Memory of Hypertrophy." *Scientific Reports* 8, no. 1 (2018). https://doi.org/10.1038/s41598-018-20287-3.

Segar, Michelle. *No Sweat: How the Simple Science of Motivation Can Bring You a Lifetime of Fitness.* New York, NY: Amacom, 2015.

Seligman, Martin E. P. *Authentic Happiness: Using the New Positive Psychology to Realize Your Potential for Lasting Fulfillment.* New York, NY: Atria Books, 2004.

Seligman, Martin E. P. *Flourish: A Visionary New Understanding of Happiness and Well-Being.* New York, NY: Atria Books, 2012.

Seligman, Martin E. P. *Learned Optimism: How to Change Your Mind and Your Life.* New York, NY: Vintage Books, 2006.

Sherman, D. K., & Cohen, G. L. (2002). Accepting threatening information: Self-affirmation and the reduction of defensive biases. *Current Directions in Psychological Science*, 11(4), 119–123. https://doi.org/10.1111/1467-8721.00182

Simpson, Richard J., John P. Campbell, Maree Gleeson, et al. "Can exercise affect immune function to increase susceptibility to infection?" *Exercise immunology review* vol. 26 (2020): 8-22.

Sisson, Mark. *The New Primal Blueprint: Reprogram Your Genes for Effortless Weight Loss, Vibrant Health, and Boundless Energy.* Oxnard, CA: Primal Blueprint Publishing, 2009.

Snowdon, David. *Aging with Grace: What the Nun Study Teaches Us About Leading Longer, Healthier, and More Meaningful Lives.* New York, NY: Bantam, 2002.

Steen, Juliette. "We Found Out If It Really Takes 20 Minutes to Feel Full." HuffPost. Last modified November 10, 2016. https://www.huffpost.com/entry/we-found-out-if-it-really-takes-20-minutes-to-feel-full_n_61087613e4b0999d2084fcaf.

Stein, Achina P. *What If It's Not Depression? Your Guide to Finding Answers and Solutions.* Las Vegas, NV: Lifestyle Entrepreneurs Press, 2021.

Stevenson, Shawn. *Sleep Smarter: 21 Essential Strategies to Sleep Your Way to a Better Body, Better Health, and Bigger Success.* Emmaus, PA: Rodale Books, 2016.

Taubes, Gary. *The Case Against Sugar*. New York, NY: Alfred A. Knopf, 2016.

Tomova, Livia, Kimberly L. Wang, Todd Thompson, Gillian A. Matthews, Atsushi Takahashi, Kay M. Tye, and Rebecca Saxe. "Acute Social Isolation Evokes Midbrain Craving Responses Similar to Hunger." *Nature Neuroscience* 23, no. 12 (2020): 1597–1605. https://doi.org/10.1038/s41593-020-00742-z.

van der Kolk, Bessel. *The Body Keeps the Score: Brain, Mind, and Body in the Healing of Trauma*. New York, NY: Penguin Publishing Group, 2015.

Vernikos, Joan. *Sitting Kills, Moving Heals: How Everyday Movement Will Prevent Pain, Illness, and Early Death -- and Exercise Alone Won't*. Fresno, CA: Quill Driver Books, 2011.

"Via Character Strengths Survey & Character Reports." VIA Institute On Character. Accessed January 24, 2022. https://www.viacharacter.org/.

Walker, Matthew. *Why We Sleep: Unlocking the Power of Sleep and Dreams*. New York, NY: Scribner, 2017.

Watson, Christopher J., Helen A. Baghdoyan, and Ralph Lydic. "Neuropharmacology of Sleep and Wakefulness." *Sleep Medicine Clinics* 5, no. 4 (2010): 513–28. https://doi.org/10.1016/j.jsmc.2010.08.003.

Whiteman, Honor. "Five Ways Reading Can Improve Health and Well-Being." HuffPost. Last modified October 13, 2017. https://www.huffpost.com/entry/five-ways-reading-can-imp_b_12456962.

NOTES

Introduction
1. Csikszentmihalyi, M. (2002).
2. Lyubomirsky, S. (2008).
3. Achor, S. (2018).

One
4. Lyubomirsky, S. (2008).
5. Cheatham, L. (2012).
6. Snowdon, D. (2002).
7. Brickman, P. (1978).

Two
8. Neal, D. T., Wood, W., & Quinn, J. M. (2006).
9. Durant, W. J., & Durant A. (1935-1975).
10. Haidt, J. (2006).
11. Baumeister, R. F. & Tierney, J. (2012).
12. Fogg, B. J., (2020).
13. Gollwitzer, P. M., & Sheeran, P. (2006).
14. Baumeister, R. F. & Tierney, J. (2012).
15. Bem, D. J. (1967).
16. Greitens, E. (2015).
17. Oettingen, G. (2015).
18. Oettingen, G. (2015).
19. Duhigg, C. (2014).

Three
20. Ben-Shahar, T. (2009).
21. Brown, B. (2010).
22. Parkinson, C. (1955).
23. Godin, S. (2020).
24. Godin, S. (2020).
25. Ben-Shahar, T. (2009).
26. Collins, M., & Civia, T. (1990).

Four

27. Dweck, C. S. (2007).
28. Maguire, E. A. (2000).
29. Dweck, C. S. (2007).

Five

30. Hanh, T. (2017).
31. Cigna Report. (2020).
32. Barreto, M., et al. (2021).
33. Tomova, L. (2020).
34. Peterson, C. (2006).
35. Lyubomirsky, S. (2014).
36. Eker, T. H. (2005).
37. Gable, S. L. (2004).
38. Keysers, C. (2011).
39. Rizzolatti, G. (2005).
40. Hardy, D. (2021).
41. Frederickson, B. (2009).
42. Kashdan, T. B., & Biswas-Diener, R. (2015).
43. Fredrickson, B. L. (2001).
44. Frederickson, B. L. (2009).
45. Frederickson, B. L. (2009).
46. Dicket, R. (2010).
47. Exline, J. J., Lisan, A. M. (2012).
48. Carter, C. (2011).
49. Alden, L. E., & Trew, J. L. (2013).
50. Frederickson, B. L. (2013).
51. Neff, K. (2011).
52. Gutman. R. (2011).

Six

53. Sisson, M. (2016).
54. Breuning, L. G. (2012).
55. Zak, P. J. (2013).
56. Breuning, L. G. (2012).
57. Harvard Medical School. (2016).
58. Habib, N. (2019).

Seven

59. Hyman, M. (2020).
60. Kirkpatrick, B. (2018).
61. Mukerjee, et al. (2018).
62. Hyman, M. (2010).
63. Lustig, R. H. (2013).
64. Perlmutter, D. (2015).
65. Fuhrman, J. (2013).
66. Habib, N. (2019).
67. Taubes, G. (2016).
68. MacGill, M. (2014).
69. Prager, C. (2020).
70. Milano, S. (2022).
71. Perlmutter, D. (2013).
72. Pollan, M. (2009).
73. Mosconi, L. (2018).
74. Steen, J. (2016).

Eight

75. Stevenson, S. (2016).
76. Mass, J. B. (2011).
77. Lotker, M. (2020).
78. Watson, C. L. (2010).
79. Huizen, J. (2020).
80. Dimitrov, S., et al. (2019).
81. Pratt, E. (2019).
82. Kornblatt S., (2010).
83. Walker, M. (2018).
84. Stein, A.P. (2021).
85. Hassan, S. M. (2020).
86. Lewis, D. (2009).
87. Stevenson, S. (2016).
88. McKeown, P. (2016).
89. Breus, M. (2021).

Nine

90. Gauthier, et al. (2015).
91. Bratman, G. N., et al. (2015).

92. Pillay, S. (2016).

93. Ronn, T. (2013).

94. Seaborne, R. A. (2018).

95. Aguilera, M. (2020).

96. Simpson, R. J. (2020).

97. Stein, A. P. (2021).

98. Nieman, D. C. (2019).

99. Sandoiu, A. (2017).

100. Habib, N. (2019).

101. Kok, B. E. (2013).

102. Otto, M.W. (2011).

103. Nieman D. C. & Henson D. A, et al. (2010).

104. Goleman, D. (2015).

Ten

105. Peterson, C. (2006).

106. McGonigal, K. (2016).

107. Greitens, E. (2106).

108. Centers for Disease Control. (2020).

109. Seligman, M. E. P. (2011).

110. Hanson, R. (2009).

111. Korb, A. (2015).

112. McGonigal, K. (2016).

113. McGonigal, K. (2016).

114. VIA; Values in Action. (2004).

115. Pennebaker, J. W. (1997).

116. Seligman, M. E. P. (2006).

ACKNOWLEDGMENTS

The day-in, day-out process of writing a book I'd be proud to put out into the world was not an easy feat by any means. Luckily, I had two very important things. One, I had my Inner Giggle as a tool to guide me through the hard work of writing – and more often than not I found the process both meaningful and pleasurable. Two, I had the loving support of great friends and family. Like many other significant projects, no great book can happen in isolation, and *Happier Being* was no different.

To my late grandmother, Hannah: Thank you for being a steady force in my life, anchoring me to my own responsibility of becoming happier, and showering me with kindness. Though you grew up as an orphan with very little, your abundance mindset and endless wish to give taught me resilience and empowered me to be of service to others in this world. Although your presence is greatly missed, your spirit and wisdom still guide me today – writing included.

To my late dad, Zevi: In the spirit of your ways, I will keep it short: Thanks for your triumphs, may you rest in peace.

To my mother, Nehama: No words can express my gratitude to you (and still I will say just a few). Thank you for encouraging me to spread my wings and for always being there when I need you most. Your constant love and support ease my difficult days, and add vibrancy to my good days. You showed me firsthand the benefits of consistent work, and with that I was able to finish this book. I love you to the moon and back.

To my husband, Haimi: Thanks for always supporting my need to expand my learning, to seek new experiences, and to be in service to others. Thanks for believing in me, this book, and providing me with a space to work on my Happier Being.

To my daughters, Shani and Noam, who always tell me things the way they are: You expanded my heart to measures I could not have dreamed of. You changed my life (yes, for the better, since you asked....).

To Shani, my oldest: Thank you for all your encouragement to write, and for reviewing my manuscript. Your insightful comments were filled with grace and compassion, and your artistic talents assisted with creative aspects of the book. Your ability to see every scenario in life from different angels has always inspired me to listen deeper and look wider. It also allowed me to take your gentle, humoristic yet pointed feedback and elevate this book.

To Noam, my youngest: You are all over this book. Without your constant edits and yes – sections of the book that reflect your insistent energy – this book would not have been made whole. Your invaluable dedication, support, and effort on all aspects of this book's creation is a testimony to your smarts and resiliency. Thank you for your confidence in my authoring, despite my tech challenges, and your patience in showing me, over and over, where I saved my last draft. Your innate will to endure and master any skill you embark on made this book ever more powerful – though your perfectionism still needs work :). After hours of laughing together, even if at my expense, you made this process so much more enjoyable. What would I have done without you?

To my brothers, Moshik and Udi: I am thankful that despite our geographical distances we still manage to keep each other so close to our hearts. Nothing like having siblings who share a familiar past and can discuss or laugh about the unpredictable future. To my sisters-in-law, Ariella and Liat, what unbelievable additions to our lives you both are. And to all my nephews and nieces who followed, your amazing little souls inspire me. All of you, and your love and support, mean the world to me, always.

To my aunt, Dorit: Thank you for sharing your love of books, your editorial input, and your whimsical soul. Since I was young, you admired anything I have ever created (not subjective at all!). I am grateful for your continued confidence in my ability to write this book, your endless support of me, and how your love of writing encouraged mine.

To my late uncle, Yehuda: Words cannot express the impact you had on my fascination with psychology and my love of learning. I am grateful that your voice guides my writings. You are forever missed.

To all my loving and supportive relatives: There are too many of you to mention here, but you know who you are! Thanks for reminding me of the importance of family bonds, and for expressing your love, care, and support through the years.

To my faraway childhood friends: Thank you for always making me feel that I still belong. And to my local friends and colleagues who accept me just the way I am (yes, please feel free to smile!). I cherish the connections we have – you are all so dear to me. Your feedback on this book has been marvelous.

To my clients: I am grateful for your willingness to trust me with your pains, and your courage to do the deep work together. Thank you for both believing in the process of becoming a Happier Being, and exemplifying its limitless ripple effects in your lives! You never cease to inspire my life's work.

To my book team: Noam (yes, again), I am grateful for the amazing journey we went through together bringing this book to fruition. Thank you to Maggie, who joined in on the final edits, sharpened my writing, and made the book publication-ready. You assured me that there were many readers out there who would benefit from this book. Thank you also to my amazing launch team who expressed their support in the book's message and helped me spread the word.

ABOUT THE AUTHOR

Dr. Tal Leead, PsyD, is a psychologist, author, and founder of happierbeing.com. She received her doctorate in clinical psychology from Alliant International University. She is dedicated to improving the well-being of others, and does this through her work with individuals and groups. When she's not writing, she's probably trying on a new hat or making her daughters laugh. Occasionally, you can find Dr. Tal driving on a racetrack – fulfilling the wilder side of her Happier Being™!

www.ingramcontent.com/pod-product-compliance
Lightning Source LLC
Chambersburg PA
CBHW070855160726
48004CB00003B/1089